One of Ours

ONE OF OURS

Timothy McVeigh and the Oklahoma City Bombing

Richard A. Serrano

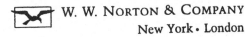 W. W. NORTON & COMPANY
New York · London

Copyright © 1998 by Richard A. Serrano

All rights reserved
Printed in the United States of America
First Edition

For information about permission to reproduce selections from
this book, write to Permissions, W. W. Norton & Company, Inc.,
500 Fifth Avenue, New York, NY 10110.

The text of this book is composed in Trump Mediaeval
with the display set in Berthold City
Composition by JoAnn Schambier
Manufacturing by Quebecor Printing, Fairfield Inc.
Book design by Charlotte Staub

Library of Congress Cataloging-in-Publication Data
Serrano, Richard A.
    One of ours : Timothy McVeigh and the Oklahoma City
bombing / Richard A. Serrano.
        p.   cm.
    ISBN 978-0-3933-3465-4
    1. McVeigh, Timothy. 2. Terrorists—United States—
Biography. 3. Right-wing extremists—United States—
Biography. 4. Oklahoma City Federal Building Bombing,
Oklahoma City, Okla., 1995.
I. Title.
HV6432.S47   1998
976.6'38053'092—dc21
[B]   98-9479
                                                      CIP

W. W. Norton & Company, Inc., 500 Fifth Avenue, New York,
NY 10110
http://www.wwnorton.com

W. W. Norton & Company Ltd., 10 Coptic Street, London
WC1A 1PU

1 2 3 4 5 6 7 8 9 0

For those who died in Oklahoma City,
and those who continue to suffer.

Contents

1. Almost Home 1

2. Beginnings 11

3. Bad Company 25

4. Alienation 47

5. Waco: God Sees Your Lies 65

6. The Road to Oklahoma City 81

7. Ode to Oklahoma 99

8. Going for It 105

9. From Intellectual to Animal 117

10. Final Days 127

11. Patriots' Day 153

12. Patriots and Tyrants 175

13. Betrayal 199

14. The Why 217

15. Playing Rough 227

16. The Order of Battle 247

17. Meet John Doe No. 2 259

18. Trial 273

19. One of Ours 293

20. Life After Death 317

My thanks to:

Colleagues and editors at the *Los Angeles Times*, particularly Doyle McManus and Tom McCarthy, who gave me the time and push to continue chasing the story;

Literary agent Ronald Goldfarb, for his support, and at W. W. Norton, editor in chief Starling Lawrence and his assistant, Patricia Chui, for their patience;

Fellow reporters and friends in Oklahoma City and Denver, particularly Nolan Clay, Sally Garner, and Terri Watkins, for their guidance and expertise, and Mary Marsh too;

And especially my family, Vincent, Nicholas, Mark, and Elise.

One of Ours

Chapter One

Almost Home

Another thirty minutes and Timothy McVeigh would be gone. He was sitting on a wooden bench waiting to be taken inside Judge Danny G. Allen's courtroom, and all he had to do was listen to the prosecutor make a short legal presentation: the judge would grant bail, and then he could gather his belongings and be out the door.

For two days he had been tucked safely inside the eighty-year-old Noble County Jail in little Perry, Oklahoma, while the world's eyes were trained on Oklahoma City, some seventy-five miles down the road. No one would think to look for him in a fourth-floor jail cell atop this small-town county courthouse, a face unrecognizable among the town drunks and petty thieves and other local miscreants. What better place to hide?

He had been arrested Wednesday morning on a stupid charge of driving without a license plate. Of course, the Oklahoma highway trooper had also found the loaded assault pistol concealed under his left arm. So he was taken to jail on traffic and gun charges, and he would have gotten out Thursday but for the unhappy circumstance that Judge Allen was tied up with a messy divorce case that took longer than anyone expected. The judge held over until Friday the hearing for McVeigh's bail.

But McVeigh was usually a patient man. For the past several years he had been a drifter; he had no home, really. He had lived with friends in Michigan and Kansas and Arizona, and he had rented a trailer home for a while, and sometimes he would stay a week or two in cheap motel rooms.

He liked being alone. Not that he was unsociable, although he was somewhat withdrawn and did not make friends easily. It was more that he embodied the restless spirit of so many young men in America today, restless to the point where some become disillusioned about the way their lives are turning out and begin to seek new roads to travel. It is never easy to get your life on track. McVeigh had tried and stumbled repeatedly.

But he never seemed in a hurry. He owned a succession of battered old used cars, and he logged so many miles on these "Warriors," as he called them, that one after another they would give out and their odometers would turn no more. He had had a tiny gray four-door with a red-and-black National Rifle Association decal on the window, but four months ago it had been rear-ended in Michigan. He had bought a roomy blue Pontiac station wagon, not a young man's car, and it had clunked out a week ago in Kansas. He had traded the wagon in for a 1977 Mercury Marquis, a big yellow sedan, and it was the car that had gotten him into the trouble that put him on the bench here waiting for court to begin.

Sometimes he slept in his car. On warm nights, particularly out in the desert Southwest, he would veer off down a dusty side trail and pull out his bedroll, the evening stars the last flickers of light he would see that day. Still wearing his flannel shirt with the sleeves rolled halfway up his forearms, he would lay his hands behind his head and dream. He once had been a soldier and had fought great battles in the sands of another land. In the future, he vowed, he would fight again.

By this Friday morning, about to be escorted into Judge Allen's courtroom, he was tired and restless and eager to push on. For two nights McVeigh had slept precious little, recalled fellow inmate John Seward, a local in for burglary. "He would act like he went to sleep," Seward said. "But he didn't sleep at all. When they took him out of here he had them black bags underneath his eyes."

McVeigh was waiting on the bench next to another inmate, Dana Charise Haynes, a young woman from Kansas City being held on marijuana charges. It was almost ten-thirty, and the judge was about to take the bench. McVeigh could reach out and almost wrap his fingers around freedom.

Sheriff Jerry Cook, a tall man, soft-spoken and slow-moving and yet at the same time possessing the distinct mark of authority, had not even seen McVeigh until the phone call came in. His office is on the first floor, past the hallway with the posted bills about the upcoming spring food drives and the pending farm auctions around this part of rural, flat north-central Oklahoma. There is an outer lobby where his small support staff works, and past them in the back is Cook's own little office. The room is cluttered, and the sheriff's chair and desk are pushed up snug against the wall.

The telephone on that desk rang. On the other end of the line was an agent from the federal Bureau of Alcohol, Tobacco and Firearms. Government investigators had been calling around the Midwest since the night before, desperate to locate a Timothy James McVeigh, date of birth April 23, 1968, wanted for questioning in the bombing two mornings ago of the Alfred P. Murrah Federal Building in downtown Oklahoma City.

Do you have him? the agent asked.

Cook took a moment to run his finger down the names on his daily inmate roster. McVeigh was halfway down the list. Yes, he said. He's here.

"We got him!" the agent shouted to his colleagues. Then he spoke into the phone again. Hold him, he said.

Cook hung up and took a breath. He bounded up the stairs and into the offices of Mark Gibson, the Noble County district attorney. He told Gibson the incredible news: the man the whole nation had been seeking was in their courthouse.

Gibson, not your normal county prosecutor in the Oklahoma Bible belt but rather a young man who sported long hair and dark sunglasses, was skeptical. "That's BS," he said.

But it's true, said the sheriff.

Gibson shook his head. "You're playing games with me, Jerry," he protested.

We've got the bomber, Cook said again. Federal agents are on their way here.

Then Gibson blanched. It suddenly struck him that right that minute McVeigh was sitting outside Judge Allen's courtroom and would more than likely be released very soon.

"Take him back up to jail," he instructed the sheriff. "Until we get something figured out."

Cook found McVeigh and Haynes sitting on the bench, quiet, patient, waiting. The sheriff fumbled for something to say.

"They don't want you right now," he told McVeigh.

He took him by the arm and they started toward the jail elevator.

"Well," McVeigh asked, "do you have any idea when I'll be going to court?"

"No," Cook said. "But it'll be sometime today."

Haynes was left sitting there. "They took him upstairs so fast," she recalled. "Then everybody kept saying he was the bomber."

The sheriff's phone rang again. This time it was the FBI, which placed a federal hold on Cook's instantly famous prisoner, Inmate No. 95-057. Cook was back downstairs in his office. All day long he would be up and down the courthouse building; all day his phones would be ringing.

He shut down the jail telephones and set up a security perimeter around the courthouse square. Gibson conferred with Judge Allen and the judge decided it was best to proceed as scheduled, so they brought McVeigh down a second time and escorted him into the courtroom, alone, without a lawyer.

Gibson and McVeigh approached the judge's bench. Gibson was nervous. He wanted to be as far from McVeigh as he could be. As the session began, the prosecutor could not help but study the man standing next to him. He's one cool customer, Gibson thought. I've never seen anyone so unreactive. So military-like. He's a void. Not macho; not tough-guy. Just no reaction at all.

By now everyone in the courtroom, and almost everyone in the courthouse, and even some among the crowd that was forming outside realized that McVeigh faced considerably graver problems than these piss-ant misdemeanor gun and traffic charges. But in the courtroom all of them, Judge Allen too, carried on as if nothing at all were out of the ordinary.

The judge asked McVeigh if he would be able to secure a large bond.

"I'm unsure," he said. "I only have a couple of grand cash. I don't know about a bond. I don't know what to do."

Other concerns? the judge asked.

McVeigh said he was confused about why he had been charged with both carrying a weapon and carrying a concealed weapon. "It looks like a doubling up," he said. "Isn't that the same thing? I was carrying a weapon and it was concealed."

"Thank you," the judge said. "You may very well have a point, but I don't know without getting into the facts of it, and it may be something that you would want to talk with your counsel in regard to."

Gibson requested a total bond of $5,000. "Mr. McVeigh was born in the state of New York and in visiting with him just prior to court, says he has a mailing address in Michigan, but that's not actually a residence," the prosecutor told the judge. "According to what he told me before court, he has no residence at this time. He's traveling."

The judge turned to McVeigh. "Where do you presently live, sir?"

"I have a mailing address of Michigan."

"Michigan, okay. Are you presently employed, sir?"

"No."

Judge Allen mentioned the high bond recommended by the prosecutor. "Mr. McVeigh," he said, "do you have anything you wish me to consider in regard to bail?"

What had brought him here? Almost twenty-seven years old, a typical American kid from a middle-class background, a decorated army veteran and a hero of the Gulf War, and now this. What had gone wrong? He had never been arrested before and certainly had not seen the inside of a jail cell. He had spent the last two days with three other male inmates, cramped inside a concrete-walled tank containing four metal-frame beds and a commode. Now he was standing before a judge and was keenly aware of the commotion building up all around him.

In the past he could always find a way out of scrapes and other minor troubles, matters as small as lying about his name or where he lived or what he did for a living. He was good at things that did not matter, like cheating motel owners when he lied about how many would be staying overnight. He was persuasive. At the last motel he had stayed in, up the interstate in Kansas, he had talked the owner down eight whole dollars because it was Easter weekend and she found him to be a pleasant and nice enough young man. That was something he had learned to do a few years ago, a talent he had discovered selling firearms and other weapons on the gun show circuit. He could turn on the charm when he had to.

"Just . . . just that I've never tried to do anything as far as illegal in any way," he told the judge. "You know, I didn't intend for it to be illegal, and I've never done anything illegal."

"Thank you," the judge said. "I appreciate that."

He set bail at $5,000, and McVeigh was sent back upstairs. Shortly after noon, a phalanx of FBI agents helicoptered into Perry and landed over by the local YMCA building. More teams of government agents were coming. News of the arrest was flashing around the courthouse square. The curious were collecting out front; so were the media, with reporters abandoning their "satellite city" encampment in Oklahoma City and rushing to Perry. Up in his cell, McVeigh was trying desperately to telephone a local lawyer, but he could not get through.

"Why isn't this phone working?" he asked Farrell Stanley, one of the sheriff's jailers.

Stanley wasn't sure what to tell McVeigh. He didn't want to lie, but he also didn't want to admit that his boss had ordered them shut off.

"Guess they're out of order," he said, shrugging.

McVeigh gripped the phone receiver hard in his hand and smashed it into the cradle on the jailhouse wall. "That's the only time I ever saw him show emotion," Stanley remembered later. "He slammed it down like he was mad."

Emotions were pouring through the young man. His first concern was his safety. He hated the national government and he despised federal law enforcement. He believed that if the FBI was coming here, as surely he knew they were, he would never be safe. Ever since his final days in the army, when he washed out of a once-promising future as a career soldier, he had learned to mistrust the government he had once served so proudly. After several years of reading extremist propaganda and staying up to listen to the vitriol of the fanatical right on late-night shortwave radio, he had heard plenty of horror stories about the FBI. Phony confessions. Broken promises. Trumped-up charges. Torture.

He had for some time believed that the government in Washington planned to disarm the American public through gun control, particularly the dreaded Brady bill, and turn the United States into some kind of a dictatorship. And then the twin evils of law enforcement abuses at Ruby Ridge, Idaho, and Waco, Texas, aroused his anger, and he was convinced that when the FBI came calling, no man was safe, not even behind the four walls of his own home. He was so certain of this that once, while living in a small house in the Arizona desert, he kept loaded rifles by his door and stacked wood out front to use as a berm, in case federal agents tried to storm his living room. And he always, always, carried a pistol. But now he was unarmed and defenseless in a county jail in a tiny prairie town, not far from federal agents eager to avenge the dead in Oklahoma City.

McVeigh looked up, and it was Sheriff Cook again. "There's some people who want to see you," he said.

The sheriff brought his prisoner back down the jail elevator and through his lobby and into his own cubbyhole office, and McVeigh saw them—a pair of federal agents with the familiar dark blue windbreakers with the letters FBI printed across the back. Agents James L. Norman, Jr., and Floyd M. Zimms started the conversation. Or tried to.

The room was crowded, and Cook squeezed into a corner. The sheriff's top priority was that no one, McVeigh included, be hurt, and that was a chief concern because, he said later, "there were rumors going around that we had snipers." He strained to look at McVeigh and was amazed that the young man was able to obscure his image, to deny his inquisitors any show of concern about what was happening here. It was the same blankness that had struck District Attorney Gibson when he noticed the emptiness of McVeigh's face, the totally unresponsive look in his eyes, the absence of any human emotion. "I was looking and I didn't see any," Cook recalled.

The FBI spoke first. "Do you know why we're here?" one of the agents asked.

"Yes," McVeigh said, blurting out his words. "That thing in Oklahoma City, I guess."

He cut off any more questions. He wanted a lawyer, he said. He would give only his name, age, and other routine information. He would not tell his place of birth.

"I will just give you general physical information," he said.

The agents attempted to pry him open. "Our investigation has revealed that you have knowledge about the bombing . . ." they said. "We have identified other individuals connected to the bombing. . . . You are the only one who can decide whether or not you want to cooperate."

McVeigh recognized this instantly as FBI entrapment. Where was the advantage in placing yourself in the arms of the enemy? No, he decided. Better to say nothing than to trust the devil. And his concerns were shifting. Now he was no longer even listening to the agents. He seemed instead distracted by the increasingly angry crowd forming outside. He imagined the man who ran the local hardware store with a hammer in his hand, the aproned mother weeping as she thought about her own little ones in preschool, and the beefy farmer in the big blue overalls who had left his fields to "come here for the hangin'."

The three hundred people outside were getting noisy. Many of them knew somebody who had been hurt or killed in the bombing in Oklahoma City, where McVeigh knew the FBI was going to take him, and they all wanted more than just a glimpse.

He implored the agents, "Take me out the roof."

What do you mean? they asked.

"Jack Ruby," he said. "You remember what happened with Jack Ruby."

He meant how easy it had been for Jack Ruby to get up close to President Kennedy's assassin that day and shoot him. McVeigh had no doubt that the Dallas cops had let Ruby slip into the police garage. He believed in conspiracies—didn't all Americans believe in government conspiracies? Why would anyone trust the government? Why should he expect anything different here?

But the agents assured him that he would be well guarded. Enough people had been hurt or killed already, they said. No one was interested in any more casualties. They meant to assure his safety, but they also meant to assure their own. A rifle shot aimed at McVeigh might hit an agent. Someone else in the crowd could be a friend to McVeigh.

James Adams, the senior assistant special agent in charge of the FBI's Dallas office and a former Marine Corps helicopter pilot in Vietnam, had flown up to Perry with the others, and it fell to him to make a decision. He determined that the roof was not suitable for a chopper landing—there were too many trees and power lines. The best alternative was to use the sheriff's van to transport the prisoner to a helicopter. They could back the van up to a courthouse entrance and walk their man out. But they would have to move fast. "We were concerned about an assault with a rifle,"

Adams said. "And the bulletproof vests that we have don't stop a rifle round. And quite frankly, I didn't think to put a bulletproof vest on him."

Louis Hupp, a senior FBI agent from Washington, stepped forward to take McVeigh's fingerprints. He placed a layer of tape on a countertop, poured out some ink, and with a roller spread out a fine, light-colored film. Then one at a time, beginning with the right thumb, he rolled McVeigh's fingers, knuckles, and palms across the sheet of ink, recording for history the hands the FBI would say had been wrapped around the steering wheel of a yellow Ryder rental truck.

The jailers escorted McVeigh back to his cell, through the sheriff's reception area, where a TV set was showing live pictures of the crowd outside the Perry jail, the reporters speculating about the man inside. McVeigh again tried the phone, but it was still dead. He could lift himself high up on the windowsill to see some of the ground below, but not who was out there. He began ranting to Tiffany Valenzuela, a female inmate from Tulsa sitting in a nearby jail tank.

"I don't know what the deal is," he said. "I don't know what the deal is. . . . This sketch of a guy who bombed the federal building . . . they say it looks just like me. . . . But he's got a double chin and bigger ears than I do. . . . That's not me."

Still trying to peer outside, he hollered across the jail area to Valenzuela and asked whether federal agents in business suits were patrolling outside.

"Be my eyes," he said. "Are there any suits on the roof? Are there any suits outside?"

Valenzuela was annoyed. "If you didn't do anything, you shouldn't be scared," she told him.

"But I might be a Lee Harvey Oswald."

"Just sit down and relax," she said. "I'm sure they got the wrong man anyway."

He breathed deep. "I'm not scared," he said. "I'm not scared right now." But then: "Oh, I'm getting kind of paranoid now. . . . Everybody's out there. . . ."

By midafternoon, Royce Hobbs, an attorney with law offices on the west side of the courthouse square, who had been trying for some time to get in to meet with McVeigh, a man who he knew desperately needed legal help if anyone ever did, was finally allowed in the building. He was permitted inside only after filing a hasty petition with Judge Allen alleging that McVeigh was being held incommunicado. Then the judge granted another short hearing, McVeigh was brought down, and the judge asked the prisoner if he wanted to meet with Hobbs.

"In regards to what?" said a confused McVeigh.

"In regard to what you appeared before me earlier today," Judge Allen said, "on transporting a loaded weapon and carrying a concealed weapon."

McVeigh did not hesitate. "Yes," he said.

Lawyer and client were given a private room; they spoke briefly, and Hobbs presented the standard lawyerly advice: say nothing.

Then Hobbs was gone; McVeigh was alone again.

And now the agents were coming, ready to present him to the throng outside and the rest of the country—a nation in disbelief that the tremendous destructive force in Oklahoma City could come from a deep anger born and nurtured within our borders. McVeigh was handcuffed and his legs were put in irons, and he began muttering to himself. "I'm not scared," he said. "I'm not scared now."

Then he was walked out into the late-afternoon sun and the angry jeers from the crowd. "Killer!" they shouted. "Baby killer!" McVeigh did not appear to hear them. He seemed detached, disinterested, showing neither fear nor remorse, neither guilt nor innocence. He stared straight ahead, his eyes not moving. The nation was watching live on television, and Timothy McVeigh, army veteran, Gulf War hero, the modern revolutionary, gave the United States of America a first-class display of his iron countenance. He gave the thousand-yard stare. He was hurried into a van, then to a helicopter, then to Oklahoma City.

Soon he was on the cover of *Time* and *Newsweek*, on the front pages of national and local newspapers. Who could forget this image? The television news footage of Timothy McVeigh walking out of the Noble County Courthouse was played over and over and over in the years that followed. His was the face of terror.

Chapter Two

Beginnings

When he was young his eyes would sparkle. He had bright blue eyes and lived in far-western New York State, up nearly to Canada, in a small town rich in great open spaces and wild, wonderful woods. In the summertime he would run barefoot through the neighborhood, up Meyer Road and down Hinman Street in little Pendleton, New York. Like all small-town boys he dreamed of someday going as fast and as far as his feet could fly. He knew his friends so well and their parents too that he would just come roaring through their front doors without so much as a knock.

When he was older, in his twenties, his eyes had turned cold. Bitter cold, some said. He smiled less; his dreams were darker. He wore shoes, big black heavy combat boots usually. His boyhood friends had all moved on; he had lost them, and his family too. His father never knew where he was; he seldom talked to his mother. He wrote home only occasionally, came home even less. He wore his hair clipped very short, military-style, in a tight buzz crew cut. He was alone and often, very often, angry.

His change was not swift, but it was sure and constant, and over two decades, his first twenty years, it transformed McVeigh into someone few would have foreseen. Outwardly, in the neighborhood, at school, he was the cut-up kid. He seemed well-adjusted, studious, intent on success.

But his family was breaking apart. Tim's mother began leaving home for long stretches before he was ten years old; by the time he graduated from high school, his parents' divorce was final. His teenage years were troubled with the twin angst of abandonment and raw nights alone at home, and so he entered manhood eager to please others while at the same time unsure how to please himself. He craved attention, and he would find it, but he would never find himself. He grew to distrust authority because he felt that those he had once loved and respected had let him down. When he ultimately left Pendleton, he did not take with him the comfort of his family, his hometown, or his roots. He went alone into the world.

Perhaps it was fitting that he came from a town founded by a man who also hated the federal government.

Sylvester Pendleton Clark led an antigovernment movement in western New York in the early 1800s, a group of people who decided they no longer wanted to pay taxes. Clark was a rowdy fellow, and his followers preferred to be left alone. They settled on Grand Island near the mystical Niagara Falls that separate the United States from Canada. They set up their own government and sought to live in peace as separatists, away from the still-new government at Washington called the United States. The people at Grand Island chose Clark as their first governor.

But their community was short-lived. In 1819, the haven was attacked by a state militia. Their homes burned and their land lost, some in the group slipped north into Canada. But Clark went east. He purchased land again, this time in Niagara County. Ten years after he and his followers first raised their fists against the United States, Sylvester Pendleton Clark established another small community. In honor of his mother's maiden name, he called it Pendleton.

The town thrived because of the Erie Canal. Some of the men who dug its channel stayed on to raise families. A sense of history still hangs over the area, and children here grow up to respect their heritage.

In the days before the Civil War, the community served as one of the last way stations along the Underground Railroad. At nearby Lockport, fugitive slaves paused only long enough to take one final look at the United States in their flight to Canada and freedom. They too were running from a government and a set of laws that they could not tolerate.

Today Pendleton is a predominantly white, Christian, blue-collar community some distance north of Buffalo. But urban sprawl is slowly crowding in, and new houses are claiming the once vast side yards that in past years made endless playgrounds for young children.

Timothy James McVeigh arrived in the ficklest of weather. The day before he was born the mercury hit seventy-five degrees, an unusually warm spring day in 1968. He was born at eight o'clock the following morning, April 23, and by that time it was snowing.

His grandfather was Edward W. McVeigh, a keeper of the rugged individualism of the Pendleton past. The old man had learned to hunt as a boy wandering wide-eyed into the magic of the North Woods. In his teenage years he tamed wild horses on a local ranch. As a man with a new family, he worked as an ice cutter, hauling loads of frozen pond water to the railyards and then helping to hoist it onto refrigerated cars.

Eddie McVeigh was tough and handsome, and he threw both of his strong arms around life. America was his home, the good home, and gladly he gave back to his community the blessings he had received. A proud Catholic, he joined the Knights of Columbus, and he served with the local volunteer fire company. When his wife, Angela, died in 1972, succumbing to multiple sclerosis, he continued to donate his time and energy to the needy and the ill. He drove a van for the Red Cross, and like so many of the men around Pendleton and Lockport, he bowled.

He had two boys, William and James. The brothers grew up with Catholic educations and clean hearts, and they too came to understand that hard work brought good money. It was the 1950s. The two big wars in Europe had ended, and ahead awaited their future. A sense of vigor, of renewed promise, crackled in the air. But where the father was an outgoing man, the son Bill was quiet, introspective, and shy, painfully shy. He served two years in the army, working in the unglamorous motor pool as a truck driver, and then he came home. Unlike his own son, Tim, he seldom ventured far away again. Instead, he slipped on his work pants, picked up his lunch box, and headed off each day to the local assembly plant where they built car radiators. He loved to garden, and he grew shoulder-high corn, big red tomatoes, and zucchini. He shared his bounty with his neighbors and they baked him zucchini bread, and like his father before him, he bowled.

In 1965 he married Mildred "Mickey" Hill. She hailed from Pekin, a burg even smaller than Pendleton, a tiny rural spot near the south shore of the great Lake Ontario. A country girl, she rode horses up and down the wide corn and hay fields that covered the countryside. She met Bill at an alumni party for graduates from his high school. While she was precocious and lively and eager for fun, he was silent and withdrawn. But he managed to summon the nerve to buy her a drink at the school reunion, and when they were married at the Immaculate Conception Church, in another village called Cambria set between their two hometowns, they were surrounded by a large, rambunctious group of family members and friends, good Catholics every one. They honeymooned in the Adirondacks, then returned home to live in a small apartment above a garage in Lockport.

Timmy was their second child, their only son, a boy with pale, mushroomy skin, a long chin, a thin nose, and jug ears. Relatives remembered him for what he did not do: he did not cry, did not fidget, did not whimper. At first he seemed to have his dad's silent demeanor, his father's love of conformity and desire to stay put.

But there also was a generous dose of Grandpa Eddie in the young boy. Just as Eddie's father had taken him along on hunting trips up in the Bear Ridge woods as a boy, he passed on the thrill of the hunt to his grandchild. Tim learned to fish and how to toss a baseball, and later, when the family grew, the McVeighs moved to a single-family home popular throughout the neighborhood for its backyard swimming pool. How American their lives: Dad at work at the plant, or spending evenings at the local bowling alley or bingo parlor; Mom raising the children and also pursuing a career as a travel agent. How American was the way the family ended up: Dad always at work, Mom gone, the children raising themselves.

Eddie McVeigh cast a wide influence on his grandchildren's young lives, his imprint felt at almost every turn of their journey toward adulthood. He lived up near the canal, and there Tim, his sisters, and their friends would run and play and climb the bridges that spanned the slow-moving, ever-churning waterway. His grandfather took them grocery shopping or out to dinner, or over to the Kmart in Lockport to let them feast their eyes on the new line of Star Wars figures. He drove them to Kenan Arena for ice-skating, and they thought him so wonderful when he gladly reached into his big pocket and paid their fifty cents admission. Tim skated while his grandfather and father bowled.

On summer vacations they all drove out to Darien Lake, and each of the kids chose a friend to bring along. Tim invited Steve or Vicki Hodge, or sometimes both of them, and they fished and raced bicycles and camped outdoors. Here he learned to sleep under the sky, to feel the wind in his face, to be alone and beholden to no one.

At home in Pendleton, the Hodges lived across the street, and there they loved to play King of the Mountain. Tim was always the resourceful one. He may not have been the first or the tallest or the best at anything. But he had his own way of getting along—selling gum to neighborhood kids at a quarter a stick, putting on the annual Halloween haunted house, or getting baby-sitting jobs.

"He was a clown, always a happy person," recalled Vicki Hodge. "He went through that awkward stage where his arms and legs were longer than the rest of his body and he was kind of a gangly kid. But growing up, he was always someone who had a good scam going to make a little money."

When the younger kids followed Tim and his buddies around, he came up with a keen idea for how to ditch them: he tied their bicycles high up in the trees. But other times he would delight the younger children. At Halloween he turned his parents' basement into a haunted house, stringing sheets over the pipes and dividing the cellar into secret rooms. He played the tour guide. For a quarter he slowly escorted them through each room until they stumbled upon the great finale—a phantom ghost sliding down the stairs on a hidden string, a trick that never failed to draw wild shrieks from the little children.

"The kids in the neighborhood always thought it was great," Hodge said. "They'd come back a couple of times and we'd always try to figure out another way to change it just a little bit so we could scare them again."

To her, McVeigh was like a second brother. "He lived over there, but he made himself at home with us. First thing he did when he came in our house, he'd go open the refrigerator and help himself. He made himself at home. It was home for him."

If he was not at the McDermotts', he was over playing at the home of his cousins Kyle and Kenneth Kraus. Their mother, Linda, was his godparent, a place of honor to any young boy growing up Catholic. "Tim would stop by and he would never call," she said.

"He'd just stop by and walk in the house and get a can of Coke out of the refrigerator and sit down and we'd chat."

At the Drzyzgas', four houses down Meyer Road, Tim played with their sons too and on holidays, he brought their mother, Lynn, her favorite chocolate-covered candies. Once while putting on a garage sale at his house, he came running over to the Drzyzgas' and presented her with an old tin cup that had a fancy flip lid. He knew that "Mrs. D" collected tins.

"Tim enjoyed running down the road barefooted," she said. "One day he was sitting on the couch and I noticed the bottoms of his feet were very black." She told him he was always welcome, but that he must wear socks in her home. After that, he either came flying down with his socks in his pockets or she kept an extra pair handy. "It became a routine," she said.

In 1977 came the Blizzard, a massive January snowstorm that was fierce even for this part of the cold Northeast. Several people froze to death in Buffalo, found later in their cars along the side of snow-banked roadways. Thousands were stranded at home or at work. Mickey McVeigh, Tim's mother, had gone that evening to a local hotel in Lockport for drinks with friends. The night deepened and the snow fell, and she telephoned home and said she would not be able to make it. So the rest of the family huddled together, and Tim began to learn to adapt to times without his mother.

The blizzard defined the eight-year-old boy. The storm dragged on for days, and afterward few around Pendleton could be sure that they could ever be prepared adequately. Once the snow had let up and the roads were passable, Tim was out with his shovel, digging out his neighbors' cars. Meanwhile the McVeighs began stockpiling canned goods and bottled water and other supplies. The basement, his magical cellar, became a fall-out shelter.

He seemed at ease in his childhood, so much so that even when he reached his teens, he still seemed to enjoy being around children. The McDermotts lived next door, and Tim was a half-dozen years older than their small children, Molly and Paul. "We had Tim baby-sit our kids very often, and he was wonderful," said Elizabeth McDermott. "I mean, the kids loved him because he spent time with them. He played with them. Yes, he was super."

Molly remembered him as "the best baby-sitter we ever had." He was, she said, simply fun. "He would come over and ask what we wanted to do. He would bring all of his plastic aliens over and he would set them up and have wars and pretend they were all going to Mars."

But change was coming, and he would lose his carefree sense of the world. Soon he was no longer Timmy; he was Tim, and the toy action figures of his childhood gave way to something even more special. Grandpa Eddie gave him his first gun, a .22-caliber rifle.

Tim was all of thirteen. His grandfather was a gun collector and Tim the novice, but he was anxious to learn how to fire, load, clean, and store the weapon. Grandpa Eddie taught him to shoot at pop cans. Suddenly here was power, real power. He loved it all, the firepower of the gun, the feel of the handle, the pull of the shot, the tension, the aim, the spark, the smoke, the sting . . . all of it, down to the first click of the trigger and the last squeeze of the finger. It all took him in, filled him with awe, blessed him with purpose. The rifle stock pressed against his shoulder, the barrel squared, the squint of his eye, the glimmer of the target, and then, more than anything, more than bullet or boy, the sound of its voice. Here was true freedom.

Sometimes he brought one of his guns to school, and dazzled the other boys. He bragged about his cool rifle. In a career-day survey at school, when other boys said they hoped to become doctors or truck drivers or simply to follow their fathers into the factory, Tim had other dreams. To the question "What do you want to be when you grow up?" Tim wrote: "Gun shop owner."

His love of guns filled the sudden hole in life at home. Mother was leaving. Even before she met Bill, she had sought the night life, was often out late at parties or at dinner with friends. She kept leaving and returning, uncertain about what to do, creating a whipsaw of emotions for the young boy. Then by the time he was in high school, she was finally gone to Florida with his two sisters, Pat and Jennifer. Feeling deserted, angry, and afraid, Tim would later disown his mother. A bitch, he would tell friends.

Mickey McVeigh saw it differently. "My children had a choice on whether to stay with their father or go with me," she wrote years later to the *Fort Pierce Tribune* in Florida. At that time her son was in terrible trouble and she herself was hounded by the news media trying to gauge what impact her departure had wrought on his personality. "Tim chose to stay with his dad," she wrote.

She also struggled to explain her own decisions in life. "I had a day job with a travel agency and my husband worked swing shift at a local GM factory," she wrote. "He worked six days a week, fifty-two weeks a year with no vacation time. I traveled for my job about every four to six weeks. They were one- or two-day trips. When Tim was eleven, I did leave for six weeks."

Kids can be resilient, and Tim tried desperately to internalize his feelings. But the turmoil at home made it all the more impossible to carry on as the spirited young boy wandering on bare feet through the neighborhood. He felt hurt, and he also felt betrayed.

He tried to be the same. He still played football in the yard, and he still loved the feel of grass between his toes. In the house at night he made up "flashlight games" and wandered through the hallway and bedrooms scaring his father and friends. Now starting high school at Starpoint Central, he brought home good grades, but never really applied himself. He felt at times as if much of the zest had been kicked out of his spirit.

But he was discipline-free, a good kid, and according to Principal Jim Allen, he was awarded an "honor pass" his senior year. It allowed him to meet with other high achievers in the school lobby to study and socialize. He also earned a Regents Scholarship, a hard-to-get step toward college, if he would take it.

While he may not have been the most memorable in class, few forgot him, and many of his teachers from the mid-1980s would recall the struggling, sometimes happy, other times moody student and shake their heads at how he looked so completely un-Tim-like years later, on that spring day in 1995 when he was under arrest and being marched out of the Perry, Oklahoma, courthouse.

Deborah Carballo taught him freshman Spanish; she remembered that he "never shut up." He was a "nice-looking boy, a nice kid. He liked to be liked. You'll never find a person at Starpoint who can say a bad thing about him." Her impressions were that Tim was fairly "well balanced for a child from a broken home." She did not see the obvious signs—the daydreaming, the fatigue, the failing grades that often follow a divorce. But she did notice that his father came alone to open houses at school; she recalled nothing about his mother.

Later, when he was a graduating senior, she helped him pick out a quotation from *Bartlett's* that he felt best summed up his outlook on life. Advancing into adulthood was serious business, she told him and the other seniors. "I warned them that there should be no mention of violence or sex, or no rock-and-roll lyrics. They should pick something that represented their high school career, or something about themselves that they believed in or that reflected their ideas. And we were very strict about this. They could also only pick a certain number of words."

Tim chose nine words. "People are able because they think they are able."

To him, the operative word was not "able" but "think." That word, conjuring up mind-set and dedication and purpose, was what would drive him. Focus, stay focused. Here he was acknowledging the virtues of commitment, hard work, and loyalty to a cause. Think, and it will happen.

"He changed," said Carballo, unable to reconcile the senior yearbook picture with the television image of her former student in handcuffs and leg irons in Oklahoma. "He looked different. He wasn't the same. He looked like something bad had happened to him."

Carballo thought that Tim's younger sister Jennifer was someone who "had a chip on her shoulder." To her, Jennifer was "rebellious, angry, argumentative . . . a piece of work." Once, she said, Jennifer became unmanageable over what she wanted for her picture in the school yearbook. She preferred a "glamour shot," but that would violate school policy, and Carballo told her no. So Jennifer insisted that a blank space run where her picture belonged. She seemed to like that idea; maybe because it was different, but certainly because it was rebellious.

Carballo later told the FBI that she could think of only five Starpoint students who over the years showed some sign of imbalance and who might have gone on to be involved in "something of this sort." But Tim would never have come to mind. "Jennifer was more likely to do it than Tim," she said.

At school, where other kids doodled in their notebooks, he drew guns. At home, he collected comic books and hoped one day to resell them and pay for college. John McDermott, the father of Molly and Paul, knew a man who ran a comic book store, and he took Tim down there one day to explore whether he too might want to become a small businessman someday. He could be independent and work for himself. "They hit it off quite well," McDermott said. "He was buying comic books for his future."

His mother gone from the home, his father always away at work, often on the night shift, the teenaged Tim sought comfort in his own pursuits. His father would later be surprised to learn how captivated his son had become by firearms and exotic weapons, and how he threw himself into the art of knowing how best to make it on your own. It grew into an obsession; Tim would always be prepared.

Along with his comic books, he began collecting magazines like *Guns & Ammo*. He fantasized with his friends about a World War III, and they put together their own survivalist team to weather the atomic holocaust they were sure was coming. Tim told his father that a "big package" was going to be delivered to the house. A day or two later, it arrived—two plastic fifty-five-gallon barrels—and Tim stacked them along with other materials in the basement. Bill McVeigh was perplexed. "That's when I realized he had this cabinet, and he had all this stuff," he said in one of his rare interviews, this one to ABC News. "He had gunpowder in there, whatever he thought he needed. If everything went haywire, he'd have it there. You know, he was into survival."

Bill McVeigh asked his son for an explanation. "What are the barrels for?"

"Water," Tim said. "If we need it."

It was a simple answer; the young McVeigh was thinking even then in the simplest of terms, how best to face an unfair world. But his father never dug deeper. He did not press his son, nor did he peer further into his boy's makeup to see the changes that were slowly taking hold. Had he looked, he would have seen Tim was showing early signs of insecurity. More important, he would have noticed the trademarks of many who end up on the fringes of American society—those who believe in government conspiracies and demon threats, and who trust no one in authority. For them, one makes it through life relying on basic instincts.

As a teenager, Tim McVeigh embraced fantasy rather than accept the reality of the breakup of his parents' marriage. Sometimes he could not move beyond his mother's exit from his young life. To shore up his defenses, he built a fortress in his secret basement world.

Still the question nagged at Bill McVeigh: why did he keep barrels of water down there? "I guess he thought that someday a nuclear attack or something was going to happen," he said. "That was my feeling. You know, he was ready for anything."

Dave Darlak, a high school chum, recalled how Tim threw himself into preparedness. The boys had met in the ninth grade, and later graduated together in 1986 from Starpoint High—the same year his parents' divorce was final. "We used to shoot guns," Darlak said. "If we were at my house, we played basketball. I had an ATV. We'd ride that. A three-wheeler. Just hang out and talk." Later, after high school, they pooled $7,000 and purchased nine acres near Humphrey, New York. It was some fifty miles south of Pendleton, just a small tract on the side of a mountain with plenty of trees and hidden trails. Tim had fancy plans for the wooded property, and he talked openly about how he was going to transform their wooded refuge. "He wanted to build a bomb shelter there," said Darlak. "Concrete blocks. . . . I kind of got the impression that he was afraid of nuclear war."

Tim was easily impressed. Certain movies took hold of him and he would act out their story lines and imagine himself in the center of the plots. *The Last Day* told the story of the effect of World War III on a small town. *Red Dawn* was about a school football team that takes to the hills to battle an invading Soviet army. For a while, Tim began calling himself "the Wanderer," after the old 1960s song by Dion and the Belmonts. He was skinny, and other kids sometimes picked on him. Some called him Chicken. "Chicken McVeigh," they said, a reference to his awkward strut around school. He loved to eat, but he could not gain weight. He dug rock and roll—mostly heavy metal, Van Halen, the Scorpions, the garage-band sound full of throbbing bass and screeching lyrics. Gradually he was trying to open up more, talking to his friends, speaking to his teachers. At his high school graduation, he was voted "most talkative." But the subject of his mother rarely came up, and he led others to believe that he could make it without her.

He did not run from his problems; he chose rather to ignore the fact that all was not perfect in the McVeigh house. Sometimes he showed up at school red-eyed and tired. In his last high school yearbook, he wrote in jest that he made up for lost sleep by napping in class. He wrote in the yearbook that he planned to "take life as it comes . . . buy a Lamborghini . . . California girls."

While in high school McVeigh had worked at a local Burger King. But now he was graduating, and at the end of the Reagan years jobs were not easy to come by. Local employers like Bethlehem Steel and General Motors were downsizing, and could no longer offer steady work to graduating seniors. For many, college—if you could afford it—and the military—if you could stand it—were the available options.

He enrolled at a business college in Williamsville, New York, not far from home. But he found boredom in the classroom, not a challenge, and he dropped out after the first semester. He wanted something quicker, something bigger.

Guns were what most interested McVeigh; they were his passion. He was reading a book called *To Ride, Shoot Straight and Speak the Truth*, a primer on firing a .45-caliber. The work is a classic among gun enthusiasts, used by some law enforcement agencies to teach basic gun-handling techniques. "Knowledge of personal weapons and the skill in their use are necessary attributes of any man who calls himself free," went the pitch on a sales promotion for the book. McVeigh would say it was the most important book of his youth. He began to visit gun stores, to check out military gear, and to pick up extra hunting supplies.

In 1987, a year out of high school, he was issued his first permit to carry a loaded handgun. By now he was spending more time on the wooded tract he owned with Dave Darlak and was becoming proficient at target shooting. He could be spotted in camouflage, running up and down the woods, his woods, firing his guns, a grown boy playing army.

To get the gun permit he needed signatures from several adults, so he hit up the parents of his childhood friends around Pendleton. He turned to Elizabeth McDermott, whom he had baby-sat for when her children were small. Like many still around McVeigh, she thought it odd that he seemed to be making himself so completely different—darker, more sinister perhaps—from the barefoot kid of his childhood past.

"It wasn't so much that I didn't want to sign it for him," she said. "It's just that I didn't see why anyone would want one. But, you know, if Tim wanted me to, I would. I think I did give him a little sermon on my views, but, yes, I did sign it."

The permit got him hired at the Burke Armored Car Service in the Buffalo area. He spotted an ad and went down to the security company office; there he passed a background check and a polygraph test, and, of course, now he had the gun permit. His job was helping to transport large sums of money, sometimes as much as several million dollars in cash. Vincent Capparra, a Burke supervisor, remembered Tim McVeigh as a "good, honest employee."

"He did his job," Capparra said. "He was left to run the truck, and he made all his stops on time, got there and got back, never had a loss in his truck." McVeigh also ran "specials"—so called because they were extra, last-minute runs when a bank might need some cash right away. He was reliable, and he phoned in sick only twice. The only complaint filed against him was from two older workers who were upset about his sometimes playing rock and roll as they moved money around the area in the armored vehicles. "He would turn the radio all the way up and put earplugs in his ears and just drive with the music blasting," Capparra said.

Another time Capparra invited McVeigh out to his house because he was having problems with neighborhood boys throwing ice balls at the windows. The balls were big, with eggs inside them, and the kids were unruly and difficult to catch. So Capparra, McVeigh, and another Burke employee lay in wait one night, hiding in a trench until the boys returned with their ice balls. Then the young men sprang up from the trench and nabbed some of the boys. They decided to scare them.

Capparra held one of the boys pinned to the ground. "Tim came over and he said he wanted to know his name, that he could really blow his house up," Capparra said.

The threat frightened the boy, but left the two young men laughing out loud. "We just thought it was funny, and he was joking," Capparra said. "Just to scare them. And they've never thrown ice balls again."

But other times McVeigh unnerved even Capparra. Once he told him about his wooded lot south of Pendleton, saying that he wanted to build a bunker there. "He was a survivalist," said Capparra. "That's what he told us. He said if they ever blew up a bomb or anything, you know, if we ever were bombed, he would have a place he could put his stuff and be safe."

McVeigh was fascinated by the heavy materials that went into the armored vehicles they drove, especially the concrete walls and the half-inch steel rods that kept the cargo safe. That made for a "good bunker," he thought; maybe he would use similar reinforced materials to build his own fortress out in the woods.

His last months with Burke he worked as a supervisor, but even as a boss, he continued to startle others. A coworker, Jeff Camp, was amazed at young McVeigh's love of guns and preparedness. One day, Camp said, McVeigh showed up at work in camouflage clothing and crossed bandoliers of ammunition. It was another joke, this one played on a supervisor, but it left a lasting impression at Burke. McVeigh was again restless and looking to move on. Working with a loaded pistol hanging from his hip was a dream job for such a gun enthusiast, but he wanted more.

Feeling little encouragement from his family to improve himself, he sought the counsel of others, among them Richard Drzyzga, who also had signed his gun permit application. The father of two boys of his own, Drzyzga wanted to establish a separate paternal relationship with Tim, particularly now that Tim seemed so vulnerable. Tim kept showing up at their house, and Drzyzga, sitting in the living room or at the dining-room table, kept prodding him to take the big step.

"Tim, you've got to do something with your life," he coached him. "You've got to focus. Why don't you join the service, get into the military? It's a perfect solution for you. You like weapons. They can give you all the weapons you want. And you can learn something besides, and maybe you can bring something home and be useful."

At the same time, Dave Darlak showed him an army recruitment brochure and said he was planning to join up. That at last was the trigger; it moved McVeigh to act fast and beat his friend by enlisting first that spring of 1988.

Timothy McVeigh came home one night and abruptly announced to his father that he had no plans to try college again. He said he was through with the security job as well. Nothing at home or in Pendleton held his interest any longer. He told his father he was enlisting in the morning. At daylight he drove to Buffalo, alone, with his birth certificate, Social Security card, and high school diploma in an envelope on the passenger seat. The date was May 24, 1988. He stepped inside the recruiting office and left his childhood behind.

Chapter Three

Bad Company

Posing for his official portrait soon after he entered the army, strong-looking and handsome in his dress uniform, he looked the picture of American pride. It was a glorious point in his life, and as he always did, Timothy McVeigh threw himself into the moment. He arched his shoulders back, held his chin up, and looked squarely at the camera. He did not smile for the photographer—soldiers do not smile. But it was clear he was happy, satisfied with himself: there was no doubt that he had made the right decision. Above all, McVeigh projected confident determination. He was new here in the army; difficulties would surely come his way. But he was prepared; he was ready.

When he left the service three years later, he was covered in a rainbow of recognition. His chest was still thrust forward, and he wore the green crest of the 2nd Battalion, 16th Infantry. His breast displayed the colors of the Presidential Citation, the Unit Citation, and the Meritorious Unit Citation. On his right shoulder was the Big Red One patch, a sign to all the world that he had gone to war as a U.S. Army infantryman. Sergeant stripes graced his arm, and then came more insignia—the Combat Infantryman Badge, a musket on a blue background, showing that he had not just gone to war but had fought there too. Pinned to his front was the Bronze Star for valor, and then the Army Commendation Medal with V Device and

Oak Leaf Cluster, again for courage. And more still: the Army Achievement Medal, the Good Conduct Medal, the National Defense Service Medal, the Expert Rifleman patch, and the school and Southwest Asian ribbons. Finally, he had three service stripes, one for each year he was a member of the United States Army.

In each photograph, standing in uniform and at attention before the American flag, the color of his eyes blended in with the tiny blue splotches of the banner he had pledged to defend against all enemies, foreign and domestic. He seemed one with his country.

From the first day of basic training at Fort Benning, Georgia, Timothy McVeigh relished army life—the grueling hikes, the one hundred push-ups at dawn, the tasteless chow, the crew cut, the backpack loaded with rocks, the black lace-up boots. He loved it all: scrambling under barbed wire, slogging through mud in dirty green camo, firing on the run, yelling out over the flat, treeless, blue-green horizon:

"Kill! Kill! Kill!

"Blood makes the grass grow!"

He was determined to work hard, to do whatever it would take to make the grade. He nurtured a secret goal on those long, hot hikes that continued even after he was transferred from basic training to infantry and tank school at Fort Riley, Kansas. One day, he told himself, he would become a Green Beret, a member of the fabled Special Forces. His childhood fascination with survival tactics and basement hideouts would hold him in good stead when he made his way, and he knew he would make it, as one of the army's elite covert jungle fighters.

But first he must prove himself a soldier.

He advanced quicker than others in his class, making corporal, then sergeant while the rest at Fort Riley were still grumbling about when was the next weekend off. When his army buddies headed out Friday nights to carouse in the local bars, McVeigh often stayed back in the barracks to clean his weapons.

He was not the most athletic, nor the toughest in individual combat, but he was the first and last on the rifle range, and he led the climb up and out of the foxholes, rallying the others to rush the next ridge. He loved living, sleeping, breathing the outdoors, training under the prairie sky and through the tall weeds. He was not afraid of dirt or mud or thorns or brambles. At dusk, McVeigh trooped back to the barracks wearing the thickest coat of dirt, and he left the biggest mud puddle on the shower-room floor. But on inspection day, he was the soldier whose boots sparkled with the best shine.

Even after he was gone, and even before his picture was made famous, he had already left his mark as a soldier; the United States Army remembered Timothy McVeigh.

Just as he had been a trickster as a kid, for a while he ran his own small loan-sharking operation on post, lending cash to other enlistees at high rates. He was able to do so because he saved his money while others spent it on lap dances at the strip bars in nearby Junction City; $50, $100, he had the money on hand. He hoarded much of his cash, spent little, and circulated some around in transactions that brought in more cash, with interest.

But McVeigh—in a world of weapons and armaments—was much more widely known around the post for his deep interest in exotic firearms and assault-style rifles. At the command quarters desk or in the troop recreation hall, he repeatedly was spotted buried in the gun magazines: *Guns & Ammo, S.W.A.T., Gun World, Soldier of Fortune*—he read them all.

He particularly devoured *Soldier of Fortune*. To him it was the handbook for a Green Beret.

The magazine is a bible for the far right, a must-read for the gun lovers of America. Its lifeblood is revealing U.S. military operations and tactics at such remote army outposts as Haiti and along the Korean peninsula. Nearly 100,000 subscribers are thought to take the monthly magazine, which also sponsors a convention and three-gun shooting fest each September in Las Vegas. It is read closely by the CIA and the federal Bureau of Alcohol, Tobacco and Firearms, and in almost any issue they could find articles on thermal warfare in Iceland or the latest on American POWs allegedly still lingering in Southeast Asia.

For McVeigh, who loved guns, loved the army, and dreamed of wearing the black scarf of an army ninja, *Soldier of Fortune* became an adult comic book. But more than that too, because peppered throughout every issue were an ever increasing number of articles criticizing the federal government and advertisements of antigovernment propaganda. He would stay a loyal reader, and eventually he would devour the sensational stories about federal law enforcement abuses at a place called Waco, Texas. He would find ads for publications that revealed the often simple recipes for building homemade bombs.

He also was mesmerized by a book called *The Turner Diaries*, a thin paperback potboiler heavy on racist overtones and long on imagination. It told the impossible story of an uprising of civilian militias that strike back against a U.S. government bent on confiscating the property of the gun owners of America. The book actually landed him in some trouble, and he was chided by his superiors for carrying it around in his rucksack and sharing it with other soldiers on long quiet nights in the barracks.

What he liked about the book was how deeply the heroes felt about their right to carry guns. The Second Amendment was McVeigh's most cherished freedom; soldiers around the company could see that in the young man. He stored firearms in his barracks and in his car and, later, in a small house he rented off-post. "You never know," he told friends. Sometimes he sold weapons to other recruits, or traded one for another, and he was popular for giving impromptu lessons on the proper way to take them apart and clean them.

It was on the rifle range firing those guns during long afternoons of target practice that a friendship took hold with another recruit. Terry Lynn Nichols had come to the service later in life, a dozen years older than McVeigh, and the men of Fort Riley called him "the old man." He had first met McVeigh during basic training at Fort Benning, and then the two of them, along with another army recruit, Michael Fortier from Arizona, were transferred to Fort Riley in Kansas.

Fortier was young like McVeigh, but brash and cocky, and he was in the army only because it was tradition among the men in the Fortier family to join the service; it was expected. He would much rather be at home swilling beer or smoking pot. He did not like the army and he complained of a bad shoulder; he was one of those soldiers just marking time.

Nichols tried to make a go of army life. He hated the structure and the strict authority thing, but he loved the guns and he bonded quickly with McVeigh. Nichols had a wife and a son, and he held deep, harsh feelings about life and his country. He had been through hard times on the family farm in Michigan, and the army now was a last attempt to make something of himself. But it did not work; his wife gave up on him and moved away. Nichols took a hardship discharge, and he left the service to raise his son.

McVeigh would keep in touch. They all shared an interest in survivalism and guns, and Nichols could talk for hours about how he did not trust the government, about how authority in any form was corrupting. McVeigh began to buy into some of it, particularly the talk about the evil gun control lobby and the fear that liberals in Washington had hatched some hidden agenda to disarm the American public. He clenched his teeth at the thought of ever having to surrender his weapons.

Sergeant Bruce Williams followed McVeigh from Fort Riley to the Gulf War, and he rode with him in a modern-day army tank known as the Bradley Fighting Vehicle over the sand dunes of Kuwait, marveling at McVeigh's intense interest in firearms. He was amazed too at his total devotion to soldiering.

"Why did you enlist?" Williams asked him once.

They were alone together, one of those rare, quiet moments when men could talk about the forces in life that had brought them together—here in the middle of the country, on a Kansas parade field caked with the footprints of hundreds of thousands of soldiers who had marched before them.

The two men had very little in common. Williams was several years older. He was not from a small town like Pendleton, but from Jamaica, in Queens, on the asphalt end of Long Island, and he was black. He also was married, and the father of a baby girl. He joined the army not to win medals or become a stealth warrior. He enlisted because of the influence of a strong, loving figure in his life—his mother.

Williams enjoyed the military life so much that he served four years and then reenlisted for another term. It was during his second stretch that he met McVeigh. He wanted to know what made McVeigh such a good soldier. Why had he enlisted?

"I like weapons," McVeigh said. "You know what? I'm quite fond of them."

Williams noticed something unusual about McVeigh. "I remember he used to walk around without a sling on his weapon."

Most soldiers, Williams too, hoisted their rifle sling over the shoulder and carried the weapon across their back. More comfortable that way; goes easy on the march too. It may look kind of slouchy, but who said war was pretty?

So on another summer march Williams sidled over to McVeigh and asked him, "Tim, where is your sling?"

"I don't have one," McVeigh said. "I took it off so I can't carry it on my back."

Okay, so McVeigh was lazy, Williams thought. Or just trying to be noticed.

Perhaps McVeigh sensed that his friend still did not understand. "An infantryman always carries his weapon in his hands," he explained.

His biggest weapon was the 25mm cannon atop a Bradley Fighting Vehicle. He was training with a tank crew too, learning to ride the armored horse. In a combat situation, the gunner sits in the pivotal position above the Bradley. "It's what we like to call putting steel to steel," said Staff Sergeant Robert Daniels. "Fire and hit the target, whatever he's aiming at. He's got to be able to hit fast and quick, and kill it quick and get gone and search for another target."

The main goal of a gunner was to score one thousand points on the weapons test. Gunners were scored for alertness, fire commands, timing, discharge, targets, and accuracy—a whole range of abilities. A score of one thousand brought a Top Gun status. McVeigh made Top Gun in several shooting contests. Of fifty-six gunners at Fort Riley, McVeigh outshot them all.

Those who soldiered by his side would never forget his enthusiasm.

"Tim shined. He was motivated. He was better than other soldiers. He was a top-notch soldier," said Williams.

Said Captain Jesus Rodriguez, "He did what he was told. He anticipated what had to be done. He took pride in his work. He had a genuine care for how we looked in front of the company."

"He was an outstanding soldier," said Sergeant Charles Johnson. "He stood out among the entire company. Everybody spoke highly of him, and everybody took notice."

It was more than show. As his stomach hardened with sets and more sets of sit-ups, so too did his resolve. Let's go another mile, boys. Let's take another hill. "He was what we call high-speed and highly motivated," said Johnson.

In the military world, most spoken praise is reserved for the entire unit, not any one individual, and such commendations for a single solder are exceptional. "He didn't get into the kinds of trouble that a lot of young soldiers get into," Johnson said. "He really liked what he did when he was in the army. It's very obvious because there are a lot of people who don't like what they're doing."

So intense was McVeigh the soldier that some considered him bizarre and overbearing. Others thought him an aberration, some kind of Audie Murphy throwback, a Sergeant York for the nineties. He was certainly a loner, and that can be a problem in an army unit that is built on team cohesiveness. First Sergeant Major Bob Harris recalled occasionally chastising McVeigh when he caught him alone on weekends at Fort Riley. "I told him to get out of the barracks," he said. "He was there on Saturdays and Sundays inspecting the equipment and wall lockers to make sure that everything was correct."

As he was promoted, eventually making sergeant, he took an increasing interest in those whom he commanded. He was barely in his twenties, but already a father figure to the men in his group. Many of them had come into the service with him, they were his age and his class, and now he was their leader. He commanded respect, and he was loyal in return. That was the hinge, his basic belief about life: give good, and good will be given back. He led by example, and he taught the men in his squad—as many as fifty soldiers by the end of his enlistment—what he had learned just a short time ago in high school. Think that you are able, and it will be done. Above all, stay focused.

As a leader, he worked at not being overly harsh. Attention, notice, appreciation—those were values McVeigh had sought most of his young life. If he held them dear, so too must his men.

McVeigh was increasingly sure that he had found his life's calling in the military. He expected to grow old with the army, expected that the government would support him and, should he marry, his wife and children. "Tim and I both considered ourselves career soldiers," said Specialist Ted Thorne. "We were going to stay in for the twenty-plus years, hopefully make sergeant major. It was the big picture of retirement."

At Fort Riley, the home of warrior legends, where names like Custer are still revered and men are famous for their accuracy on the rifle range, McVeigh made his own reputation. He was called Top Gun, the Man, the It, the Top Dog of the Company. He could shoot well, and ultimately he won one of the most vaunted positions on the post—he was the lead gunner on the Bradley Fighting Vehicle assigned to the first platoon. In the army, he had found stardom.

His written evaluations were superb. Page after page in his army jacket was covered with exceptional ratings. He "displays absolute loyalty to superiors and to the unit . . . and a high degree of honesty, loyalty and integrity." He "inspires soldiers to win. Mission is always first." He was, according to his superiors, "an inspiration to young soldiers."

Everything was looking up. His army career was moving faster than even he could have hoped. So he applied to the army's Special Forces training facility at Camp McCall in North Carolina. He sent in the paperwork because he now was ready to make the leap, to move past the world of army grunts and into a new phase in his life's work. He wanted to wear the green beret, just as he had promised some of those at home in Pendleton. This was the summer of 1990, he was twenty-two now; what better time to make the cut and move upward? He thought he was able, and so he could do it.

Then came the war.

Saddam Hussein invaded Kuwait, and the United States began mustering in Desert Shield to push him back into Iraq. McVeigh, the lead gunner in the first platoon, was shipped overseas.

He would now have his chance to prove his worth, but if he could have chosen, he would have opted for the Green Berets over the ground war in the Persian Gulf. He did not seek combat glory; rather, he saw himself behind the scenes, the unsung soldier, the night ranger. But he had not heard back from Camp McCall, and now there was a war to fight, what his friend Williams called the test of being "an American."

"Even if at first it didn't seem like a war," Williams said. "We kept getting messages from the government that everything was okay. They told us they had Saddam on the phone and were working things out."

But McVeigh was going; he was sure of that. So positive was he that on leave from the army before heading out to the Saudi desert, he went home to Pendleton and told his friends about what he faced in the weeks ahead.

One stop was at the Drzyzgas'—Richard, who had encouraged him to join the army, and Lynn, his replacement mother, the one he gave chocolate candies and the little tin with a flip lid. He was devoted to them, and he was eager to share his excitement, his apprehension too. There was no oak tree in their yard, so the Drzyzgas wrapped yellow ribbons around a large maple. Lynn told no one in town who it was for; she and McVeigh shared the secret.

He came by their home one evening in the crisp early fall of western New York. There they visited, as on so many days gone by now, and he told them that soon he must return to Fort Riley. Then it was off to a staging area in Germany, and from there, Saudi Arabia. He returned to Pendleton only to drop his car off with his father, he said, because he did not want to leave it unattended while he was in the Middle East. And now as he looked around the Drzyzga home, the scene of so many pleasant childhood memories, his emotions began to upstage his tough, warrior facade.

"There was a serious tone about him at the time," Richard Drzyzga recalled. "Serious because he was telling me about how he had to go and rearrange his will. You know, make sure that he was in order, and they were talking about the insurances and everything else. And they had meetings about some of his guys weren't going to be coming back, and that kind of concerned him, although he was trying to be brave, and he kept a stiff upper lip."

As he was leaving, Lynn Drzyzga followed him out on the porch. She wished him well.

"How hard this must be for you," she said.

She sat on the front stoop, and as he started down the stairs, he suddenly turned and looked back up at her parting smile.

"Mrs. D," he said, "I'm coming back in a body bag."

"No, you're not," she said. "You must get those thoughts out of your mind."

Through her tears she could see his. When she looks back on that day, it still touches her deeply. "He hugged me, and he walked away very slow. And it was just like my own son was leaving at that moment."

In January 1991, the men of Task Force Ranger, Charlie Company, 2nd Battalion, 16th Infantry, were flown from Kansas to Saudi Arabia. Their mission: liberate Kuwait. It would be a short war, not a particularly bloody war, but combat nonetheless, the first real smoke and bullets since Vietnam. It would be a war remembered for how quickly it was over, whereas Vietnam was America's longest. Also unlike Vietnam, American soldiers would come home heroes.

McVeigh sat atop a Bradley Fighting Vehicle, a million-dollar troop transport. The men called it the steel coffin, though it was built of aluminum. If the pale-green box took a direct hit with the hatches closed, the men inside would be incinerated. Should the gunner miss . . . should the gunner not react . . . should the gunner forget . . .

Sergeant Timothy McVeigh held the lives of a half-dozen men directly in his grip. Where once he had fired at trees on the old wooded lot, now he was belted down at a 25mm cannon that shot armor-piercing shells. He commanded enough firepower to blast through layers of reinforced concrete. When he pressed his forehead against the padded viewfinder, the desert profile lit up in a red glow. He could spot the slightest movement hundreds of yards away. It was video game warfare come alive, Mortal Kombat for humans, Pac-Man in real time.

He had named his Bradley, christening it with a song that he had loved in high school: "Bad Company." It worked as a metaphor for his squad of soldiers, and he had the name painted in big block letters on the side of the tank. Its message was unmistakable. He could plug his Walkman into the Bradley intercom and play his song, his heavy metal, and he could hear the music thump-thumping around in his head as the Bradley rumbled across the desert, pounding upon the sand, his hands always on his weapon, the big weapon.

McVeigh was not scared, nor arrogant, nor particularly bloodthirsty. But he was prepared. He would be the one guarding the crew as they dismounted and inched forward on foot into Kuwait in the ground offensive, searching out enemy Iraqi soldiers in hostile territory this time.

"He was the overwatch, the overseer," said Williams. "While we were on the ground, he had to be ever so alert to see far out in the great distances. He was our eyes and ears."

The Bradley is tight—another six metal seats in the back, two in the hole—and it is very confining. The infantry would sleep in tents on the ground, or up against the Bradley for support. But McVeigh never left his gun parapet.

"He slept in the Bradley," Williams said. It was terribly uncomfortable; a cold steel back, a seat as hard as iron that would not pull down. So McVeigh slept sitting upright. "To be ready," Williams said. "We were in a combat situation. It was a real-world situation."

"The 25mm was really a monster," said Sergeant William Dilly, a fellow gunner. "It was so heavy, but you would have to take the insides out to clean it. It was packed with grease. Over there, the sand was murder. As a matter of fact, we'd even wrap our machine guns in plastic. We tried to keep the 25mm clean too, because we knew there couldn't be a speck of dirt on anything."

Cleaning the giant artillery piece could be a drudgery. Said Dilly, "You would have to take the barrel out, and then you would have to go inside and take the body of it out and then disassemble the body of it to bring the insides out where all the grease and the packing and the chain was. It's a chain gun and you had to keep that greased up. That's where you really get dirty. So it was a long-drawn-out thing, three hours maybe."

McVeigh cleaned his cannon daily, working against the blowing sand and burning sun and struggling to ensure that no piece of his weapon would be less than perfect. He broke it down one part at a time, pulling out the chain with two grease-smudged hands and then plastering it with gobs of more lubricant to keep it mobile and loose. And ready.

The war came for McVeigh in a blistering flash in February 1991. He had been promoted to sergeant just three weeks earlier. Months of gathering men and machines in Saudi Arabia for Desert Shield was now turning into Desert Storm. An intense air barrage of Iraqi positions in Kuwait would be followed by the ground attack. He was part of a massive troop movement lunging across the border. In one of the first strikes of the ground offensive, his company and dozens of others swept the soft brown horizon, forcing thousands of Iraqi soldiers from their dug-in positions, bringing them up out of the sand either to surrender or to die. For a hundred hours the action raged, and when it was done, several thousand enemy soldiers were either dead, many buried alive as the Bradleys and other U.S. war machinery rolled over them, or popping up out of the sand, their hands waving little white flags.

His viewfinder scanned the red mist of oil wells burning in the desert wind. The sky was aflame day and night, and below it, the enemy continued to rise to the surface. Amid the squawk of radio traffic, the drone of the tanks and the Bradleys in front and behind

him, the rush of the music, the *Bad Company* pushed on, solemnly
conducting the business of America—eliminating the enemy.

Once he keyed into an Iraqi soldier some two thousand yards off
on the horizon, locked in his position, and set the trigger. Then
McVeigh blew the man's head off. He targeted another Iraqi soldier
and killed him with an equally impressive burst of fire.

PFC Royal Lamar Witcher, Jr., the radio transmitter operator on
McVeigh's Bradley, was among the crew that would dismount as
the tank pushed forward to smash the enemy's defensive lines. Like
McVeigh, he was amazed to see so little resistance, and how
quickly the enemy surrendered in droves.

"Some were in the trenches," he said. "But for the most part they
were all out and walking in groups toward us with their hands up
with white flags and just giving up. I think it kind of shocked most
of us. We had thought that they were our enemies, and then for us
to encounter something like that with a mass of people giving up."

But some Iraqi soldiers held tough in their bunkers. The American tank gunners greeted those who did resist with cannon fire.

Pushing across the desert's shifting floor, Witcher looked up at
the figure perched above the Bradley. There was McVeigh, the gun
lover, the all-day soldier, the oddball back home at Fort Riley, but
nevertheless the only one the crew would have wanted in that position behind the giant gun. He was their safety, Witcher thought.

Through the din of tank treads slewing in the sand and the sand
itself whirling into their faces, Witcher could see the panic of those
among the enemy trying to fight back. They did not have to shout;
they did not even have to raise their voices. Their wild eyes, their
gaping mouths, their outstreched hands said it all. Witcher, walking along the Bradley looking up at the gunner, could hear McVeigh
shouting.

"I got 'em!" McVeigh screamed.

"I got 'em!" he screamed again.

But McVeigh would not remember the war as some fast-action
shoot-'em-up. Five years later, in a prison cell in Oklahoma, he saw
war differently. By then the gunner's viewfinder was gone; there
was no more red-tinted vision, no more rose-colored confidence.
Life was as black and as white as the bars of his cell.

"We were falsely hyped up," he said in a letter to freelance writer
Jonathan Franklin, who has written extensively about McVeigh's

war exploits for *Spin Magazine* and other publications. "And we get there and find out they are normal like me and you. They hype you to take these people out. They told us we were to defend Kuwait where the people had been raped and slaughtered. War woke me up. War will open your eyes."

He remembered the surrendering Iraqi soldiers. "They were regular guys. I felt the army brainwashed us to hate them."

The American infantry had been warned that their own casualties that first day of fighting could reach as high as 80 percent. It fell to him, Sergeant McVeigh, to steady his Bradley crew. "I knew what everyone was thinking, that you could die tomorrow. I decided to bring it out in the open, just so people wouldn't be frozen by their fears. Everyone was pretty much numb to it by that time, I guess."

And then the mission was go, and the Bradleys were rolling. "No one knows what the feeling is like to know that any second you could be hit by a bullet or shell from indirect fire or from a tank. In that one second without even seeing it, you could be dead. Basically, you are just working yourself out of all emotion, saying that if it is going to happen, it is going to happen. At the same time you are keyed up beyond comprehension, observing your environment around you like never before."

Finally, combat. "The first day we fired one shot into a bunker, actually burned and destroyed a tank behind it to get them to come out, and as soon as we did, they raised their white flags and started marching out. The second day we hit a unit that was ready to resist, but we broke their backs quickly."

From Saudi Arabia, his letters back home to the old Pendleton neighborhood were equally descriptive, although what was missing was the blood and the dying. He did not write about dead soldiers; he left that part out. McVeigh saw war as a total experience, one single panoramic scene encompassing color and noise and human suffering. In his letters, he could easily blend jokes about cookies from home with the faces of starving Iraqi children.

"This is definitely the 'real stuff' now," he wrote to Jack and Elizabeth McDermott. "We had an alert yesterday; everyone had to get into their chemical protective gear and wait. I'll write more later; and send you some sand!"

When the McDermott children whom he had baby-sat sent him cookies and, of course, comic books, he wrote the family again.

"The first thing I thought when I opened the cookies was 'Oh man, Jack made these!' I guess I could give them to the enemy, then they'd all get sick and couldn't fight a war! . . .

"Right now we're 17 miles deep into Iraq, sitting in a small farming community. A major 6-lane highway runs through here, and we've set up a blockade to deter the movement of supplies from south to north. It's not like a movie, where a car crashes through the middle of two others to get through. Try crashing a Toyota pickup through two 46-ton M-1 tanks. Not pretty.

"Anyway, we've got these starving kids and sometimes adults coming up to us begging for food. Because of the situation, we can't give them any. It's really 'trying,' emotionally. It's like the puppy dog at the table; but much worse. The sooner we leave here the better. I can see how the guys in Vietnam were getting killed by children. Thank God this isn't that way."

He also wrote Vicki Hodge.

He bragged about the small number of "kills" to American fighting vehicles in the short war, and he said his battalion had returned to Charlie Company headquarters, bringing him much-needed relief as a young army supervisor. "The officer-induced stress is gone," he wrote, "but the same old bullshit is back."

Comfortable writing to his childhood friend, he began indulging in vulgar descriptions. At one point, he lost his concentration ("dropped my damn pen in the sand!"), but he carried on, seemingly unconcerned about the harsh language he used with a female. For McVeigh, never known to be at ease in social graces around women, it was a sign of his awkwardness with the opposite sex.

He wrote that his supervisor recently had gone home on emergency leave, and that he took it upon himself to start handing out army-issue Meals Ready to Eat packages to the hungry children. "I'm in charge of the Bradley for the rest of the time we're over here. Since I'm in charge, I gave the locals 6 cases of MREs before we left. Is that good or bad? you ask! I just hope they don't get sick eating something their stomachs aren't used to. I know they'll definitely be farting a lot!"

But it was not all silliness. In another letter to Hodge, McVeigh anguished over how tough it was to sort through his guilt, saying how he hated Saddam Hussein because he made him shoot soldiers whom he—McVeigh—felt did not want to fight at all.

"Saddam . . . Saddam, if he ever showed up . . ." McVeigh railed. "He didn't, chickenshit bastard. Because of him, I killed a man who didn't want to fight us but was forced to."

At the close of the war, a very popular war, McVeigh had learned that he did not like the taste of killing innocent people. He spat into the sand at the thought of being forced to hurt others who did not hate him any more than he them. That was how he felt then, believed then.

His supervisor, Jesus Rodriguez, then a lieutenant, recalled a night when McVeigh was pulling security duty. "He was one of the better soldiers I could rely on not falling asleep," Rodriguez said. "Because one of the things I pitched to my guys is you stay alert, you stay alive. You don't put your guard down until you're back on neutral soil."

But this night, Rodriguez could not sleep. Around three in the morning, he rose and drove out to sit with McVeigh. The moon hung over the desert ground, the air was calm. It was a good night to talk, and to listen too.

"Hey, sir, what are you doing here?" McVeigh asked.

"I just feel like pulling security with you."

"Why's that?" McVeigh said. "You're an officer."

"That doesn't mean anything," Rodriguez told him. "I'm a soldier just like you. When the bullets are flying, we've got to rely on each other. If you don't mind, I'll just sit here for a while."

They talked a bit longer. The ground war was over; now it was mop-up time, waiting for the final surrender ceremony and the trucks and armor to be loaded up and the long trip home. McVeigh would be returning with a chestful of colors—the Bronze Star and a host of ribbons and other medals. With the moon as his lamplight, he could see far out into the vast flatland. He had joined the army not to fight other men's wars, though fight he did. He had enlisted rather to accomplish his other goal, to become a Green Beret. Still no word yet on his application, though. Had the army forgotten him out here in this desolate landscape?

Suddenly there was radio chatter, some kind of Red Cross message, and that meant trouble for someone. The two men drove back to the command tent. "It was ironic," Rodriguez remembered. "That day we were trying to figure out when people were going home and everything. So we drove back in the dark and I was expecting to receive a Red Cross message for one of my soldiers. But what happened was the Red Cross message was for me, and I found out my brother-in-law was killed."

His brother-in-law had died in a paragliding accident. "He was really close to me. It was like the brother I never had. And the problem I was facing was that I was ordered to go back home, and I was pretty distraught, just pretty upset, and the commander told me to go home."

Rodriguez returned to his vehicle with McVeigh and another soldier. But it was McVeigh whom he would always remember that night, McVeigh who was "just really compassionate."

Speaking of it today, Rodriguez still struggles for words. "Good soldiers are judged by the buddy system, and when a soldier acts upon his own accord and he just . . . What he did was he just grabbed all my gear, I mean, and this is in the pitch dark, you know, and he grabbed my stuff and he gave it to me, and I had to give him my weapon, all the sensitive items. And it was the first time he . . . he just kind of . . . you know, he . . . Sympathetic, you know; he was just there. He showed he really cared."

Rodriguez left the Gulf. He also filed an engagement report outlining his command's activities in the war, and in those pages he singled out McVeigh for praise. "His faithful execution of the mission was a display of true professionalism," Rodriguez wrote. "His performance showed confidence, involved sacrifice, set the example for others to follow," and, he added with emphasis, "reflects great credit upon himself, 1st Infantry Division, and the United States Army."

Sergeant McVeigh, his army boss said, "energetically maneuvered against Iraqi defenses, showing the true character of an American fighting soldier."

After war, peace. At a ceremony on March 3 to negotiate a cease-fire, McVeigh and his unit were honored with the privilege of providing security for General Norman Schwarzkopf as he met the Iraqi command at a makeshift tent city. He stood in line to greet the general, his helmet strapped tightly onto his head, his pocket camera in hand. He was enjoying the greatest moment of his life. He felt the pride of America. Later he developed his snapshots— there he was in the honor guard for the general. There also were photos he had taken of dead Iraqis.

Ecstatic, he wrote home that he had even met NBC anchorman Tom Brokaw. "Did you see me on the news!" he asked. "They filmed me shaking hands with Gen. Schwarzkopf!"

But that was not what excited him most. On March 28, at last, he received the long-awaited orders to report to the Selection and Assessment Course for the Green Berets. But things were happening too fast; he worried that he was nowhere near ready. He had been laboring in the Gulf under grueling desert conditions for the last three months. Physically, he was spent. His field gear was shot, and his trusted combat boots had recently been replaced with new, still-unbroken-in boots. He was not alone; many of the soldiers were frazzled. Some, like his fellow gunner William Dilly, had lost as much as thirty pounds.

"We had no facilities to do real PT," Dilly said of the lack of physical training in the desert. "We would do jumping jacks and try, but we couldn't run. We could do no running because of the sand. We would do approximately fifteen minutes of PT in the morning. So he was not in very good condition."

McVeigh felt he had no choice, though; now was the time to go. He packed up and moved out of the Gulf, and on April 5 he arrived at Pope Air Force Base in North Carolina. He headed for Camp McCall.

There he joined several other recent Gulf War veterans trying to make the Special Forces. But all of them were worn thin, and they were wary of what lay ahead. Once, McVeigh recalled, he and other Desert Storm soldiers were pulled from a training formation and asked if they wanted to cash out, maybe try this some other time after a long rest. Maybe return if they could get their bodies back in shape. But one of the Gulf War veterans insisted that they all were ready now, and so none of them raised their hands in surrender. None quit.

But by his second day, McVeigh feared that he could not continue. His feet were sore, his head jumbled, his will drained. The first part of the course had been a lengthy physical examination, followed by brief psychological tests. There were sentence-completion exams and an adult personality review.

Next the soldiers were ordered to complete an obstacle course— something McVeigh felt he did well. After lunch the volunteers formed up and were told they were about to start out on a forced march. They were not told where, or how long, or even when they would be back. They were ordered to fill their backpacks with whatever necessities they thought they could use, and told that their packs had to still weigh more than forty-five pounds when they returned—whenever that might be.

McVeigh packed regular infantry gear and tossed in several extra pairs of socks. His feet were killing him. He poured sand into ziplock bags to meet the weight requirement. Then he and the other applicants headed out.

Five miles into the march, his new boots blistering his feet, he paused at a brook to refill his canteen. The water was cool and refreshing; he drank and poured water down the back of his neck. The forest was lovely. Its trees were large and comforting, offering him shade and relief from the relentless demands he had placed upon himself. The trees would be here another thousand years for all the soldiers who were yet to come passing by. High above, the leaves were still.

It was then that he knew it was over, that he could not go on. He had been mentally prepared, but physically it was too much. It was so quiet in there; and in the silence he told himself that the army had not given him the time he needed to complete the training. He acknowledged to himself that his six feet three inches of bone and tissue, his big hands and iron countenance, were just not enough.

He walked back to camp, dejected, hurt, confused, asking himself why the army had let him down. And he dropped out; he saw no other recourse. He filled out a voluntary withdrawal form, and he wrote, "I am not physically ready, and the rucksack march hurt more than it should have."

He was gone before his written exams were ever reviewed or graded. He returned to Fort Riley that spring, and he continued to advance in gunnery. He scored another one thousand perfect points on the 25mm Bradley cannon, and he once again was awarded the Top Gun title.

But what were more prizes when he had already gone to war? Once he had been the lion in his unit, the man in the gun turret, the baddest of the company; but he had failed the one test that really mattered. Special Forces was so elite, so exclusive, that he knew second chances were not likely. All he had worked for, had hoped for in an army career, had vanished.

Bruce Williams saw the change. He no longer thought McVeigh resembled the statue of "Iron Mike" at Fort Benning, the model infantryman gesturing his comrades onward. McVeigh was no longer the follow-me guy.

"I'd hang out and go to the parties and drink Budweiser," Williams said. "Tim just stayed in his room playing Nintendo."

In August, he moved off base, something he normally would never have done. He left the army family, as they called it, and he rented a small house with Witcher in Herington, Kansas, some forty miles south of Fort Riley. It fit him because he now felt half the soldier he had been. He still had his guns, the ones he had bought for his own personal use, but the house was tiny and his bedroom had but the barest of essentials. There was a bed and a dresser, and little else. He pinned a poncho liner over the window for a curtain, and a laundry bag sat rumpled on the floor. He no longer slept on army-issue sheets or under a green wool blanket. He instead bought children's sheets with orange pictures of Garfield the Cat—something to cheer him up. His uniform hung limply from a peg on the wall.

At work—and it was work now—he spent more time hanging around the post rec center, more time devouring the gun magazines. He began to visit Junction City, not to check out the bars but to stop in the gun stores and pawnshops. He made no secret that he would be out of the army by the year's end; nor did he hide his feelings any longer about his family. He began to openly deride his father's dull life as a factory worker. His mother he dismissed curtly. "A bitch, a whore," he said.

He still enjoyed mornings on the rifle range, alone with his weapons. Other friends were packing up or had already left. Terry Nichols, the "old man" in the company, had gone home to Michigan; Michael Fortier had returned to Arizona. Many of those leaving the service felt no better off than their first day at boot camp, no more prepared for adulthood and a civilian job than the day they enlisted.

"The war ended so quickly and then the drawdown started," said Master Sergeant James Hardesty. He had served in the Gulf War with McVeigh, and he had been badly injured.

"They were just dumping people left and right, trying to get people out," he said. "Some people were getting early-outs, where they

were given severance pay and asked to leave. Some people were just
not given the option for reenlistment. They started a point ratio
system where people couldn't meet the points to stay in. 'Cause it
does get very disillusioning when you go there, you know. You're
sacrificing for your country, and all of the sudden you come back
and you're discarded baggage."

McVeigh loaded up the trappings of his military career—his certificates, his medals, his uniform, his guns—and at Christmas 1991,
he moved back in with his father. He took his old bedroom, at least
until his sister Jennifer came back from Florida and moved in too.
Then he slept on the old worn sofa in the front room.

But he was not yet rid of the army, or the war either. He stopped
by to visit Linda Daigler, his godmother. They sat around her
kitchen table and he talked about sleeping in his Bradley after
pulling work details that could last as long as seventeen hours. "He
felt sorry for the children there because they would be begging for
food," she recalled. "And they were unable to give them food. And
he told me that he had killed an Iraqi soldier at close range."

He was not bragging; she thought he felt some remorse.

Another evening he went over to the Drzyzgas'. Together, they
took the yellow ribbons down from the maple tree, and then they
all went inside and he told them about the war.

Richard Drzyzga, who had encouraged him to enlist almost three
years earlier, would never forget their conversation. "He was telling
about all the action that was going on and the fact that there was a
lot of carnage out there, that the sights that we had on our tanks
and equipment were so far superior to what the Iraqis had, and that
they could actually see through the clouds of burning oil.

"It was virtually a turkey shoot," Drzyzga said. "It was an unfair
advantage. And coming from somebody that was pulling the trigger,
you know, that kind of struck me."

Drzyzga also was touched by McVeigh's vivid memories of the
starving children and his helpless feeling when the U.S. government would not allow him to feed the little ones. Coupled with
that was the humiliation of never earning a green beret.

"I knew that Special Forces was something that he wanted,"
Drzyzga said. "He was disappointed because he really—I guess the
time in the desert from a physical standpoint kind of wore him
down a little bit. Didn't have a chance to recoup his energies or

build himself back up for whatever test he had to go through to get into the Special Forces. And the only thing I knew was that he washed out after a couple of days."

McVeigh left, and in the years that followed, the Drzyzgas would rarely see him again. They stayed in Pendleton while he wandered throughout the country in one old car or another, in search of himself, looking for his place in America. He was out of the army, but he kept the crew cut and the heavy lace-up boots. His love of guns grew, and so did his imagination.

One of his last times to visit the Drzyzgas, he walked up to their front porch and he knocked. He was not barefoot and he did not come charging right into the house; he was not a little boy anymore. He knocked; and when they opened the door, they saw the bright blue eyes and the shiny black boots; they saw a fat wide grin and on his shoulder, where he had placed them for a joke, a pair of white socks.

If he had learned anything in the army, they thought then, hoped then, maybe it was how to act as a grown-up. "Can I come in?" he asked.

Chapter Four

Alienation

By the spring of 1992 he was back in uniform as a private security guard, wearing a single badge on his chest and a small gun on his hip, a dark-colored pistol in a brown leather holster. He wore it high; he liked the feel of it that way. It was good to show off his weapon.

The job was not what he had wanted. McVeigh came home to Pendleton and it seemed as if his old world had shrunk. Many of his friends had moved on. Even David Darlak, who had first shown him the army brochures, had left the service and was painting signs for a living; he soon would open his own sign company. Darlak was doing well, even after spending ten months in the army brig and taking a bad conduct discharge for an alcohol-related accident. McVeigh had visited him in jail, and now Darlak was the one getting ahead.

McVeigh's sister Jennifer came home from Florida, and she soon would try college. His younger cousin Kyle Kraus went to work at Johnson's Country Store, the local gun shop, a job McVeigh would have loved.

Time and his friends had slipped past him; the familiar feel of home and boyhood was no longer there. The house was empty most of the time, but then he had to give up his bedroom for his sister, and the front-room couch did not fit his long legs. He would get up in the morning and head out the door looking for work, but he

could not seem to hit a groove. He took the hiring test to become a
New York turnpike toll-taker, but the state officials over at Albany
never called. He checked out a job with the United States Marshals
Service; that went nowhere.

He took the best position he could find, which was this job with
the Burns Security Company in Buffalo. It was honest, steady work,
a salaried job, and he rose quickly in the company, just as he had in
the army. He was promoted to inspector. He took on assignments
guarding plants and other worksites around the area, even working
a while at Buffalo International Airport. But most of the time he
stood sentry at the sprawling Calspan Corporation, an aerospace
research complex in Cheektowaga, near Buffalo. He would help
man the guard posts at the four plant gates. It meant long hours,
and plenty of boredom.

In the army, on those warm nights in the Persian Gulf, he had
worked security shifts as a company sergeant and dreamed of someday wearing the camouflage of the Special Forces. Here in Buffalo
he was merely a rent-a-cop, clocking his eight-hour shift, sipping
Seven-11 coffee to keep himself awake at night.

He told people that it was not his fault he was back among them
with a regular job, and he blamed the army for the step backward
he had taken. Specifically, he blamed the federal government. From
his first day on the job, he came to work with an attitude.

His most lasting impact was on a fellow guard named Carl
Edward Lebron, Jr. Like McVeigh, Lebron was a conservative man.
Also like McVeigh, he had a great talent for remembering details
and those who played a significant part in his life. He would not forget McVeigh, or the eight months they worked together.

It is through Lebron's recollections that the change in McVeigh
begins to come clear. He would recall how spiffy McVeigh looked
in his security guard uniform, always starched and ironed, his boots
polished. And of course the crew cut. McVeigh rarely talked about
his family or a girlfriend; he was not proud of the first, he did not
have the latter. But what he did discuss, and often, was authority.
He had not had good parental figures at home, the army leadership
had let him down; who was there left to trust? he wondered.

He became increasingly disturbed about the direction of the U.S.
government. It began with gun control and spread into politics;
soon McVeigh was knocking off remarks in a scattergun fashion,

criticizing Washington for some new law or regulation or another government proposal he did not like. Often the two men worked together, holding forth in late-night discussions about the state of America, a pair of young men trying to make sense of the national scene. They would share coffee and rub their hands together and by the morning sun's arrival they would have talked through a broad range of world affairs. The next day, McVeigh would be eager to hash it out again.

As Lebron recalled it, their conversations dealt mostly with "politics, secret societies, some religion and conspiracy theories." McVeigh felt that the federal government had too much power and that federal law enforcement officers were becoming too involved in "police actions."

Sometimes McVeigh would get himself so lathered up that Lebron thought his friend might belong to some secret sect, that maybe he was some sort of a "weird" Freemason. His political views were decidedly "right-wing," no doubt about that. Most of the time, Lebron felt, McVeigh was just trying to impress him, going for the "Wow!" factor, saying anything that won him attention. He might show him a Ku Klux Klan newsletter. He would come to work with a pocketful of gold coins, some printed with an American eagle, others minted across the falls in Canada. Which is more valuable? he would ask. Which is backed by their government?

He talked about unidentified flying objects, and he was convinced that they were real. The only questions were where they came from and what they wanted. "They're from another dimension," he declared.

He worried about Project North Star, a federal task force that coordinated trade and antidrug efforts along the U.S.–Canadian border and had offices in one of the buildings he and Lebron guarded. McVeigh claimed to have seen a document in the building that convinced him the federal government was bringing drugs into this country. He theorized that the shipments were probably making it in through some river on a miniature submarine. The river was "some place down South," he warned Lebron.

But when Lebron asked to see a copy of this document, McVeigh said no. "It can't be copied," McVeigh said. "It's on some kind of special paper."

Once they were working a security gate and Lebron secretly

slipped a microcassette player into the pocket of his windbreaker and taped their conversation. He was growing increasingly concerned about his friend, and he decided the bosses at Burns Security should know more about who they had hired. "I thought something was not right and wanted him to say what he was up to," Lebron remembered. "It was bothering me what he was talking about."

His larger worry was whether McVeigh was still suited to work in the security business. Should he be carrying a gun? It turned out that most of McVeigh's comments on the tape were harmless gibberish, just him carrying on about the government and his belief that "some people" were out to get him.

Who? Lebron asked.

I don't know, McVeigh said. The people at Project North Star maybe.

Lebron tried another approach. After work, he wrote down notes of some of their conversations. He kept them as a sort of road map through McVeigh's shifting psyche.

They talked about secret societies. "I brought in two books on Freemasonry to share with him," Lebron wrote. "We got into a debate on this. It became heated. I was claiming that Freemasonry was behind communism. When I told him this he said, 'Communism!' His face lit up a little and he said it like it was a wonderful thing. He might have been mocking me. But I don't recall him laughing."

They discussed guns, of course, and Lebron wrote that down too. "When talking about the military he mentioned that it would be very easy to rob a base of guns. He said two people could get away with it." McVeigh told Lebron that he had a particular army post in mind where he believed he could score a cache of M-16 rifles.

"There's only one guard on duty," McVeigh said. "And it's not that far from a fence line."

At the end of eight months, he was bragging about heading off for new adventures. When he quit, he told Lebron and others that he had lined up a civilian job painting army trucks in Kentucky. He told them that maybe he was going to rob that army base after all.

There was no job painting trucks, but he quit the Burns Security Company all the same.

"I got to get out of this place," he announced on one of his last days there. "It's all liberals here."

His political evolution—his alienation, really—had begun before he came home from Fort Riley. Some of the antigovernment rhetoric he had picked up from his army friends, Terry Nichols and Michael Fortier. Some of it was born in the barracks, and nurtured in a world of guns and young men.

Mostly, McVeigh's fervor came from *The Turner Diaries*. So mesmerized was he by the two-hundred-page adventure novel that he spent the next several years constantly recommending the book to others, lending it out, selling it, giving it away if he had to. He was its greatest publicist, and if he had written it himself, he could not have better understood its message. Read this book! he would insist. Read it!

At Fort Riley he had given it as a gift to Fortier. Back home in Pendleton, he passed it around to old high school friends.

At Christmastime in 1991, Kyle Kraus received a package from his cousin Tim. It was a copy of *The Turner Diaries*. At a family Christmas party at the McVeigh home, they talked at length about the book, ending up in the basement, that secret hiding place of Tim's childhood.

"Isn't it great?" McVeigh kept asking.

"It's just a very powerful book," Kraus told him. "And it would be very, very frightening if it really did come to this."

McVeigh seemed delighted.

Kraus kept his copy in his second-story bedroom. There it remained for three years, until one spring evening in April 1995 when he walked upstairs and read some of the pages again and, in his own disbelief, feared that some of the story indeed had come true. He telephoned the FBI, and his book—the one his cousin had given him—became Government's Exhibit No. 1 in *United States of America v. Timothy McVeigh.*

The 1978 novel, which has been called the bible of the racist right, was written by William Pierce under the pseudonym Andrew Macdonald. Pierce, a former physics professor, has at various times been linked by authorities to the American Nazi Party and the Christian Identity movement—the latter holding that whites are chosen by God but that Jews and blacks are "mud people," the children of Satan.

Pierce's work of fiction tells of an underground resistance movement that attacks Washington and bombs FBI headquarters. They are a violently racist band, a group of white supremacists who trigger a race war in order to overthrow a United States they believe has become totalitarian. The hero, Earl Turner, believes that federal employees are expendable.

Page 1: "I'll never forget that terrible day. . . . Four Negroes came pushing into my apartment before I could stop them. . . . My first thought was that they were robbers. . . . The one who was guarding me flashed some sort of card. . . . They were searching for firearms, he said. I couldn't believe it. It just couldn't be happening."

Page 37: "With our original plan, we drive a truck into the main freight entrance of the FBI building and blow it up. . . . We can wreak havoc in all the offices. . . . Several hundred people will be killed."

Page 42: "It is a heavy responsibility for us to bear, since most of the victims of our bomb were only pawns who were no more committed to the sick philosophy or the racially destructive goals of the System than we are. But there is no way we can destroy the System without hurting many thousands of innocent people—no way. . . . We are all completely convinced that what we did was justified. . . . Americans have for so many years been unwilling to make unpleasant decisions that we are forced to make decisions which are stern indeed."

McVeigh told Kraus that if the government maintained a stranglehold on the public, then someday it could possibly come to this. If Washington continued to pass repressive legislation, he said, if it continued to intrude into our daily lives, then it someday could trigger a new civil war in America. The people must stand up to a government bent on marching into private homes and confiscating guns.

He gave Darlak a copy when they visited a gun show in the Buffalo area. Read it soon, he told him. Months later, McVeigh still was asking him about the book, but Darlak was not interested. So McVeigh took it back and passed it on to another friend. Armed with his book and his guns, McVeigh sought solitude from the noise of an America he was becoming more and more skeptical about. "We would shoot guns, talk, go out to bars," Darlak said. "We went bear hunting one time."

McVeigh was often spotted hanging out at Johnson's Country Store, looking over the new line of firearms and talking to his cousin Kraus, also a hunter and sportsman. Gun control was a hot topic then, particularly the Brady bill, a new proposal before Congress to create a "cooling-off" period before a handgun could be purchased and legally registered.

In February, still just a few months home, the McVeigh that people considered unremarkable suddenly acted. Increasingly upset with the antigun movement, he dashed off a note to a local congressman, John LaFalce of Buffalo. He wrote it out in longhand, covering several pages, and the power of his own words made him feel important.

He mailed the letter from his father's home. "Recently I saw an article in the *Buffalo News* that detailed a man's arrest," he wrote, "one of the charges being possession of a noxious substance (CS gas). This struck my curiosity, so I went to the New York State penal law. Sure enough, section 270 prohibits possession of any noxious substance, and included in section 266 is a ban on the use of stun guns.

"Now I am a male, and fully capable of physically defending myself, but how about a female? I strongly believe in a God-given right to self-defense. Should any other person or a governing body be able to tell another person that he/she cannot save their own life, because it would be a violation of a law? In this case, which is more important: Faced with a rapist/murderer, would you pick to

"a) die, a law-abiding citizen or

"b) live, and go to jail?

"It is a lie if we tell ourselves that the police can protect us everywhere at all times. I am in shock that a law exists which denies a woman's right to self-defense. Firearm restrictions are bad enough, but now a woman can't even carry mace in her purse!?!"

Anxious because his letter prompted no immediate reaction, he wrote another, this one to the *Union-Sun & Journal*, his hometown newspaper. Headlined "America Faces Problems," his letter to the editor complained about the rising crime rate, overcrowded prisons, and criminals who laugh at ever being really punished. "Taxes are a joke," he wrote. "Politicians are out of control. . . . No one is seeing the big picture.

"What is it going to take to open up the eyes of our elected officials? AMERICA IS IN SERIOUS DECLINE! We have no proverbial tea to dump; should we instead sink a ship of Japanese imports? Do we have to shed blood to reform the current system? I hope it doesn't come to that?"

A second letter to the newspaper took up the issue of hunting. "A good hunter enters the woods and kills a deer with a clean, merciful shot. The deer dies in his own environment.

"To buy your meat in a store seems so innocent, but have you ever seen or thought how it comes to be wrapped up so neatly in cellophane? First cattle live their entire lives penned up in cramped quarters, never allowed to roam freely, bred for one purpose when their time has come. Would you rather die while living happily or die while leading a miserable life? You tell me which is more humane."

McVeigh was reading more, listening to the sounds around him, trying to educate himself on the problems he saw in the country. Visiting gun shows in the Buffalo area, he began to pick up the ideas of others who viewed the world through a single black-and-white prism. They shared a common belief—that the government meddled far too much in individual lives, that the enemy since the end of the Cold War had been Washington itself, and that unless people like themselves stood up to this new domestic threat, no one would be safe.

Such people are the great disenfranchised. They believe in giant government conspiracies. They are convinced there was a second rifleman in Dallas, that political leaders in Washington are involved in secret drug deals, and that Clinton White House aide Vincent Foster did not kill himself. They come to their conclusions slowly, usually after some significant episode has spun itself to a wretched conclusion in their own personal lives. Perhaps it was a family farm that failed, or a small business that went under. For others, it's too much time reading the tabloids, or too much angry talk radio. All of them know someone who knows someone else who was burned by the system.

For the most part they are harmless. Even federal agents who infiltrate their ranks see them primarily as all mouth and no fist. They print up leaflets and sell bumper stickers at gun rallies and preparedness expositions. Some have enough money to buy airtime and spread their vitriol over the radio waves. Others publish broadsheets and magazines and books that spell out their dire warnings about a government-orchestrated doomsday. But few, very few, ever act on their passions. And most of those who think of trying are caught first.

And yet at gun shows around the nation, where local hotels and community halls are jam-packed with visitors craning their necks over the sales tables, they meet and talk and their numbers grow. They are extremists; they like the sound of that word. Their old hero Barry Goldwater told the nation that their kind of fervor in the defense of one's country is not extremism at all, but patriotism. They see themselves as today's patriots, and they like that word too. They liken themselves to the Green Mountain Boys of the American Revolution. Their catchwords are guns and ammo, stand and fight. They simply want Washington to stay the hell out of their lives. They are angry about illegal immigration, upset at growing violence in the nation's cities, determined not to let the United States join a global economy. They hate the New World Order—that catchphrase from the Bush administration which they translate to mean one giant and evil force that wants to subjugate America and rule the globe. Above all, they absolutely despise any form of gun control.

Into this world walked McVeigh. His eyes lit up—guns, man against authority, hardball politics. It made him feel good; it made him feel important; soon he embraced it all. But where the others would just talk, McVeigh would reach inside himself and feel around for a way to turn his anger outward.

In time he would become a part-time gun dealer, working erratically for others or selling his own merchandise, occasionally popping up behind sales tables at gun shows around the country. His first was in Monroeville, Pennsylvania, just east of Pittsburgh. It is a large show, so popular among the far right that it is held about four or five times a year. Vendors working the sales tables lay out a rich display of guns and armaments: antique arms, collector weapons, military surplus, automatic firearms, all kinds of ammunition, explosive devices and targets—a virtual firearms flea market.

Gregory Pfaff, owner of Lock & Load Distributors, was working one of the tables in early 1992. He sold special-application ammunition, the type that is not used for standard target practice or hunting: explosive-tip ammunition, tracers, incendiary rounds, even prefragmented bullets. He had been in the business for two years now, a real specialist. He is a balding man with a black beard who later would drop out of the gun circuit and open a small delicatessen in the Shenandoah Valley of Virginia. The gun trade was tough, with long hours and lots of travel, and Pfaff worked the Eastern Seaboard, from New York and Connecticut down into the Carolinas. He was seldom home, and he was never away from his fellow gun lovers. He was typical of many in the crowd—antigovernment, anti–gun control, anti-anything that was not right by them.

One afternoon at the Monroeville show, up walked McVeigh.

"We spoke about ammunition and different firearms," Pfaff recalled. "We spoke about Desert Storm and him being in the service."

He sold McVeigh some ammunition, including armor-piercing incendaries, the kind with a magnesium compound that, upon breaking apart, ignite with enough heat to penetrate metal.

In the summer, McVeigh showed up at another Pfaff sales table, this time at a Buffalo gun show. They spoke again for about a half hour; Pfaff even let McVeigh run his table while he stepped away to the rest room. When he returned, Pfaff and McVeigh shared coffee and talked some more.

McVeigh was more than just chatty. He had a few items of his own for sale. Pfaff bought some small blast simulators; they were made of two pieces of wire and made the sound of a small explosion, like a noisemaker or an M-80.

Pfaff also paid McVeigh for some military-style smoke grenades, and asked him if he knew where he could get some more.

"He said that he did," Pfaff recalled, "but that he had them with some other things that he owned buried in the woods. In case he ever needed them, you know, he knew where they were and nobody else did."

In November, McVeigh telephoned Pfaff at home. He had the blast simulators. They met at another show in Monroeville, and there talked for another half hour. Pfaff bought some of the simulators. McVeigh also had brought with him a punctured plate of steel, and he showed Pfaff the difference between what a standard round could do and what the armor-piercing incendiary bullets did.

To Pfaff, it was clear that McVeigh was moving smoothly into the gun show circuit. McVeigh even gave Pfaff some atropine and asked him to sell it for him on consignment. Atropine is an antidote to chemical warfare, and when Pfaff later unloaded the material, he sent some of the proceeds to McVeigh.

McVeigh's mind was reaching beyond the bullets and simulators and exotic weaponry at gun shows. He was interested in the antigovernment propaganda that was for sale too. He ordered books from Paladin Press, a mail-order operation that catered to the far right. For $25, he purchased *The Big Book of Homemade Weapons*, and *Improvised Explosives* for $10. For $16, *Homemade C-4: A Recipe for Survival*. The book's promotion literature promised that readers would learn that "for blowing up bridges, shattering steel, and derailing tanks, they need C-4."

All of it fascinated McVeigh: guns and bigger guns, tracer bullets that light up the sky, metal projectiles so deadly they can break through a piece of steel. As a boy he had experienced the thrill of wrapping his small fingers around his first rifle. As a young soldier he had steadied his large hands on the wheel of a tank cannon. Now home in Pendleton, he knew he would never again feel that same rush working nights as a private security cop.

On one of his last days at Burns Security, toward the end of 1992, he met Lebron at the Calspan complex to say so long.

"Stay out of trouble," said Lebron.

"I can't stay out of trouble," said McVeigh. "Trouble will find me."

And so he just disappeared; one day he was gone.

"He wasn't drifting before he left," said his father, Bill McVeigh. "He was out looking for some place to live where he could get a job, I thought. He told me he was sick of New York State taxes. He was going to live somewhere else."

Timothy McVeigh never found another home; he never stayed anywhere long enough to settle down. For the next two years and then some, he wandered America, crisscrossing its highways and soaking in the nation's undercurrents of frustration. Time was all he had. Occasionally he would work the gun show circuit, staying in cheap motels or sleeping in whatever old beat-up rattrap of a car he happened to be driving then. Sometimes he wrote his father or his sisters, but he told them little about his changing ideology.

Often he mailed political leaflets to friends, attaching a short note of his own. "Read this article," he would insist. "It's good stuff." In other letters he talked about his work on the gun circuit and described selling ammunition to people he considered "responsible." He offered Lebron copies of videotapes he had about flying saucers. He said he could get them from an organization called the Citizen Agency for Joint Intelligence, an outfit promoted, he said, by William Cooper, a short-wave disc jockey heard in the Arizona desert.

Increasingly these were his fellow soldiers now, those who cherish their firearms and jealously protect their individual freedoms. They will say it, too. They are the voices heard on small-budget radio programs, where low-watt preachers spew hate into the night. They sell their message on the Internet, in how-to books on bomb-making, even on C-SPAN; the cable network once televised Montana militia leader John Trochmann ranting during a hearing before the United States Senate. Trochmann was by then a hero to the far right.

Montana was the home of the Freemen, where a group of belligerents would refuse for months to surrender on tax and other federal charges to the FBI and the U.S. government they did not recognize. Georgia was where a mystery group would set off a cheap bomb during the summer Olympics. In Arizona, a train would be derailed and, in a separate case, a band called the Vipers would plot to blow up buildings.

They, the angry, the disillusioned, are the John Browns of today, the firebrands at the close of this American Century. So angry are they at the direction they see the government going that they are calling up new civil violence to take back the freedoms they believe they have lost. Adopting the spirit of the country's forefathers, anointing themselves the real American patriots, they have sounded the trumpet call against government encroachments they cannot tolerate, and especially against the federal authorities who have taken an oath to enforce those laws.

They warn about secret government intrigue; they are convinced that global satellites spy on us; they see black helicopters that hover in the night; they say the government has polluted our waters and contaminated our air; and now they believe that they alone can save an America in peril.

This was McVeigh's new army, but he did not become a member of a weekend militia, nor did he parade in front of the TV talk show cameras. He was not quoted in the militant newsletters, nor did he attend antigovernment rallies or pass out literature on street corners. But like the Vietnam veterans who tossed away their medals when they came home from their war, McVeigh too felt that the government had turned against him despite his sacrifices as a soldier.

He had a lot of time to think as he drove alone around the country, and as his association with the far right hardened, many of those he came to know, among them a man named Roger Moore, would only push him further into his conviction that the federal government was the enemy of the people.

Roger Edwin Moore is a beefy man with wild eyes and receding curly hair. He claims to have made a million dollars as a young man building boats for the U.S. military during the Vietnam War era. He has been an accountant, a rancher, and a small businessman; most of all, he collects, trades, and sells guns. When he ventures out, he sometimes wears disguises, and he often uses an alias. Bob Miller, he likes to call himself, or just plain "Bob from Arkansas." He can be loud and boisterous, his eyes darting about, his anger boiling up through his words, talking faster than most people are able to listen. He is full of his own importance and, once wound up, boastful about his hatred for the government of the United States. There is no room for debate on that subject.

"You can go to gun shows and find some angry people," he said once. "You can go to south Florida and find people who are losing their tomatoes because of NAFTA. There's angry people all over. So what do you do? Well, I'm a serious patriot. And a patriot is a person who loves his country. I've heard that word used on talk shows and Larry King, and I'm a patriot because I love my country."

Like so many in the extreme right, he brags about starting a "war" against the government but never fires the first shot. His excuse, he said, is that his girlfriend in Arkansas, Karen Anderson, will not let him become too involved. So his mouth remains his biggest weapon. "I don't give a shit," he said. "I'll put on my flak vest, take a bunch of goddam guns in my van, and if I get in a firefight, so be it. I wanna run around and dig up a lot of stuff, but she will not let me go anywhere."

Moore, like other extremists, strongly distrusts authority, and he particularly hates talking to the police, especially federal agents. "They don't tell you nothing, man," he said. "They ask questions. And there's always four or eight of them in the room and before you think of the answer, they've asked two more questions in a row. And by the time you're done answering them, another man with a clipboard and notes . . . he asks a question."

Authorities have had plenty of reasons to meet with Roger Moore.

In 1986, he reported that a housekeeper had stolen $11,000 in cash bundled in bank packets. The woman was never found—alive; she killed herself in Arizona. Later that same year, a ranch hand asphyxiated himself in the farm garage while Moore and Anderson were away.

Ed Smith, a local Garland County deputy, never got to the bottom of either of those incidents. What role Moore may have played in the missing money, if any cash was gone at all, he never found out. But he did collect a stack of complaints from neighbors who were fed up with Moore's shooting off guns on his property, with the automatic rifle fire and bullet tracers that exploded in color.

"There's a lot of things law enforcement would like to know about him," said Smith.

In 1993, Moore found himself again talking to the police, but this time the glare was on him. He was arrested by a highway patrol officer just over the state line in Wagoner, Oklahoma, for shooting out the back window of a car carrying four people on a state turnpike. He had been returning from a gun show up in Tulsa and he said he was carrying $3,850 in cash, two firearms, and twenty-three different kinds of pills for everything from ulcers to sleep disorders. He was angrily trying to pass other cars, and he reached under his seat, picked up a 9mm Browning automatic, and fired a tracer round that lit up the night sky and shattered the glass in their rear window. Then he nonchalantly continued on down the turnpike in his big white Ford LTD.

Moore tells it in typically boastful fashion: "I'm driving sixty-three miles an hour on cruise control, listening to the World Series and it's the seventh inning. The guy from our side—I can't remember who was playing—he just hit a homer and all of a sudden I look in the mirror and there's blue lights from the cop car."

He spent the night in the Wagoner County jail. He telephoned Anderson; she scooped up a bundle of money, chartered a plane, and flew to Tulsa. Then she drove down to Wagoner, strutted into the county sheriff's office, and flashed them $50,000 in cash to make his bail.

Sheriff Elmer Shepherd, like any good small-town law enforcement officer, could not believe what he was seeing. That kind of cash just doesn't walk into his courthouse. "We looked at all that money and it would have taken us all day and all night to count it," he said.

So Moore made bail. He hired a local lawyer and then he went around trying to convince everyone that he never shot out the back window of that other vehicle. "They wouldn't let me go back and see the window," he complained. "My friend who used to be a bail bondsman down in Muskogee went down and found the glass shop. He asked his buddy at the glass shop how'd the car come in. He said it came in with no window in it at all!"

What did that tell Moore, if he was innocent? "That highway patrol guy kicked the window out," he said. Why did they pick on him? "You got me. You have good luck all your life and then . . ." Why tie up all that $50,000 in cash for the bail and spend so much on a charter flight? "She wanted to get me out of there 'cause we'd always discussed this for a long time. If anything ever happens to either one of us, don't waste a second. Get me out of there."

His Wagoner attorney was Richard McLaughlin, a short, round, bearded man who was pleasant enough about people—until he met this client. "He was a piece of work," McLaughlin recalled. "He's real volatile. He has an antigovernment attitude about everything. He has no respect for the court, or anything. He's loud and obnoxious, and you couldn't tell him anything. He was a loud-mouth in court. He talks in riddles; he talks nonstop. Even after the case was settled, he still turned in complaints against the trooper."

Moore entered a plea of no contest to a reduced charge of transporting a loaded firearm—the loaded 9mm that the highway patrolman had found hidden in a bag under the seat. There was a loaded clip in the gun, and the first three rounds were tracer bullets. Moore was given a $200 fine, and he left Wagoner—all in all a pretty good deal. But he continued to telephone McLaughlin, repeatedly, and then, two years after the arrest, with the case settled and Moore having paid his fine and having been returned his firearms and pills, he suddenly showed up again in McLaughlin's office. He sat down and began complaining that the lawyer's fee had been too high.

"I didn't get treated right up here!" he yelled.

McLaughlin was genuinely scared for his safety. He placed a hand on his desk drawer, where he keeps a loaded handgun.

"This town is nuts around here!" Moore was screaming.

McLaughlin stood up. "Get your ass out of that chair!" he said.

Moore rose up. The two men faced off: the beefy Moore and the squat McLaughlin. Then Moore caved in. He finally shut his mouth

long enough to allow McLaughlin and his secretary to escort him
outside.

McVeigh and Moore met at a gun show in Fort Lauderdale, and
McVeigh eventually would visit Moore's ten-acre horse ranch on
three stops during his endless wandering. They would sit up for
hours, sharing their disgust with the state of their country. Some
nights, when Moore was too worn out to talk any longer, the
younger McVeigh would sit by himself, devouring the latest edi-
tions of *Shotgun News* or *Guns & Ammo*. Or he would slip on the
headphones and listen to the nightcasts on the shortwave radio,
hearing the arguments of others equally disillusioned with the government, their voices rattling around inside his head as he sat alone
in the dark.

Said Moore, "Of all of the guys you've ever talked to, he looked,
he acted, the most normal. You'd never think anything. Clean. Spit
and polish. Talks nice. An absolute gentleman. Yes sir, no sir. The
whole nine yards."

Their late-night discussions centered on the Cause. Both men
believed Washington was selling the country away. McVeigh told
Moore that the government was spying on him. He said that when he
arrived in the Persian Gulf and was given an inoculation, the army
actually had implanted a tiny plastic transmitter in his buttocks.

They also talked guns, and sometimes Moore would notice
McVeigh outside the farmhouse loading and reloading his weapons.
"He carried one with him wherever he went," Moore said. "He
slept with it under his pillow. He was never without it."

When morning came, McVeigh would announce, "I gotta be
going."

"He just always wanted to travel," Moore recalled. "To New
Mexico and up the coast and through Wyoming and back to New
York. Just go."

Anderson, who with Moore also worked the gun circuit selling
ammunition, and who shares Moore's distrust of the government,
never felt threatened by McVeigh. He seemed to be a hurting
young man, a loner, a rambler, but not violent. "You just knew he
was radical," she said. "But you have to remember that going to
gun shows and talking to the ammunition people we met with, a
lot of people are."

There were others out there McVeigh would meet; some he would live with for a short while. His old army pal Michael Fortier was back in desert-hot Arizona, and whenever McVeigh breezed through town, they would pick up their friendship. Or when McVeigh was headed the other way, slicing north and east, he would stop over at Terry Nichols's family farm in rural Michigan.

There was much to talk about. In late 1992, the gun magazines and other tabloids, and some of the legitimate press too, were in full chorus questioning what had happened to a mountain man named Randy Weaver and his family at Ruby Ridge, Idaho. Weaver was wanted on illegal gun charges, and the FBI had surrounded his property and was ordering him out. Instead a gun battle erupted; Weaver lost a son, the FBI lost an agent. Then an FBI sniper killed Weaver's wife, Vicki, while she held one of her babies in her arms.

The rifle shot flashed across McVeigh's consciousness. Was this the country he had fought for? Was this foreshadowed by Earl Turner in his diaries? He studied photographs of Weaver in his mountain cabin with long hair, and he compared them to later pictures of Weaver in federal custody with his hair cut very short. McVeigh believed that the government had shaved Weaver's hair to demonize him, to make him look to the American public like some kind of evil monster.

Soon his attention was drawn elsewhere, to a place called Waco and a date, April 19.

Chapter Five

Waco: God Sees Your Lies

They all came to Waco. Protesters lined the farm roads chanting slogans and hoisting signs that warned doomsday had arrived. Opportunists set up vending booths and sold books, tapes, and magazines that criticized a federal government they said no longer answered to the American people. Some were just curious, pulling off Interstate 35 in north-central Texas to see for themselves why the nation's eyes were fixed on this spot of sagebrush near the Brazos River. Others were lured here as part of a self-initiated pilgrimage, to feel the dirt under their feet and the dust in the crisp air and to let the FBI know that America is a land of people with little patience for government misconduct. McVeigh came for all these reasons.

Through March and most of April of 1993, with winter turning to spring, a religious cult called the Branch Davidians was dug in at their rural complex of farm buildings called Mount Carmel. They were surrounded on all sides by the Federal Bureau of Investigation, with their SWAT team forces and their Bradley Fighting Vehicles capable of lobbing gas grenades at the compound. The cult's leader, David Koresh, was a self-styled rock-and-roll guitar-player-turned-prophet whom the government suspected at the least of stockpiling illegal weapons, at the worst of sexually molesting the children of his flock.

Koresh had warned his followers that one day the government

would be at their door. Now they were here. A gun battle between federal agents and Branch Davidians had erupted on February 28 when a raiding party of the federal Bureau of Alcohol, Tobacco and Firearms assaulted the compound that Sunday morning. The firefight, much of it caught on network television and zoomed around the world, took the lives of four agents and six cult members. The scenes were chilling: federal police trying to force their way into a private home, climbing up on the roof, smashing windows, and firing machine gun bullets at the occupants inside.

It was a mismatch—men, women, and children against the better-trained, highly equipped federal agents. But the Branch Davidians, firing their guns from the safety of their own four walls, beat the federal agents back, and a long siege followed.

Waco would burn long after the last lights had gone out with Randy Weaver's surrender in Idaho. Here in Texas, America was unsure which side it was on, divided over who was right and who wrong. The agents killed in the line of duty, ostensibly trying to enforce the laws of the land? Or those trapped inside, asking only to be left alone to practice their own peculiar form of religion?

Over the next seven weeks, the situation at Waco ground inexorably onward. March turned to April and there seemed no comfortable end to the prolonged standoff. The FBI could not persuade Koresh to come out. Koresh could not get the feds to go away.

As the new Clinton administration in Washington bought time, many in the nation's growing antigovernment movement began to talk about Waco as the epitome of the very FBI misconduct that they had been railing against for years. Big government had surrounded a religious community. The federal authorities had broken into a private residence, spilling blood on the doorway. Angry at the violation of a man's fundamental right to his personal freedom, people were coming here to pledge their support for those trapped inside. The protesters were religious zealots, malcontents, the paranoid, the ultraright, the fringe element. They were arriving in Waco one and two at a time, or in larger groups, staying for an hour or an afternoon, stopping long enough to sell their propaganda and preach their warnings along old farm-to-market Road 2491, which led past the compound. They came to Waco to find out what had gone wrong with America.

McVeigh came at the end of March. The signs led him here. East of Waco off the interstate, before the little Mount Carmel hilltop, the homemade signs posted by those before him had sprung up like early Texas wildflowers.

"David Koresh: The Great National Diversion," proclaimed one. "What Is The Mark Of The Beast?" asked another.

The FBI waged psychological war against the Davidians. When night fell, they shined huge bright floodlights on Mount Carmel. Each dawn they startled the cult members awake with raucous music blaring from giant speakers. Or they played Tibetan chants, or the piercing screams that rabbits make when they are being slaughtered. They cut off electricity and water. And always they drove the tanks and Bradley Fighting Vehicles around every side of the complex, circling the hilltop, crushing cars, smashing bicycles, and tearing up the garden vegetables.

To McVeigh, there was no mistaking those Bradleys. He too had ridden one to war, and the FBI SWAT teams prowling the Waco perimeter were bitter reminders of the secret Green Beret squads he had once dreamed of for himself.

On the first day of the siege, the battle call was sounded by Koresh himself. "You need to call the president of the United States and explain to him what you have done," he said to local police authorities on a 911 telephone call from inside his encampment. "You've ruined this country. You've ruined this nation."

Toward the end of the siege, aware that the world was watching, Koresh and his Davidians tacked a sign high on a compound wall that announced, "FBI, God Sees Your Lies."

His followers also sought to lock arms with a famous victim of police brutality when they hoisted a second banner that proclaimed, "Rodney King, We Understand."

McVeigh took their message to heart. He embraced their courage to fight against the machine. He could personalize their anger toward the government because he no longer trusted authority either. He now knew that with Waco, here it was at last, the final nightmare: no man in America is safe in his own home.

The voices from inside the compound did not escape the nation's ears. A growing section of the public, both around Waco and throughout the nation, began to question what was unfolding. Koresh had often left the encampment before the raid. If the federal government wanted him so badly, why hadn't they simply arrested

him on one of these trips? There were suspicions that the Davidians were stockpiling weapons. But they had been there in some
form or another almost sixty years, and neighbors, except for dis-
missing them as eccentric, seldom felt threatened by their current
leader, Koresh, and his group.

If there were sexual offenses occurring on Mount Carmel, hadn't
the parents themselves freely chosen this lifestyle? And some of
the children who had been released during the standoff were later
examined by health care professionals who found no evidence of
physical abuse. The children, they said, for the most part seemed
well adjusted. If they were at all disoriented, it was because they
were anxious to be reunited with their parents.

These were the questions being asked outside the compound.
The country road was crammed and hard to manage. Television
satellite trucks and radio antennas lined either side. With little
news of what was happening inside the compound, the press turned
to those outside to find a fresh headline.

Linda Cox and two business partners were hawking T-shirts
from a makeshift tent in front of a small farmhouse. They had ventured down to Waco when it became pretty clear that the FBI stale-
mate was going to last for a while. They sold T-shirts with
screaming messages like "Mount Carmel Erupts!" The shirts did so
well that they followed them up with a new line of hats, and then,
another set of shirts. The new ones said, "David Koresh: Let's Get
It On." The sign behind their stand promised that $1 from every
sale would go to the federal Bureau of Alcohol, Tobacco and
Firearms, the agency that had launched the first raid and taken the
casualties.

McVeigh parked next to Cox. He dragged his hand across the
back of his neck and grimaced. It had been a long drive to get here,
and he was beat. But he was not interested in helping the ATF, the
federal government's law enforcement branch responsible for polic-
ing, among other things, the ever-widening universe of illegal
firearms and explosives.

He wore a red-checked flannel shirt, the long sleeves rolled
halfway up the forearms the way he liked them. He had blue jeans
and a camouflage cap. His hair was cropped short, and even though
he seemed weary, he still managed to project the military bearing
he had learned as a fighting soldier.

He stuck a handmade sign under his windshield wiper. His bumper stickers were $1.50 each, or four for $5.

He stacked them neatly on the hood of his car.

"A man with a gun is a citizen. A man without a gun is a subject."

"Fear the government that fears the people."

"Politicians love gun control."

That last one was a particular favorite. Drawn on either side were replicas of a hammer and scythe, and the Nazi swastika.

McVeigh could talk tough, but he did not scare. He smiled easily, and still seemed the picture of youth, just a few weeks away from his twenty-fifth birthday. He was in a mood to talk, something unusual for the increasingly silent, brooding McVeigh who felt more and more uncomfortable around strangers.

Michelle Rauch, a student reporter from Southern Methodist University in Dallas, a twenty-two-year-old coed not far from McVeigh's age but vastly different in ideology and life experience, walked over and opened her notebook. Rauch had come down on her spring break. For twenty minutes she talked with the young man with the bumper stickers. Three years later, when the FBI was cataloguing every day of McVeigh's life, she remembered that she had interviewed him. She dug through a bag in her closet and found a lost copy of her article for SMU's *Daily Campus*. It was a big break for the FBI. It put McVeigh at the very spot of his defining anger: Waco.

At the time, Rauch was amazed that she and McVeigh had grown up in the same country. She had been raised in a privileged home. She was not angry, nor was she aimless. The future for her still held opportunity. But who was this McVeigh? He seemed articulate and purposeful, not menacing at all. Rauch's photographer, Lauren Aldinger, thought him nice enough too, not ranting or crazy like some of the other government protesters who summoned themselves to Waco. But it also was obvious that he had been sleeping in his car.

"He was just a guy," Aldinger said. "He wasn't scary. But I didn't want to date him either."

McVeigh told them that the eighty heavily defended followers of Koresh inside the compound were well within their constitutional rights to bear arms. He was sorry for the government agents who had died in the initial raid, he said, but the ATF had "no business" being there at all. He talked about his own war adventures pushing the Iraqis out of Kuwait. His army years had taught him what freedom is really all about.

He climbed up on the hood of his car; better to be seen up there, better to make it about himself.

"I'm out here to make a statement," he said.

And so he talked.

"I think if the sheriff had served the warrant, it would all have been okay," he said, placing his trust in local police over federal law enforcement.

"It seems like the ATF just wants a chance to play with their toys paid for by government money."

He derided the ATF, chiding the agency as nothing more than a government bureaucracy with guns, incapable of planning a paramilitary exercise, and certainly inept at carrying out the raid against the Branch Davidians.

"They're not tactical," he said, again reminding Rauch of his own military exploits in the Gulf. "They are government employees."

Working for the federal government, he said, was the unpardonable sin.

"The government is afraid. Afraid of guns people have because they have to have control of the people at all times. Once you take away the guns you can do anything to the people."

Rauch was taking notes, and McVeigh was digging the attention.

"You give them an inch and they take a mile," he told her. "I believe we are slowly turning into a Socialist government. The government is continually growing bigger and more powerful, and the people need to prepare to defend themselves against government control."

He said the government is only out to waste taxpayer dollars, and that Waco just gave them another opportunity to spend money. He said constitutional laws were being broken here, and that U.S. military resources like the Bradley tanks should never be used against American citizens. The Koresh standoff was only the beginning, he warned. Beware of government's role in our lives.

Rauch closed her notebook. "He appeared calm and very articulate," she remembered. "He appeared well versed on what his beliefs are."

McVeigh did not hang around long. Soon he was off again. He

would tell others about what he had seen and heard there, and how the drama at Waco had so influenced his own thinking.

Back in Pennsylvania, he dropped in on the Monroeville gun show and stopped by a sales table managed by Pfaff. He stayed long enough to boast about being at Waco, a subject still captivating many on the far right. He was very angry, sensationally angry.

"Down there the federal agents had a perimeter fence around the compound so nobody could go in or out," he told Pfaff. "But I crawled up to the fence and crawled back without being seen by any of the agents."

He said he could not comprehend why the government that he had defended as a soldier would act this way. Before he left, McVeigh gave Pfaff a stern warning.

"This," McVeigh said, "could be the start of the government coming house-to-house to retrieve the weapons from the citizens."

From Pennsylvania he drove north, up the thumb of Michigan, past the rich and vast farm fields of the flatlands and toward the moist air of the Great Lakes. Here he stopped in Decker and visited his army friend Terry Nichols, "the old man," then working with his older brother James on the family farm. Fellow patriots, they talked about gun control and hidden government agendas, but the real subject was Waco.

By the middle of April, McVeigh and Terry Nichols had resolved to drive down to Texas together. McVeigh wanted to experience Waco again, Nichols to see it for himself.

Terry Lynn Nichols was the son of Robert and Joyce Nichols. The family controlled one of the largest rental units in the thumb of Michigan, in Lapeer County up north past the auto plants of Flint and nearly to the cold harsh waters of Lake Huron. His father insisted on the best tractors with plenty of creature comforts—accouterments like air conditioners and tape players. Farming was hard enough; why make it unbearable? he told his boys. When the children wanted new clothing, they charged it to their mother. They went on skiing vacations and rode go-carts, and they were given guns at a young age and allowed to fire the weapons on the family property. They also worked hard, drawing forth from the ground bushels of wheat, corn, soybeans, oats, navy beans, and sunflowers. The children were raised with high hopes, and they were taught to think and act for themselves and to be open to new ideas. Be different, their parents told them.

But not all was idyllic. The oldest Nichols boy, Les, was badly burned in a welding accident and nearly died. Sparks from the welding iron had ignited a gas tank and it had burst, the heat searing off his ears and nose. People said imprints of his hands could be found on the concrete floor where he crawled madly away, his body afire, trying to get away from the flames. Then there was a divorce; parents Robert and Joyce split up. The family was falling apart, much like the McVeighs in New York. Neighbors told about hearing arguments on the Nichols farm late at night, and of seeing Joyce drinking into the early morning hours. The Lapeer police chief, Bill Dougherty, Sr., gave an odd story to the *Los Angeles Times* about once stopping Joyce on a rural road. Suddenly she started tossing empty beer bottles into a cornfield. He said he walked up to her car and, to his amazement, heard the whir of a chain saw she had inside the vehicle. She was trying to fire it up, he said, and then "she throwed it at me."

In school, Terry was such a quiet young student that the other kids assumed he had a speech impediment. On the farm, the Nichols boys were making homemade bombs and other explosive devices. Terry went off to Central Michigan State University for a while and hoped to study medicine. But then his family purchased a farm in Sanilac County, near Decker, and he was called home. So he was back in the fields. Later, in the summer of 1976, he moved out west to Colorado, to the open fields around Boulder and Denver, and he earned a real estate license. At last he had found a job where he would put on a clean white shirt each morning.

But just as Pendleton's great Blizzard of 1977 stranded the young Tim McVeigh, nature's forces struck the Nichols farm in Michigan when torrential rains began falling in the late seventies. The rains turned the Michigan topsoil into Michigan mud, laying waste to crops and agriculture equipment and farm finances. Federal disaster aid relief was inadequate to help the family and many of the other area farmers. Terry's older brother, James, still working the Decker farm, had become dissatisfied with the federal government. So Terry again returned to try to boost up things at home. But the family was changing, particularly James. Terry idolized James, listened to his every word, and what he heard was James becoming fed up with the way of government programs. The seeds of dissent had been sown.

In 1980, Terry moved out again, and soon he married a local Michigan realtor. "I first saw him on a John Deere tractor," Lana Padilla would remember. "He was plowing the fields around my house."

They tried to make a go of things off the farm. They gradually built up a real estate business, buying fixer-uppers and turning them around for a small profit. They also sold insurance. Gradually they began to make a little money; things seemed good, and they were blessed with a baby, a boy they named Josh.

But Terry Nichols still fidgeted. He began to bake his own bread. He became interested in natural foods, and he pounded out organic wheat on a stone grinder, passing it around to friends. He said he was getting back to his roots, moving away from a reliance on others. He packaged and froze his own meals. Withdrawing further from mainstream society, he began to ignore his obligations. He started to doubt the solvency of U.S. currency, and that led him to a situation where creditors were hammering on his door.

His marriage was in trouble too. While he often was quiet and withdrawn, Lana saw herself in the role of the family mainstay trying to keep the three of them together. She was anxious to motivate him somehow, to find something to jump-start him back into taking an active role in their lives.

She hit on an idea about the army, and brought home some brochures. She thought a military career might lift him up. At her prodding, he went down to the recruiting station and, at the age of thirty-three, he up and enlisted. Soon he would be marching with men a dozen years younger than he.

He met fellow enlistees McVeigh and Fortier at Fort Benning. It was his bond with McVeigh that stuck first and lasted longest. Just as Terry had looked up to James, now McVeigh was admiring Terry—if only in the beginning. Nichols was a mentor type, and Lana seemd to approve of her husband's relationship with the younger McVeigh. "He was a home person, a loner," she said of Terry. "He didn't have a lot of friends. When he first met Tim, I was pleased because he needed a close friend."

Transferred to Fort Riley, Nichols and McVeigh became inseparable. They often paired up on the rifle range during the afternoons, or elsewhere on the base in the cool Kansas evenings, sharing ideas about guns and revolution. But Nichols would miss the war in the Persian Gulf, and unlike McVeigh, he would not touch glory. He worked as a chauffeur driving an army captain around the base, a mundane assignment but something he nonetheless tackled with his own elbow-grease determination. He kept the vehicle immaculate, often spreading Armor All on the body and then wiping it clear with baby oil.

But the luster was gone from his marriage. Lana announced that she was leaving him and moving to Las Vegas, where she planned to toss the dice on the booming real estate business there. Suddenly Nichols was a single father. He applied for and received a hardship discharge from the service in order to raise young Josh, and he returned to Michigan with very mixed emotions. He told his family of the great disappointment he had found in an army uniform. He had prepared so hard and had so diligently tried to make a fantasy come true. But when he came home, it was nothing. "It was a waste of time," he said.

Like McVeigh, Nichols brooded about life after the service. He too would soon pick up and disappear, eventually leaving his Michigan home for a job as a Kansas farmhand and—later still—to a small home in tiny Herington, Kansas. He would settle in the middle of nowhere; but first he wanted a new wife.

He turned far away, to the Philippines, and in 1990, when he was thirty-five, chose sixteen-year-old Marife Torres. She was still in high school, the daughter of a Philippine National Police officer. She and her family lived in a small apartment above a lumberyard. Nichols showed up as a tourist that spring and stayed at the Sundowner Hotel in Cebu City. He found her through a mail-order-bride agency, and the couple met in the downtown plaza of the bustling city. Because of their wide age difference, her parents were immediately concerned about her well-being. They told her to go slow, to be careful in her relationship with this older man from the States. Nichols was small, with short hair, and he wore large-framed glasses that slid down to the end of his upturned nose. Sometimes he sported a wisp-thin mustache.

Marife's parents, Eduardo and Calumpag Torres, questioned Nichols closely. Why did you come here? they asked. What do you want with our daughter?

He told them that a friend had said Filipino women made loyal wives and were good with children. More important, he said, "they stayed at home."

After he left the Philippines, he started to write and to call, and soon they set a November marriage date. He returned to the Philippines for the wedding but stayed barely a week. Then he went home to Michigan and she remained behind, waiting for approval of her U.S. visa application.

The visa came through the following spring. But in the meantime she had given birth to another man's child, and when she moved to America, she brought along the little boy, Jason. She and the baby moved into the Michigan farmhouse with her new husband, Terry Nichols.

So McVeigh had come to visit the farm in April 1993, with the Waco standoff still ticking along with no reasonable end in sight. There he and Terry Nichols began making preparations to head south to Texas; they planned to pull off the old farm road and get as close as they could to the FBI checkpoints. They wanted to show solidarity with those holed up inside.

On the morning of April 19, McVeigh was outside by his car when Terry and James Nichols suddenly hollered at him to come inside. McVeigh hurried into the farmhouse and the three of them stood in stunned disbelief around the television set. It became immediately clear that there was no longer any reason to go to Waco.

Terry Nichols looked at McVeigh. "We're too late," he said. The Mount Carmel complex was burning to the ground.

The siege at Waco had ended on its fifty-first day. Using tanks and CS gas, poking holes into the compound walls and lobbing gas grenades, the FBI tried to force a surrender. What McVeigh and the Nichols brothers saw on the television was an image of warfare by the federal government against its own citizens: poison gas that was highly flammable; immobilizing tactics that locked the Branch Davidians inside the complex; heavy weaponry that broke through the Davidians' perimeter and smashed their wall of resistance.

As the tanks roared in, Mount Carmel suddenly burst into smoke and fire. The two- and three-story structures of the compound were engulfed; even the tops of trees were consumed. The heat spread so fast that the government could not safely approach the doors to attempt a rescue, and those barricaded inside could not get out. Some eighty people, women and children included—the exact number of dead would never be truly known—either shot themselves, shot one another, or lay down and let the fire take them.

Someone turned off the television, and the Nichols farmhouse fell silent. For a while, not a word was spoken. Through the open windows could be heard the soft sound of the breeze in the side yard. McVeigh's tongue went dry, his body shivered, his thoughts were racing. It had happened! he realized. It had really happened! The government of the United States was killing its people; the slaughter had begun.

Soldier of Fortune magazine, one of McVeigh's favorites, called Waco a national disaster, and its reporter rushed out of a Texas jail with interviews from Branch Davidian survivors.

Avoiding bloodshed would have been simple, Livingston Fagan told the magazine reporter. The ATF, he said, could have knocked on the door. "You all come here and say you are seeking to understand us," said Fagan, a former theology professor and minister. "But do you understand yourselves? If somebody comes into your house, where your wife and your children are, and threatens you, what are *you* going to do? Roll over and die?"

The magazine ridiculed the ATF, suggesting the F stood for "F Troop." The FBI was likened to the Gestapo. The hated ATF was coming for all the guns. The DEA, chartered to enforce the national drug laws, was instead the most lucrative channel for illegal narcotics in the country.

Even the Green Berets became a target. Dale B. Cooper, a senior foreign correspondent for the magazine, wrote that after covering military actions from the Gulf War to Somalia he had learned that the U.S. Special Forces Operations were going soft because of a weak-kneed Clinton administration no longer willing to let the American military play rough.

In Colorado, Ron Cole, an antigovernment militant, was printing up leaflets he called "the truth behind one of the worst tragedies and greatest cover-ups in recent American history." His signature artwork was a shadow drawing of David Koresh in long hair and beating on an electric guitar at his waist, all the while as bullets were fired at his gyrating silhouette. GOD ROCKS, he called the drawing. NEVER AGAIN, he promised.

Believing that federal law enforcement agents would not stop, he wrote an epitaph for America. "Today I take a moment to reflect, in solemn sorrow, on a lost loved one. I remember her well as an innocent child, taken from me by a gang of thieves that used her for their own purposes. . . .

". . . Her name was Liberty, and we will together pay the price for her passing."

McVeigh was falling headlong under the spell of the articles and leaflets telling him about the perilous state of his country. He began to save much of the material; he would send some home to Pendleton for his sister Jennifer to read, or to friends or associates he met along the gun show trail. He also was collecting videotapes that sought to whip up public frenzy over the Branch Davidian tragedy. Most popular was *Waco, the Big Lie*, produced by Linda Thompson, a notorious government hater and conspiracy theorist operating out of her home in Indiana. Her tape was popular because it was so outrageous, taking Waco to the farthest extreme, laying out as facts events that strained credibility, that the government had torched Mount Carmel, intending to kill those inside, and then purposely tried to hide its sin.

Promotional ads filtering around the antigovernment community strongly urged the purchase of *Waco, the Big Lie*. "No convincing will come close if you don't actually see it for yourself," urged one. "But be warned, you may not be able to sleep again."

Waco became McVeigh's obsession. What angered him most was that children had died there. The ATF, he told others, kills kids, and from April 19, 1993, to his own day of destiny exactly two years later, Waco steered his course—it was the specter riding shotgun as he drove back and forth across the country.

He would show up at Michael Fortier's trailer home in Kingman wearing a black hat with the letters "ATF" across the top and holes drilled into it to simulate bullet holes. Fortier often offered him the spare bedroom until he pushed on again. "We discussed the legality of Waco," Fortier would recall. "We both concluded that the federal government had intentionally attacked those people and may not have intentionally started the fire, but they were certainly the cause of the fire and potentially murdered those people in Waco."

His wife, Lori Fortier, remembered it differently; she recalled that McVeigh never gave the ATF or the FBI or Attorney General

Janet Reno either the benefit of the doubt. "The government murdered those people," he told her, flatly.

He stopped by Moore's horse farm in Arkansas, and they too discussed their anger over the Branch Davidian deaths. He was, said Moore's roommate, Karen Anderson, "very upset about all the kids killed at Waco."

To his friend Lebron at the Buffalo security guard company, he mailed photographs depicting the siege at Waco. He advised Lebron that he was receiving information from "other people," but he did not explain who they were. He sent him one of the Waco videotapes, and Lebron took it home and watched some of it. But it was of such poor quality that he guessed it might have been made by McVeigh himself. The video contained an odd segment from an old *Star Trek* television episode. What did that have to do with anything? Lebron wondered. What nonsense!

Another tape was mailed to the Drzyzgas in Pendleton. It arrived about six months after the end of the Waco saga, in the fall of 1993. Richard and Lynn Drzyzga popped it in the VCR and then leaned back in their chairs. But the craziness of what they saw—the nutty diatribes, the radical leanings, the paranoia—made them worry about McVeigh.

Richard Drzyzga turned to his wife. "What the hell's he gotten into?" he asked.

Later, in July 1994, McVeigh still could not let go of Waco. In a letter to his childhood friend Steve Hodge, he broke off their long relationship because Hodge did not share McVeigh's belief that Waco must be avenged.

"I know in my heart that I am right in my struggle," he wrote. "I have come to peace with myself, my God, and my cause. I feel that I do not have to justify myself to anyone, to defend my position. Never have I felt this way before. When I found the real truth, I knew it inside."

The time to act would be in the spring, in April.

"Blood will flow in the streets," McVeigh wrote Hodge. "Good vs. evil, freemen vs. socialist wannabe slaves. Pray it is not your blood, my friend."

April 19 is the anniversary of Waco. The date also marks the start of the American Revolution, the day that shots were fired at Lexington and Concord, the commemoration of the uprising of another group of civilian militias that rebelled against its government. April 19 is Patriots' Day. It is the date McVeigh would adopt as his new birthday.

In the late summer of 1994, McVeigh was staying for a short while in a small rental home in Kingman. He was restless, anxious for the end of summer, looking forward to the date of April 19, 1995, when the revolution, his revolution, would begin.

Fortier was noticing the oddest behavior in his old army friend from Fort Riley. "He started to become more defensive, keeping weapons behind doors in his house," Fortier recalled. "He collected wood to burn in his stove. He was stacking it in his backyard. He wanted to use it as some type of berm to block bullets in case there was ever any type of Waco-style raid on his home."

In the mail one day Fortier received a letter from McVeigh. He had written that he and their other army friend, Terry Nichols, had "decided to take some type of positive action."

A week later, McVeigh was standing near the fence in Fortier's front yard. "Tim was telling me what he meant by taking action," Fortier said. "He told me that him and Terry were thinking of blowing up a building."

Chapter Six

The Road to Oklahoma City

They climbed up out of Kingman, driving east on the interstate, the two young former army pals Timothy McVeigh and Michael Fortier on the misadventure of a lifetime. Bouncing around in the backseat were duffel bags, remnants of their days as infantrymen in Kansas. Locked in the trunk of McVeigh's old blue Spectrum was an armful of bundled-up stolen loot.

The desert lay before them, vast in its majesty, a landscape golden-brown and still and haunting, one purple-pink mesa and then the next, never ending. They were headed east on Interstate 40 from Kingman to Albuquerque to Amarillo and on farther still. They were driving back to the heart of Kansas, where their friendship had first taken shape on a military parade ground a half-dozen years ago. But first there would be a little detour. McVeigh wanted to show his friend a building.

Kingman, Arizona, slowly fading now in the rearview mirror of the blue Spectrum, is a dust devil of a place on the edge of the Mojave Desert. This was mining country until the big money men decided that they had dug the town dry. Today the desert city just sits flat out there on the horizon, sizzling by day and cool at night. There are few trees for shade, seldom a breeze in the chill evening air. The red-brown landscape is more Nevada than Arizona, more boulder than brush. It is the land of the trailer park, the Wal-Mart, and the $20-a-night motel. The biggest draw is the sun, luring many

Los Angeles retirement-age couples who are thrilled to find an affordable home in their sunset years. But for those who do not stay, those just passing by on Interstate 40, Kingman is just another gas stop along the road.

Andy Devine Avenue is where Route 66 used to roll through town. Devine is the town's favorite son; he went on to become a Hollywood backlot actor, three hundred pounds of Falstaffian character with a gravelly voice. He played the bumbling rube of the Old West, the television character Jingles on the old Wild Bill Hickok show, and like Kingman itself, he was never center-stage. But unlike Michael Fortier and the occasional visitor Timothy McVeigh, he never gave Kingman a bad name.

Four months had passed since McVeigh leaned over Fortier's fence and whispered his plan to avenge the dead at Waco. Fortier did not realize it then, but his friend believed he was going to spark a revolution. McVeigh had convinced himself that the rest of the nation was as incensed as he was over the FBI's final deadly assault on the Branch Davidians, and that a strike in retaliation would awaken the great sleeping middle class into action. Now winter was fast approaching. They left Kingman on December 16, 1994, their journey begun halfway between the time he had decided in August to take action and the two-year anniversary next April of what McVeigh called the Texas massacre.

There was plenty to hash over in the car during the next few days. For some time McVeigh had been popping up in Kingman. He would take odd jobs, work for a while as a security guard or a landscaper, sleep in motels or rent a small cinder-block house in nearby Golden Valley. But he would never settle down. He would sometimes vanish just as quickly as he arrived. Fortier could see his friend changing. Most notable was his heightened indignation against the government.

There were two reasons to skip town. McVeigh had removed a cache of stolen blasting caps and other explosive materials from his storage locker, and he wanted to transport them east in order to unload them on a Chicago dealer. More important, hidden away in a central Kansas storage locker was a much larger prize—a bounty of priceless guns and other firearms taken in a separate robbery.

Fortier was in it for the second part. If he would help fence the stolen guns, it would mean a walletful of instant money for the young man with a wife and new baby. He was earning just $200 a week as a bookkeeper at a Kingman hardware store. He and his wife, Lori, limped along with help from her parents. Aside from that, all they could count on was their federal tax refund next month.

Then along came McVeigh.

"How much to help you?" Fortier asked.

McVeigh grinned. He loved suspense, mystery, chance. His blue eyes found some of their lost sparkle. "Ten to the power of ten!" he said.

The math was wrong, but Fortier knew what McVeigh meant by the phrase: $10,000.

So he lied to his boss that he needed some time off to pick up a car in Florida, where a group of friends was working the gun shows. Then he and Lori dashed out to the Wal-Mart and bought some tape, Christmas wrapping paper, and a couple of boxes, just as McVeigh had asked them to do, and drove over to his room at the Mohave Motel on Kingman's Andy Devine Avenue.

"Tim took the two boxes, and he had a large box full of blasting caps," recalled Lori Fortier. "He separated the blasting caps into the two smaller boxes, and then he asked me to wrap the boxes. He wanted them in Christmas wrapping paper in case he was stopped, like anyone wouldn't think it was conspicuous because it was the Christmas season."

They talked into the night. McVeigh again asked Fortier if he was in for the game, whether he was still willing to accompany him to Kansas to pick up the stolen guns and help sell the firearms. He complained that their other army buddy, Terry Nichols, had done the robbery but that it was up to McVeigh now to get them sold. He even went so far as to say that Nichols should have killed this man "Bob" when he stole the weapons.

The plan was to drive out to Kansas in McVeigh's car and rent another vehicle there for Fortier. Then they would separate, Fortier to return to Kingman with the hot guns in his trunk, McVeigh to turn north with the stolen blasting caps.

So they left Kingman in the morning. Lori drove her husband back out to the motel, and he threw his bag into McVeigh's car. She watched them pull away in the old Spectrum, the one McVeigh called his "Warrior."

Lori was still in high school when she first met McVeigh. Michael was then in the service, and at Thanksgiving in 1988 he came home from Fort Riley with this tall, gangly fellow recruit with skin as pale as white ash. She thought McVeigh rather gentle in one instant, ghastly the next.

"He drove up with Michael because he wanted to look at some land outside of Kingman," she recalled. "It was over in Seligman, and he had it outlined on a map that had possible nuclear attack zones outlined. It was like a regular road atlas that had certain areas highlighted that wouldn't be hit if there was a nuclear attack."

McVeigh's idea in spending his holiday with the Fortier family was to purchase land in what he called "one of the safe zones." He never followed through, but he came often to Kingman in the years ahead, for a while renting a home there, or otherwise staying in various motels and, on some warm nights, simply camping under the desert stars.

Now she and Michael were married, and McVeigh had been the best man at their wedding at the Treasure Island Casino in nearby Las Vegas. Watching them driving off for Kansas this December morning, she realized how close the two had become.

Her husband was twenty-seven years old when McVeigh talked with him over the fence and told him what he meant by taking positive action. She was grown now too, at twenty-four a mother, living in a trailer park with McVeigh often as a house guest. They shared many of his stark views about the government and the far right's all-encompassing fear that someday the politicians in Washington were going to turn their country over to that global autocracy they called the New World Order. They cherished their independence and hated government intrusion. To show their colors, they flew a yellow-black-and-green Revolutionary War–era flag on a pole outside their mobile home, with the coiled snake and the warning "Don't Tread on Me" greeting anyone who ventured by.

Despite the Fortiers' own deep feelings about the United States of America, Michael and Lori would later insist that they were appalled at what McVeigh was suggesting. One evening in their living room, he had again brought up this notion about destroying a government office building. "You're crazy," Michael told him.

But neither he nor Lori could get past his eyes to tell if he was sincere about taking the crime of Waco and turning it into the spark of a new people's rebellion. "He never came to us with any violent behavior before," she recalled. "So I wasn't really sure if he was serious about it."

McVeigh appealed directly to her husband for help.

"No," Fortier said.

McVeigh pushed harder.

"No," he said again. "I would never do anything like that."

Well, maybe never. Only if a United Nations tank was barreling down the trailer park's McVicar Street and headed up to his front door.

"Then we would be at a state of war with the New World Order," he told McVeigh. "Then it would be appropriate. But not before."

Fortier would remember that whenever McVeigh did not get what he wanted, he would sulk. When McVeigh was upset, he would turn very, very quiet. When Fortier made it clear he would not help him bomb a building, McVeigh stalked off to a bedroom in the Fortier trailer and spent the rest of the night alone.

In simpler times, Fortier had simply idolized McVeigh. Fortier had lived almost all of his life in the harsh isolation of a desert community, and calling a genuine war hero one of his friends gave him special cachet around town. McVeigh had risen to the type of vaunted soldier that Fortier could only dream of becoming. He also had taken their antigovernment talk to heart.

Fortier is remembered not for what he did in Kingman but what he brought to town. He brought Timothy McVeigh.

His parents moved there from Maine when Michael was seven years old. He grew up a scrawny, black-haired, free-spirited kid, well known in school, popular at home, one of four boys in his family. A brother, John, made a career in the military. Their father, Paul, was a forklift operator; their mother, Irene, was a bit of a local character, often seen tooling around town in her bright red Corvette with an ELVIS license plate.

Much like McVeigh, Michael was the all-American kid, playing Little League baseball and doing well in grade school. Teachers never detected a hint that he could be militant or obstinate or even hard to deal with. He was the average boy lurching toward manhood.

Kingman High is where Michael turned bad. It began with beer. "I never considered it a problem," he said later. "I considered it a rash of bad luck. I would attend parties, and sometimes those parties would get busted by the cops. I didn't feel it was very safe to go running from the police like that. So I'd always just stay there; and sometimes the police would let me go home, or they would give me a ticket. And I got quite a few tickets."

He began to experiment with illegal drugs, including marijuana and crystal methamphetamine. He moved up to speed in his senior year. It was a habit he and Lori would continue to indulge in even as young parents. Eventually they began to trade guns for drugs.

His wife, Lori, had been a pretty, dark-haired high school girl whose eyes were drawn to the upperclassman. Even before she graduated, she had found herself suddenly smitten with Michael, and soon she would be visiting him at Fort Riley; later still she would be living with him out there in Kansas. She liked his bad-boy image, loved his reedy build and his scruffy goatees; and he too seemed completely devoted to his young wife. Her parents also had a little money, and they helped support the couple when they resettled back in Kingman, particularly when their first child came along. Her husband was in and out of jobs, and her dream to buy a Kingman tanning salon—in the desert, of all places—had fallen through.

Most of all, Lori was crazy about her husband's carefree attitude. "I do not put much importance on money," Michael once wrote in a school scrapbook. "So my future plans are to enjoy every minute of my life and to take events as they come."

Fortier joined the army on May 24, 1988, the same day that McVeigh walked into the recruiting office in Buffalo. But Fortier's army tour was unremarkable. He merely clocked time, waiting for weekends, then hanging out, banging on the Nintendo, eating barbecue, drinking beer, smoking dope, watching movies. He developed a sore shoulder, and that helped keep him out of the Gulf War. He came home to Kingman a different man, with even more of an attitude, the tough guy, the know-it-all with a new anger and distrust about the federal government.

Discharged in the spring of 1991, Fortier was still thin, with a long crane of a neck and dark black hair parted down the middle. He wore T-shirts with straps that come up the shoulders and a little earring, wire-rimmed glasses, and a black goatee. He and Lori paid $26,000 for the fourteen-by-seventy-foot mobile home on McVicar.

McVeigh had shared *The Turner Diaries* with him at Fort Riley, and now Fortier, a fellow gun nut, returned home bragging of his own ideas about America. He was a patriot now, he said, a Constitutionalist. In the truest sense of the Old West, he believed only in his own independence. Least of all did he trust anyone with a badge. But mostly he was lazy. He lived next door to Jim Rosencrans, a sometime construction worker and full-time drug user who also loved guns and hated the government, and they spent hours playing hearts and spades or burning the clock away hammering at video games. Fortier was in no hurry for the future.

On the other side of his trailer lived a gentlewoman named Elsie. She thought the Fortiers were a fine young family, if somewhat odd and inclined to something other than her own quiet lifestyle. She was perhaps more exemplary of much of Kingman—hardworking, good-minded people who did not seek trouble and were always willing to assist their neighbors. After Kingman heard of that bombing in Oklahoma City, and when Kingman was under attack by the nation's media because of its connection to Fortier and McVeigh, community leaders raised $11,000 and commissioned a ladies' quilting bee. They sewed 150 quilts to send to their sister city on Route 66.

It was Fortier who kept the night light on whenever McVeigh passed through town. For a short while he found his friend a job working in the lumberyard at the Kingman True Value hardware store, where he also worked in the front office.

"We spent a lot of time talking about conspiracy theories," Fortier said. "We shot some weapons and went walking in the mountains." One afternoon the two young men and Lori hiked into the hills and McVeigh exploded a silver-metal pipe bomb he had built. "He ran and hid behind some rocks," Fortier said. "And when it blew up, it took a big boulder and just slowly rolled it on its side."

One morning McVeigh came to work at the hardware store and told Fortier that he had noticed some kind of a "build-up" going on at the local National Guard armory. They snuck out there that night, cleared the back fence, and rummaged through some of the vehicles, looking for any signs of "UN activity," Fortier said. They each stole a shovel, a pick, and an ax from the undercarriage of a military Humvee. Fortier put his away in a storage shed; McVeigh painted his a sand color. More tools for the coming war, he announced.

McVeigh quit the hardware store, worked for a while at a Kingman factory, then later for a landscaping company. Nothing stuck. He and Fortier briefly fancied themselves setting up their own citizens' militia. They drove two hours over to Prescott, Arizona, and met with militia members there, hoping to learn how to incorporate and enlist volunteers. But their plans never gelled. By the fall of 1994, McVeigh was no longer attracted to the part of the far-right movement that wanted to talk tough and practice military exercises. He preferred to act.

That explained what the stolen blasting caps were doing in Christmas wrapping in the trunk of the Spectrum as he and Fortier continued on through Arizona. They were driving past Flagstaff now and into the giant Tonto National Forest, where the harsh colors of the desert suddenly turned verdant with the spires of giant evergreens.

The caps were taken from a Kansas quarry. Allen E. "Bud" Radtke had worked at the Martin Marietta rock quarry in Marion for a dozen years. He was a driller, a man who worked with dynamite and blasting caps and broke rock for a living. On Monday, October 3, he found that a trailer housing ammonium nitrate and fuel oil, along with other blasting materials, had been drilled open. "Normally, I just stick my hand up in there and feel for the key slot in the padlock," he said. But "there was no padlock there. Then I looked, and no padlock on that door. I went over to the magazine where the powder is stored and I saw no padlocks on that either."

Gone was a case of one hundred nonelectric blasting caps, another twenty-five boxes that each held ten electric blasting caps, and seven cases of sausage-shaped emulsion mix for dynamite. Marion County sheriff Lloyd Edward Davies showed up that afternoon, and Bud Radtke took him over to the trailer. Sheriff Davies noticed drill shavings on the ground from the missing padlocks. For a while he wondered if it wasn't the work of a local motorcycle gang or a fellow who had threatened to blow up a local hospital, or perhaps a group of college pranksters from around the middle of Kansas. He never solved the burglary. No arrests were made.

The gun heist was another matter. Fortier asked a lot of questions about those guns and the robbery as he and McVeigh continued toward Kansas to rendezvous with the weapons. If he was going to help sell the stolen merchandise, he wanted to know more about what had gone down. But he never got a straight answer from McVeigh. Neither did the Arkansas authorities or the FBI. The best the federal government ever could say was that McVeigh and Nichols had "caused" the robbery in order to raise funds for McVeigh's bomb plot.

The biggest stumbling block to reaching the truth was the victim himself—none other than that wild-eyed, gun-loving, government-hating friend of McVeigh's named Roger Moore.

Moore would tell conflicting stories about what happened, even changing such key facts as whether one or two men carried out the robbery. But either way, he said, whoever robbed him "was a professional."

Moore said he stepped out of his farmhouse on the morning of November 4 to feed the ducks, geese, and horses and was ordered to lie down. The hooded assailant, who carried a pistol-grip shotgun with a garrote wire, bound him with duct tape and then stole more than sixty firearms, gold bullion, and silver bars. Also taken was Moore's van. Although the vehicle was later found, missing was his list of serial numbers for the guns. Oddly enough, he maintained that he had kept the list in his glove box.

Moore and his friend Karen Anderson grew frustrated when local authorities did not make a swift arrest. So they decided to mount their own investigation. They waffled on whether McVeigh, who knew the farm and had seen where the guns were stored, might have been involved. They wrote him a series of letters in Kingman, first accusing him of the theft, then asking for his help in unraveling the riddle.

McVeigh wrote back once with some advice. Said Anderson, "He had me tramping around the farm on my ass in the woods, looking for a candy wrapper or a cigarette butt that he said would be evidence someone had been on our property."

Later Moore mailed a two-page letter to McVeigh at a postal box in Kingman. McVeigh never received the letter; he had already left Arizona by then. It was done up in code, a strange letter that works on several levels. It is either Roger Moore the patriot talking to his colleague McVeigh, or Moore the victim trying to trick his friend into returning to Arkansas so he can have him arrested.

Moore wrote about the New World Order and the "90% Solution," and he used the phrase "Better Red Than Dead"—all buzzwords among the far right.

"Plan is to bring the country down and have a few more things happen," he wrote. "This is the only cause. But the important thing is to be as effective as possible."

Moore signed the letter with the same advice that McVeigh put on his own letters: "Burn."

Was Moore simply spewing hate rhetoric? Or was he encouraging McVeigh to stay focused on some larger plan?

He continued, "After all this time, I can't believe you'd say I drive you batty as I've cooled down. You must be getting hyper."

McVeigh had an alibi for the robbery; he could show he was attending a gun show in Ohio that day. That left Nichols; his home was later searched, and some of Moore's stolen property was found.

When McVeigh talked to Fortier about the Roger Moore robbery, he always prefaced it as a "code red." That was part of the paranoia Fortier saw in his friend. "Code green" meant all clear; "code yellow" was alert. "Code red" meant trouble. Everything was always secret with McVeigh. He identified Roger Moore only as this man named "Bob" over in Arkansas.

Driving on past the national forest and now up to the rugged Navajo Indian Reservation and the New Mexico border, McVeigh told Fortier that "Terry did Bob." But even this version strained the truth.

He said Nichols, camouflaged in fatigues, boots, and a ski mask, wrapped Bob up in plastic ties and blindfolded him with duct tape. He then went about scooping up the guns. But he tired, and with one hand on a shotgun, untied Bob and forced him to help load up the rest of the loot. Then he tied him up again and blindfolded him too before leaving with the loot.

The whole story was ridiculous. What nonsense! thought Fortier. They drove on awhile in silence, into New Mexico and down the steep freeway decline into Albuquerque. But they did not stop. They pushed on into the Texas panhandle, not planning to rest for the night until they made Amarillo. So Fortier leaned back in his seat and watched the cut-and-go traffic. At one point McVeigh motioned at a Ryder rental truck they were passing.

That, he said, was the type of yellow van he was thinking of using. "Except a size larger," he told Fortier, one big enough to carry at least eighteen thousand pounds.

McVeigh turned from the wheel and looked at his friend. "I may have to stay inside and make sure that it goes off," he said.

Fortier was shaken. "Now you're talking about committing suicide," he said. "This is stupid."

If you are this angry at the government, Fortier said, try to change the system. "Stand on street corners and tell people about it," he said. "In the next ten years you'd be much more effective than doing something like this."

McVeigh shrugged him off. Fortier didn't get it. He didn't really have the soul of the patriot. "Talking doesn't accomplish anything," McVeigh said. "I'm going to sit inside the truck, and if anybody tries to stop it from blowing up, I'm going to blow them away."

Fortier knew what he meant: the Glock pistol McVeigh carried in the shoulder holster under his shirt. But neither man thought it would come to that, McVeigh firing away from the cab of the truck seconds before the bomb blew. Fortier thought back to what his wife had told him. Once when Fortier was away at work, McVeigh demonstrated for Lori how he was going to build his bomb. He called it a "shaped charge." He would assemble the barrels in a triangle shape in the hull of the truck, he told her, with most of the weight to the right side of the truck—the side closest to the building. Give it maximum impact, he said; ensure the greatest number of casualties.

McVeigh walked to the kitchen that day and removed a dozen cans of soup. Stooping down, he arranged them on the floor in tight triangles with two of the three points flush to one side. There, he said. That's my bomb.

But assembling the bomb ingredients was another matter. And McVeigh had told the Fortiers that getting Nichols's cooperation was difficult. Fortier had basically lost touch with Nichols since the army; Lori did not really know him at all. McVeigh, both in the Fortier trailer and now here on the road driving east, mocked Nichols.

"The old man was supposed to do all the talking," McVeigh said, whenever they went out in search of ammonium nitrate and fuel oil and other materials to build the explosive. But McVeigh complained that it always fell to him to make sure they had all the components.

"He was messing up," McVeigh would say of Nichols. "I will have to do it from here on out."

Nichols had nothing but time on his hands back then. His wife, Marife, had gone to the Philippines, and Nichols had quit a job working as a field hand on a large Kansas ranch. That freed him up for other endeavors.

One of their first moves—really, he said, most of their steps were quite simple—was to visit Helen May Mitchell, a Herington, Kansas, resident who kept the books for the Clark Lumber Company. As a sideline, she also helped manage a mini-storage center. On September 22, she rented a locker to a man who identified himself as Shawn Rivers and gave an address of Route 3, Box 83, Marion, Kansas—the same place where Nichols was then living and working for a local farmer.

"Mr. Rivers" paid cash for Space No. 2, a total of $80 for four months. He came in again in October and paid cash for an additional four months, through May. Now they had space to begin storing materials.

Two days after renting the storage locker, McVeigh began hunting for detonation cord. He called Greg Pfaff, his old friend who ran the Lock and Load gun dealership. McVeigh said he was living out in Arizona and needed his help. But Pfaff knew that det cord is a highly regulated item, not sold at gun shows and difficult to find. Nevertheless he promised to check around.

He also warned McVeigh that it was illegal to ship det cord in the United States.

"I'll come and get it," McVeigh said.

"Well, that's an awful long way, from Arizona."

"It doesn't matter. I need it bad."

A week later, McVeigh called him again. Still no det cord, Pfaff said. But it was like that at times—touch and go, hit and miss. Sometimes McVeigh could find what he needed with a snap of the fingers, other times it took a little work.

The Mid-Kansas Co-op in McPherson, Kansas, is a farm supply and grain cooperative, the largest in the state, with nineteen branch locations. Farmers join the co-op as stockholders, and there they set up accounts to buy feed and fertilizer and farm equipment. That fall the co-op was selling fifty-pound brown-and-white bags of ammonium nitrate fertilizer, the bags clearly marked with the words "Warning" and "Explosives."

McVeigh and Nichols came into some money by selling some of Nichols's collector coins to a Wichita dealer, and shortly afterward a man calling himself Mike Havens bought forty fifty-pound bags— weighing a total of two thousand pounds. That would be a full pallet of fertilizer. He paid $228.74 in cash. Asked if he wanted to apply for a tax deduction as a farmer, he said no.

The manager, Frederick Schlender, Jr., would only vaguely recall the purchase. But a second visit would clear up his memory. "Mike Havens" and a companion came back a second time and picked up another forty fifty-pound bags of ammonium nitrate. Again the price was $228.74, paid in cash, and as before, they turned down the application for a farmer's tax exemption.

Schlender was able to remember the blue pickup with the white camper shell. The driver came inside and made the purchase, and the other man waited in the truck. Then they brought the truck around back and Schlender worked a forklift to load the fertilizer onto a trailer hitched to the back of the truck.

Schlender remembered thinking that such a large purchase was "somewhat unusual." It had rained the day before, and farmers do not plant right after a rain. And most of his farm customers prefer liquid nitrogen fertilizer for putting in Kansas wheat. Equally curious was the fact that no individual before or since had bought so much and paid cash.

McVeigh had his fertilizer; now he needed fuel oil.

Linda Juhl answered the phone at her desk at Mid-American Chemical Inc., an Oklahoma City distributor. The man calling wanted to purchase anhydrous hydrazine, a highly volatile chemical mixture. She didn't have it, and he didn't give his name.

McVeigh telephoned Dave Darlak, his Pendleton high school chum, two days later. Darlak had a brother, Michael, who was involved in modified dirt car racing.

"Where can I purchase racing fuel?" McVeigh asked.

Darlak was curious. "Why in the world do you need that?" he asked.

McVeigh said he was busy, that he was at work and had to go. He hung up.

The next day he called Gary Mussatto in Osage City, Kansas, not far from Herington. Mussatto had run the Hutchinson, Kansas, Raceway Park.

"Do you sell racing fuel?" the man asked.

"Yes," said Mussatto.

"Do you have any nitromethane?"

"No. We don't use that type."

Mussatto asked if he was a racer.

Yes, McVeigh said. "Where can I get some?" he asked.

"Either go to a drag strip or to somebody who sells it."

Nitromethane, according to Mussatto, is "real volatile," and is used in some of the sport's most powerful race engines. He told the man about "a guy in Manhattan"—Manhattan, Kansas, not far away—who worked for VP Racing Fuels. He might be able to help. The annual Sears Craftsman National Drag Race was coming up the first weekend in October at the Heartland Park in Topeka. They would be selling nitromethane there.

Mussatto hung up. What a strange call, that a person would call a dirt racetrack for that type of fuel, he thought.

The next stop was the Sears Craftsman show in Topeka. That weekend Glynn Tipton was abruptly confronted by a man he believes to be McVeigh. Tipton was a salesman and warehouse coordinator for VP Racing, and that Saturday, October 1, he was working the pits when this stranger with short hair and two to three days' growth of beard walked up.

The man called out, "Hey boss!"

Tipton was just walking back into his trailer. He turned around. The man asked where he could buy anhydrous hydrazine in fifty-five-gallon drums. Tipton was startled. The man was inquiring about a product Tipton did not carry that day—a pure form of rocket fuel, the kind used for NASA-style rockets. The man said he had had access to anhydrous hydrazine in the past, but no longer. He wanted more, and he wanted to know the price and availability.

The man said his name was John and that he was in the process of moving from Junction City, Kansas, to Salina, Kansas. He said he did not have a phone. Tipton went into the trailer to get a business card and told the man he would check for him on Monday. "John" then asked about a similarly potent fuel called nitromethane. Tipton told him it could go as high as $1,200 a drum.

McVeigh would not be discouraged. Later that month he found what he wanted at another racetrack, this one in Ennis, Texas, just south of Dallas.

Timothy Chambers, a VP Racing Fuels truck manager, was working the Chief Auto Parts Nationals in Ennis that weekend when a blue pickup with a white camper shell pulled up. Chambers could never be sure about the man driving the truck. The pickup fit the type and color of one owned by Nichols, but the man more neatly resembled McVeigh—the hard eyes close together, the long nose down the long face; "kind of like a possum face," Chambers remembered.

The man approached the trailer and asked about three drums of nitromethane. Chambers priced it out at $925 a drum. So the man pulled the truck around, opened the liftgate of the camper, and slid down the tailgate. He paid cash and they loaded up three barrels.

Chambers asked him what he was going to do. "He said him and a bunch of his friends get together and come down once a year and buy this from this particular drag race," Chambers recalled. "He said they race Harley bikes up in the Oklahoma City area."

The man drove off, leaving Chambers shaking his head. "Well, three drums of nitromethane being sold for cash never happens," he said. "Another thing, somebody comes up to you and they are purchasing three drums and they are going to take it and split it with their friends on nitro Harley bikes? That just doesn't happen either. Harley street bike guys, if they are going to buy gas such as nitromethane from me, they will buy a gallon to five gallons. Now, nitro Harley bikes, you couldn't even afford to put one of those on the street. That just wouldn't happen."

Chambers was well aware that a Harley motorcyle filled with nitromethane can reach speeds of up to 220 miles an hour in a quarter-mile sprint. What did that guy really want with so much rocket fuel? he wondered.

McVeigh had the main bomb ingredients. It all had seemed so easy. He was proud of pulling it together too. So proud that he had showed Fortier some of the materials.

Fortier remembered that too. Driving across the tip of Texas now, their second day on the road and soon to cross into Oklahoma, the Sooner state, the winds picking up, the air cooling, he understood what McVeigh planned to put in the back of the rental truck like the one they had passed yesterday on the interstate.

McVeigh and Nichols kept a separate storage locker in Kingman. They had been sleeping out at a desert campsite where McVeigh used to go snake hunting. Nichols was only occasionally out that way; McVeigh was spending more and more time in and around Kingman. One day he called Fortier. "I want to show you something," McVeigh said.

He picked up Fortier in the Spectrum; that time he had Nichols with him, following behind in his blue-and-white pickup. It was nine o'clock at night when they reached the locker.

McVeigh shined a flashlight around the inside of the storage room, the beam dancing off the ceiling and walls and then landing on a box with an orange diamond marked "Explosives." He reached into the box and held up some explosives into the sliver of light. He squatted down before a blanket that covered other boxes, the flashlight still bouncing in front of him, and Fortier could see what lay there too: twelve boxes in all, stacked three high and two deep. All the while, Nichols was carrying the materials out of the locker and loading them into his truck.

Fortier was awestruck. He did not want to leave. He invited McVeigh and Nichols to stay the night at his trailer home. But Nichols refused; he started up his truck and drove off, alone. McVeigh, however, did go home with Fortier. That evening, in what Fortier remembers as one fantastic night, McVeigh explained the boxes of explosives in the storage locker, saying they had come from the rock quarry.

That was the start of their plans, the kick-off; use the blasting caps and dynamite for the bombing, sell the rest to keep yourself in funds to obtain the other materials. Use money McVeigh earned on the gun circuit or from odd jobs around Kingman; use money that Nichols was paid working as a hired hand out in Kansas, or money from selling precious coins or jewelry.

Fortier remembered how McVeigh drew him a diagram back then, with a box for the truck and circles for the barrels that go inside, and he described how he planned to run a fuse from the front of the cab to the cargo hold in the rear. He drew a straight line for the fuse, and said he would drill a hole through the back of the cab to run it into the hold. "He told me that he had figured out how to make a truck into a bomb," Fortier recalled. "And Tim told me that him and Terry had chosen a building in Oklahoma City, a federal building in Oklahoma City."

Why in the world Oklahoma City? Why this building?

McVeigh told him—mistakenly—that this building "was where the orders for the attack on Waco came from."

"He also told me," Fortier said, "that he was wanting to blow up a building to cause a general uprising in America, and hopefully that would knock some people off the fence and urge them into taking action against the federal government."

What of the people inside the building, the government workers, the federal agents and the military recruiters, the visitors to the Social Security office, and the children in the second-floor day care center? It was a typical federal office building in a large American city, and Fortier knew what they were like—the front doors, the lobby, the high floors, the men in suits and the women in business attire, the government at work.

"He considered all those people to be as if they were the storm troopers in the movie *Star Wars*," Fortier said. "They may be individually innocent. But because they are part of the evil empire, they were guilty by association."

And so, early into their second day on the freeway, tired, hungry, road-weary, McVeigh and Fortier reached the downtown Oklahoma City skyline. Now it was time for the little detour. McVeigh eased the Spectrum off the interstate, spun under the overpass, and drove the few blocks up to the corner of 5th and Harvey streets. Slowly they circled the nine-story Alfred P. Murrah Federal Building, past the dark black glass veneer that covered the whole north facade.

Think I can fit that large truck up at the front door? McVeigh asked.

Fortier marveled at how simple it all seemed. "You could probably fit three trucks there," he said.

McVeigh turned into an alley a few blocks away, on the other side of the downtown YMCA building. He pointed out the spot where he planned to leave a getaway car. They stopped there briefly, long enough for McVeigh to explain that he and Nichols actually were exploring several options. One had Nichols following him down from Kansas on the morning of April 19, and then the two of them, with the fire and smoke filling the city behind them, driving back to Kansas together. The other scenario had Nichols following McVeigh to Oklahoma City several days before the bombing, to allow McVeigh to drop off the getaway car and drive back with Nichols. Then McVeigh would deliver the bomb—alone—on April 19.

Fortier asked him why he did not want to leave his getaway car closer to the federal office building. "Why not down the alley more?" he asked.

No, said McVeigh. He wanted the protection of the YMCA building so he would not be hurt as he fled the scene. And he would wear earplugs too. The earplugs would protect him from the deafening roar of the bomb blast.

Chapter Seven

Ode to Oklahoma

The Alfred P. Murrah Federal Building in downtown Oklahoma City, rising nine stories up out of the flatland of middle America, was a city unto itself. It was not the highest point in the state's capital city, nor the newest nor the most architecturally pleasing. It did not hold the largest number of people either. But it was full of federal agents, military recruiters, citizens seeking Social Security payments or job applications or HUD assistance; mothers and fathers too, and their small children who attended the day care center on the second floor. The imposing entrance on 5th Street invited all those who passed by. Here the people's business was conducted; all were welcome. McVeigh was right about what he saw looking up from the street that December day. The Alfred P. Murrah Federal Building was open to the public.

It was named for the youngest federal judge to be appointed in American history. Alfred Murrah was elevated to the bench at the age of thirty-two by President Franklin D. Roosevelt. The year was 1937, at the height of the dust storms that ravaged Oklahoma. He served for thirty years as a federal judge, and two years after his retirement, Congress appropriated $13 million to erect a then state-of-the-art monument to honor his memory. The building encompassed the entire city block between 5th and 4th streets and Harvey and Robinson, prime downtown real estate directly north of the United States courthouse. It included a garden plaza in the back.

But what was unique about its design was the U-shaped, indented drive on 5th Street that allowed for quick pickup and delivery parking, and the top-to-bottom glass exterior that covered the entire front of the building. Looking up from the street you could see the people working—and the children playing—inside.

The people of Oklahoma have always been known for their grit; maybe that explains why the state has not blown away into Texas or Arkansas or somewhere else altogether. It has survived Indian wars and topsoil erosion and the tornadoes that always seem to pick Oklahoma as a good place to stir up trouble. The wind is a constant, a fact of life. When Hollywood moviemakers came here to begin making the great musical *Oklahoma!* they looked around and declared it unsuitable for filming; they packed up their cameras and moved the outdoor scenes to a southern Arizona valley near the Mexican border. There might be a bright golden haze on an Oklahoma meadow, but everyone knows that corn grows higher in Kansas and Iowa. "Hardscrabble" is too kind a word to describe this state's origins; "mean" is a better choice. Oklahomans call themselves Sooners to glorify those who cheated on the Land Rush, who got to this place before the United States opened up the land. And when the first state capital was established in Guthrie, a group of renegades broke in one night, stole the state seal, and snuck it a day's ride down south to Oklahoma City. The state was born in adversity.

Oil and gas saved it. The two main streets in downtown Oklahoma City are named Kerr and McGee after two of the biggest tycoon names to bubble up out of the ground. Route 66 came through town, and it was the Mother Road; it brought the Eastern money, the oil speculators and the wildcatters. Farmland so dry that a man could not raise a harvest because of all the hard rock suddenly was worth a fortune for what was underneath that rock. Even the state got into the act; today oil wells still churn lazily up and down on the grounds of the state capitol building. The boom came and brought the high times; the bust followed and that brought despair. Only the winds remained. The state's two most famous sons, Will Rogers and Woody Guthrie, became famous for leaving Oklahoma.

Always, the wind. When Oklahomans leave the state, they miss the wind, its sound and its touch.

That rough, batten-down-the-hatches independence survives still. People drive without seat belts here. They marry young. Most are deeply religious, and yet there seem to be more pawnshops than churches in this state. On one end of Oklahoma City there sits a modern hall of fame to the Cowboy, and on the other a working stockyard. Beef lands on every plate, and the cigarette is the popular after-dinner choice.

Richard Williams knew the Murrah building inside and out. He was a native Oklahoman, forty-nine years old, married, with two children. He had a thin mustache and wore glasses. For not quite twenty years he worked for the federal General Services Administration, the agency that oversees government property, and now he was the assistant building manager at the Murrah site.

He knew the downtown area well too. With the federal courthouse to its south, the Murrah building was also surrounded by the state Water Resources Board and the old St. Joseph's Cathedral, the Catholic church where there once had been a rectory. Williams could take a work break on the Murrah loading dock and watch the homeless knock on the rectory door. To the east of the Murrah plaza was the First United Methodist Church, and across from that the downtown YMCA.

Williams was first assigned the Murrah building when it opened in 1977, and over the years he came to know its every secret. People sought him out to fix all kinds of problems—blocked air ducts, dirty stairwells, loose doorjambs, frayed carpet. He was the Murrah fix-it man, roaming from the Social Security offices on the first floor to the ATF, the DEA, and the Secret Service stations up on nine. He was born in Chickasha and raised in Seminole, and left Oklahoma only for a short stint in the air force. He returned and worked the oil fields for a short while, and when the Murrah opened, he became its first mechanic. Asked once to describe his typical day, he said, "Walking the building, meeting the people, working with them, taking care of the system itself." Nothing grandiose, but the Alfred P. Murrah Federal Building was his baby.

His office was over on the west end of the ground floor, not far from the front doors. Each weekday morning, the first floor was bustling with people and noise, cars pulling up outside and doors slamming at the start of another busy workday. The Social Security lobby opened at eight and began processing claims by nine. At any given time, dozens of people, often whole families, would crowd into the reception area, holding numbers and waiting for their chance to meet with an adjustor. Sometimes they stepped outside to smoke and kill time; this was also a popular place for many of the building employees to take a cigarette.

Up on the second floor, directly above them, were the children. The America's Kids day care center covered almost the entire floor, with separate rooms for infants and toddlers and children up to kindergarten age. The nursery was open from six-thirty in the morning until six at night, and the mothers and fathers who brought their children here loved it for its bright colors, warm textures, and caring staff. Helena Garrett, like many of the mothers, especially enjoyed waving one last time to the children as she left the building, looking up at the curtain wall and spotting the infant bassinets or the tiny hands of children pressed up against the glass windows.

"I had heard about it through a friend," she said, "and when I went over there, I loved it. The workers were nice, and it was open and clean, and the windows . . . it was just all open and I loved it." She worked across the street, at the *Journal Record* building, close enough to take a break and visit her sixteen-month-old son, Tevin. He was born on Thanksgiving Day, and she first brought him there when he was just eight weeks old.

She visited Tevin at least twice a day. As many as thirty children a day were cared for at America's Kids, and Garrett knew them all. In the infants' room there were cribs lined along the windows, and rocking chairs too, and a sink and cabinets and a changing table. For the two-year-olds there was a big slide and riding toys and cubbyholes for their jackets, but also secret hiding places for the children to climb into and around. For the bigger kids, there were arts and crafts.

She chose the nursery because it was close to work and, equally important, it seemed the safest place of all. Everyone knew that upstairs was a phalanx of federal law enforcement teams—the ATF, the Secret Service, the DEA.

Luke Franey had been an ATF agent since 1988, assigned to the Oklahoma field office. His office was Suite 965, at the southeast corner of the ninth floor. There they kept an evidence vault and a fingerprinting room, and from there investigations into stolen guns or illegal explosives would be handled by agents working the Oklahoma region. The DEA officers put together drug cases, while the Secret Service agents handled counterfeiting cases and provided security details for dignitaries visiting the state.

There were firearms up there too, either strapped to the agents' waists or sometimes in small lockers or desk drawers. But most of the explosives evidence or large hauls taken by the ATF were stored in a bunker out at the city's air depot, a unit shared with the local Oklahoma City police and other law enforcement agencies. If anything, people working or visiting the Murrah building could take comfort in knowing the facility was roundly protected.

But most of the building was federal office space, cubicles and desks and telephones—the Department of Housing and Urban Development, the General Accounting Office, Health and Human Services. There were military recruitment offices in the building—the U.S. Army, the Marine Corps. The Federal Employees Credit Union, by its very nature one of the more popular offices in the building, took up much of the third floor.

Paul Heath, a Veterans' Affairs psychologist on the fifth floor, a graying father figure to many of those who worked at the Murrah, considered the high-rise structure a living, breathing community, a village of its own. Susan Gail Hunt, a HUD supervisor, tall and blond and with a deep Southwestern twang, knew so many people in the building and concerned herself so much with their daily lives, doing things such as arranging the flowers for employee Kim Clark's upcoming wedding, that many referred to her as the Murrah mother hen. Florence Rogers, a credit union manager, was so familiar with the lay of her office that even after the Murrah building was gone and the ground stood empty, she could walk across that flattened earth and recall exactly where each filing cabinet had stood, each desk, each person.

Michael Norfleet, a Marine Corps aviator, lived over in Stillwater and worked as a recruiter at the Oklahoma State University campus. Only occasionally would he be drawn to downtown Oklahoma City, maybe to attend a community meeting or stop by for a short visit at his command's recruiting station headquarters on the sixth floor of the Murrah.

"I tried to avoid seeing my boss too much," he would joke. But when he did appear, it was always for a round of hellos and slaps on the back. He too felt at home there among his fellow Marines.

Donna Weaver did not work in the building at all, but she knew all about the Murrah. Her husband, Mike, was a HUD lawyer on the eighth floor, his office up against the glass windows on the north face of the building. She worked as a manager for Southwestern Bell, about three blocks away. They had two teenage sons, and had moved to Oklahoma City five years ago from Texas when Mike took a job transfer.

She went into work early; he stayed late. He had the responsibility for getting the boys off to school; she made them dinner. Sometimes Donna and Mike would meet for lunch at the YMCA; she went to her aerobics class, he played basketball. Or she might take a walk through the downtown area and, when passing by the corner of 5th and Harvey streets, tilt her head of dark red hair and look up to the sky, and there, nearly to the top of the safe and secure Alfred P. Murrah Federal Building, she could see her husband.

"Sometimes he'd be at the window on the phone," she said. "I would wave and he would wave back."

Chapter Eight

Going for It

McVeigh was right: Terry Nichols was not being of much help. In fact, "the old man" had flown out of the country altogether and gone to the Philippines in search of his wife, Marife, and their baby daughter, Nicole. He had disappeared just when most of the bomb ingredients were in place, and that meant McVeigh was on his own now. But what McVeigh did not know at that time was that Nichols had left behind a note and a good amount of cash, including instructions on what to do should he never return.

For the next four months, McVeigh would be the sole proprietor of their franchise; he would have to see that everything remained in place. Even the last details would fall to McVeigh. To prove his resolve, to show the world what he was about, he left behind a note of his own, printed on a computer disk and titled "ATF Read." It may have been just a few short lines, but his words were threatening and there was no mistaking his intentions.

In Oklahoma City that day in December, McVeigh and Fortier had hung around the Murrah building and the back alley behind the YMCA facility for no more than twenty minutes. Now McVeigh was eager to push on; Fortier too. They had guns to move and blasting caps to sell. McVeigh turned the Spectrum north onto Interstate 35 and drove up past Guthrie and Perry and over the Cimarron Trail and into Kansas. Just after they crossed the state line, McVeigh sud-

denly pulled off to avoid the Kansas Turnpike. He checked his maps
and told Fortier it was not safe to travel the toll roads.

Better the backways, he said. Better to avoid the cameras that the
government mounts on the tollbooths to spy on people.

So they abandoned the turnpike and traveled north and east up
old US 77, zigzagging their way through Kansas and its great
stretches of farm country, continuing on along the western fringes
of the hardy Flint Hills region and finally closing in on Junction
City and the home next door of their old unit, the Big Red One at
Fort Riley.

They shopped at the Junction City Wal-Mart, ate at Wendy's,
and checked into a local motel. McVeigh told Fortier to hide
around back while he registered as a single guest and saved a few
dollars. It was an old game McVeigh liked to play; he always felt
good when he could beat the man. In a gesture of goodwill,
McVeigh presented Fortier with two pistols and some ammunition; for good luck, he said.

After dawn they drove out to the airport at nearby Manhattan,
Kansas. At the Hertz counter Fortier rented a Crown Victoria, chosen for its deep, roomy trunk, for they would need the extra space.
Then he followed McVeigh south and east to Council Grove, a
short sprint away, and while Fortier stood guard at the storage
locker, McVeigh went through the weapons, dividing them up
between those that Fortier would drive to Kingman and those he—
McVeigh—could not part with and decided to keep.

It took nearly an hour to get the dozens of guns safely stored and
concealed inside the Crown Vic. They were placed in barrels for
safekeeping and then locked in the trunk. What slowed the process
was McVeigh's occasional uncertainty over which weapons he
wanted for himself. He also was taking the time to give Fortier
some pointers on how best to sell the guns.

McVeigh told him that he had to win acceptance at the gun
shows or potential buyers would be skeptical about his inventory.
Look the part, he told him. Be sure of yourself, he said; think to
yourself that you can do it.

"Wear military clothing," he advised Fortier. "Don't talk in
slang. Have a military bearing about yourself."

They stopped for lunch at a Pizza Hut, one last chance to go over
their routes and for McVeigh to coach Fortier on selling weapons.

But as they split up, Fortier noticed that his Crown Vic was riding rather low. He was all too aware of the excess weight back there, and he worried that this would be a dead giveaway to any alert highway patrol trooper.

He motioned for McVeigh to follow closely behind him for a bit, just to check on the ride. So McVeigh watched the back of the big car, then pulled forward and gave his friend the thumbs-up; the car looked fine, he said. They came to a stop sign—McVeigh went north, Fortier south. Fortier drove straight through to the New Mexico–Arizona state line without stopping to sleep, and by then he was exhausted. He pulled into a rest stop and napped for a couple of hours in the car; he was not about to leave the vehicle. When he awoke, he drove on, into the next morning and early afternoon. He reached Kingman around two o'clock, stumbled into his trailer home, and collapsed into sleep.

McVeigh drove relentlessly too, but his journey northeast was more eventful. The Spectrum was rear-ended in Michigan, a collision that caused McVeigh to cringe; the blasting caps in the trunk could have detonated, blowing him and "the Warrior" across the roadway. The back bumper was bent badly and the wheel alignment twisted, but the caps had only been jolted. Nothing was lost. He nursed the Spectrum along to a truck stop in Saginaw, Michigan, and telephoned a friend.

Kevin Nicholas had known McVeigh from some years back while working as an extra hand on the Decker farm belonging to the Nichols family. He drove a spare tractor and handled other chores, and though he shared some of their antigovernment leanings, he never went so far as to turn "nutty" the way people around the Decker area thought the Nichols brothers had. He first met McVeigh hanging around the Michigan-area gun shows, and he was introduced to him under an alias McVeigh was using at that time, Tim Tuttle. McVeigh was selling Waco videotapes then, and *The Turner Diaries*, and Nicholas just considered this "Tim Tuttle" character another example of somebody who had shifted too far to the right.

Over the years he became used to McVeigh's popping sporadically in and out of Michigan. This evening his phone rang just after he finished dinner around seven o'clock. McVeigh said that he had been in an accident and asked Nicholas to pick him up right away;

he said he would be waiting behind a row of semitrailers at the local Speedway gas station.

Nicholas drove out to the Speedway in his pickup, and there he found McVeigh, just where he'd said he would be, patiently standing between two semis in the back of the station parking lot. The Spectrum was already unloaded and McVeigh had placed his bags on the pavement. With Nicholas's help, he began putting his belongings into his friend's pickup. Nicholas, in a hurry to get home, started grabbing McVeigh's packages and tossing them into the truck.

"Don't handle them," barked McVeigh. "I'll take care of the Christmas packages."

Nicholas looked at his friend. McVeigh was always acting so strange; everything was some big mystery, some big game. The guy was always too self-important, Nicholas thought. And he wasn't the only one who thought so; McVeigh had nurtured that sort of reputation up here in the thumb of Michigan, especially over at the Decker farm.

McVeigh often seemed out of place when he visited here. Dan Stromber, a farmer who ran the Mid-Michigan Rooster Ranch, recalled McVeigh's moodiness, how he often would carry on about some grandiose idea or another, and then just as quickly turn cold and start warning about the evils of big government. "If you spent an hour riding with him in a pickup, he'd keep you company and the ride would be short," Stromber would say. Another neighbor, Carl Broecker, remembered that McVeigh could suddenly become agitated at the smallest occurrence, and that he forever seemed to be imagining police cars coming down the road. "He was upset, nervous, always looking over his shoulder," Broecker recalled.

McVeigh was no farmer. He carried a gun on his waist, or strung one under his left shoulder. He could talk about farm failures and government ineffectiveness, but he was no good in the fields. He could not stand still long enough.

Loading up the pickup at the Speedway, Kevin Nicholas asked him about the Christmas packages. "What's in them?" he asked.

"I'll tell you later," promised McVeigh.

They pried loose the rear bumper on the Spectrum so he could drive better, and then he followed Nicholas over to his house in

Vassar, Michigan. They stored McVeigh's belongings in the shed, and Nicholas asked him again what was in those Christmas gifts.

McVeigh finally decided to let him in on his secret. But only halfway; the whole truth he would keep to himself. McVeigh figured that if you told someone everything, you gave away your aura.

He winked at his friend. "Caps," he said. "And I got them dirt-cheap."

Nicholas never did learn what the mystery was all about. But McVeigh later told him that he had gone down to the Chicago area to see about unloading them to a weapons dealer there. He bought another car, an old blue Pontiac station wagon, from James Nichols while staying a short while out on the Decker farm. Terry was not there; he was still in the Philippines. And then McVeigh felt the need to push on. One day he drove off; he thought he'd go back to Kingman and see how Fortier was doing selling those hot guns.

He knew that Terry Nichols wanted the money he thought due him for the firearms. In some ways, Nichols was used to being taken care of. Throughout his many misadventures, he always could depend on his older brother to keep an eye on him.

Like Terry, James Nichols had long embraced the ultraright. Both brothers for a while watched as the patriot movement gained ground in Michigan and rural communities throughout the nation. But they never joined the local militia or took the time to become involved in affairs of the right. While others spent their weekends in dark camouflage clothing practicing paramilitary maneuvers, the Nichols brothers stayed at home and amused themselves making milk-carton bombs and tossing them into the fields on the family farm.

One day, in what would be his first break with the rest of the outside world, James Nichols walked into the local courthouse and filed his own declaration of independence, stating that he was "no longer one of your citizens or a resident of your de facto government."

There was another story circulating around about James Nichols. This one came from an Indiana seed dealer named Dave Shafer.

Shafer was often on the road as a farm supply salesman, and he would work some thirteen counties in the thumb of Michigan, including Decker. Often he called on the Nichols farm, and there, he said, he witnessed some strange goings-on. Once James Nichols boasted about building a "superbomb," Shafer would say. On another visit out to Decker, this one in the late eighties, he was delivering seed on the Nichols farm and he noticed bulk quantities of fertilizer and seed stockpiled inside a machine shed. He said he could smell the heavy odor of diesel fuel in the air.

He wanted to know if James was overhauling a tractor.

No, he said. We're making cardboard bombs by filling milk cartons with fertilizer and fuel oil. "We're having fun," he said. "Milk-carton bombs for fun."

Shafer told of another visit with James Nichols around that same time, after a terrorist bomb had exploded on board Pam Am Flight 103 over Lockerbie, Scotland. "Nichols was rambling that the United States government was responsible," Shafer would contend. He said Nichols explained how much damage a bomb can do, and that the technology exists for a superbomb large enough to take down a high-rise building.

This caught Shafer's attention. "What if you had a superbomb?" he asked Nichols. "What building would you blow up?"

He said Nichols showed him a drawing from a newspaper clipping of a federal building. It appeared that the building was still under construction. Nichols said it was possible to get close enough with a bomb. This frightened the Indiana seed salesman. He thought Nichols was merely bragging, and when he looked away from the drawing and up at him, he saw that he was beginning to laugh. Then Nichols snapped, "We've got to get back to work."

Later, when he talked to the FBI, Shafer would swear that drawing was of a federal building in Oklahoma City.

James had some pretty peculiar notions. He buried special piping around the perimeter of his farm, they said, so that when the rains came, it would attract most of the water onto his fields and then he could outproduce his neighbors. And when his wife, Kathy, Lana's sister, divorced him, he buried her picture in the ground—a ritual he thought surely would bring her back.

Both James and Terry Nichols had lost their wives to divorce. But Terry tried again, after his time in the army and his return to the farm. Eventually he brought home his second wife, Marife, from the Philippines. And she came with her son, Jason.

The child would later be found dead at the age of two in his bedroom in the Nichols farmhouse. Authorities in Sanilac County said the boy died from accidental suffocation. Police reports stated that

Nichols had tried to resuscitate the child but failed. Investigators noted that Nichols at the time appeared "quiet and visibly upset." The reports also made note that helping with the attempts at first aid to save the boy was a house guest named Jim Tuttle—obviously McVeigh.

The death left Terry and Marife Nichols with just their own child, a baby girl, Nicole. But for Marife, her marriage would forever be scarred by the loss of her son. Several times she went home to Cebu City; just as often her husband flew out there to bring her back. His behavior was erratic, and he was falling headlong with McVeigh into a deepening distrust of the government.

In 1992 Terry Nichols fired off a letter to the Michigan Department of Natural Resources, disavowing any further allegiance to the United States. "I no longer am a citizen of the corrupt political CORPORATE State of Michigan and the United States of America," he wrote. "I am a natural born human being. . . ."

In May the following year, a month after the fiery end at Waco, he confronted a Michigan state judge when he was forced to court for nonpayment of $18,000 in credit card bills. During the hearing, he burst into a tirade and screamed so loud at Judge Donald A. Teeple that the official transcript came out with large blank spaces where the court reporter's fingers could not keep up.

"I don't wanna enter your jurisdiction!" he yelled.

The session ended with Nichols indicating he would pay back the money. But he sent in a phony check. On a court form, he scribbled, "How can anyone pay anything with no real true genuine money?"

McVeigh and Nichols shared a book called *Privacy!*—a self-help manual on how to go underground and resist the government; how to lose oneself in America. Among the tips: become invisible to investigators; stop generating financial records; stay out of government files; live nomadically; obtain multiple addresses; use hideouts and deep cover.

But they were seldom out of reach of each other. For a long time they shared a telephone debit card they purchased from the far-right *Spotlight* newsletter. They used the card to phone each other or to make other calls they thought would be impossible to track. After Waco, in the fall of 1993, McVeigh was back on the Nichols farm and they were experimenting with bomb-making again. Then came spring, and Nichols moved Marife and Nicole out to Marion, Kansas, where he hired on as a farmhand on a large family-owned operation cutting hay and tending the summer sorghum.

Nichols worked hard, but he had weird ideas. "He often talked about the government being too big and having too much power and that he felt that the government needed to be overthrown," recalled farm manager Timothy Donahue. "And that Thomas Jefferson had written that it was our duty to overthrow the government when it did get too powerful."

McVeigh occasionally visited Nichols on the farm, and Donahue asked about Nichols's young friend with the bright blue eyes. "He told me Tim was in Desert Storm and the government had implanted a chip into him that monitored his whereabouts," Donahue said.

Donahue never believed such ridiculous talk. And by summer's end, with Marife and baby Nicole away in the Philippines, Nichols announced he was quitting; he said he was pushing on to work the gun show circuit with McVeigh. But actually he went off to help McVeigh acquire some of those key bomb-making components. Then Nichols headed for the Philippines, after first staying a short while at Lana's house in Las Vegas in order to spend time visiting and camping with their son, Josh.

Lana drove him to the airport for his flight to Cebu City. He seemed quiet and reserved, the old Terry. In the last year or so, she had noticed the deep changes that had come over her ex-husband; much of it she credited to his friendship with McVeigh. Increasingly, she had come to distrust that old friend from Fort Riley.

Before departing, Terry handed her a package and asked her to keep it for McVeigh should he show up in Las Vegas. It was just the keys to his blue-and-white pickup, he assured her. McVeigh was having trouble with his own car, the Pontiac wagon; he'd said he might need to borrow the pickup.

So Lana saw him to the airport, but after he left, the package gnawed at her; she wondered whether her ex-husband was coming back. She turned the package in her hands and, afraid it might be a suicide note and that their son Josh would lose his father, abruptly tore it open.

Inside she found a series of letters. One addressed to her was titled "Read and Do Immediately." It instructed her to clear out a Las Vegas storage unit he had recently rented to store some of the items he had brought up from Kingman. "As of now," he wrote her, "only Marife, you & myself know what there is and where it is. I hope you will do as I have stated. Josh has just a few years before he's capable of being on his own and Marife & Nicole have many more years of support needed. There is no need to tell anyone about the items in storage and at home."

His letter also mentioned something he had hidden in her kitchen, behind the utensil drawer near the dishwasher and stove. Once again, he left detailed instructions: "There are two small levers—one on each side of drawer on rail. Pull drawer out till it stops, then flip levers down & pull drawer completely out. Then look all the way back inside. Take and push hard against back panel. Both sides & bottom are glued. After it's broke free, remove wood panel. Then remove plastic bag. All items in plastic bag are to be sent to Marife for Nicole if for any reason my life insurance doesn't pay Marife. Otherwise, 1/2 goes to Marife and 1/2 to Joshua."

Now Lana was convinced he was planning his own death. Josh would be without a father. She hurried home . . . to the kitchen . . . to the drawer. She took out the drawer and broke the panel and there she discovered a zip-lock bag. She ripped it open and found $20,000.

There were two other letters in the package, both addressed "Tim." The first explained how to enter the Las Vegas locker and where the blue pickup with the white camper would be parked, available if he needed it.

She drove out to the locker and opened the door to the storage unit. She found a box of carved jade, camera equipment, and precious stones—much of it later linked to the Roger Moore robbery—and a ski mask.

The second letter from Nichols to McVeigh turned out to be much more significant. He instructed his friend to "liquidate 40"—a reference to the Council Grove, Kansas, locker he had leased under the alias Ted Parker and where some of the stolen guns and other items had been stored. "The Parker deal was signed & dated 07 Nov 94," the Nichols letter advised McVeigh. "So you should have till 07 Feb '95. Plus 5 days grace. If close or they disagree then should pay another term period."

He gave McVeigh a warning about law enforcement: "As far as heat—None that I know. This letter would be for the purpose of my death."

He concluded: "Tim: If, should you receive this letter, then clear everything out of CG 37 [a second Council Grove locker] by 01 Feb 95 or pay to keep it longer, under Ted Parker of Decker. This letter has been written & sealed before I left 21 Nov 94 & being mailed by Lana as per my instructions to her in writing. This is all she knows. It would be a good idea to write or call her to verify things.

"Just ask for Lana.

"Your on your own.

"Go for it!!"

Nichols's attorneys would later insist that "Go for it!!" was an innocent reference to an old sales pitch he and Lana had used when working together in the early days of their marriage. The government attorneys believed otherwise. They said it was a clear indication that McVeigh was now the prime mover, that the bombing plot was in his hands while Nichols hid out in the Philippines. But McVeigh did not have to be told. With Nichols out of the country, there was no one else to push things ahead. And before the year's end, McVeigh would leave his own note behind for those who came looking for him.

In Pendleton, visiting his father and sister Jennifer, he sat in front of his sister's word processor in their small white ranch-style family house. First he typed out a letter to the American Legion, addressing it to all "Constitutional Defenders."

"We members of the citizen's militias do not bear our arms to overthrow the Constitution," he wrote, "but to overthrow those who PERVERT the Constitution and when they once again draw first blood (many believe the Waco incident was 'first blood')."

"Many of our members are veterans who still hold true to their sworn oath to defend the Constitution against ALL enemies, foreign and DOMESTIC."

He quoted John Locke about the right to slay the tyrant if government leaders force the people into a state of war. He attacked the Bureau of Alcohol, Tobacco and Firearms as a "fascist federal group" infamous for depriving citizens of their right to self-defense. He cited Waco and Randy Weaver and Gordon Kahl (another extremist hunted down by the government) as victims of the ATF "fascist tyrants." He mocked the "power-hungry storm troopers of the federal government."

"Who else would come to the rescue of those innocent women

and children at Waco?!?" he asked. "Surely not the local sheriff or the state police! Nor the Army—whom are used overseas to 'restore democracy,' while at home are used to DESTROY it (in full violation of the Posse Comitatus Act), at places like Waco."

So there was that too, the final break from the army he had loved so much such a short time ago. They had betrayed him; now he was his own Green Beret.

"One last question that every American should ask themselves," he wrote. "Did not the British also keep track of the locations of munitions stored by the colonists; just as the ATF has admitted to doing? Why??? . . . Does anyone even STUDY history anymore???"

Jennifer saw the letter; it alarmed her. She too embraced much of his ideology, having these past two years received so much of his antigovernment literature and other writings. She had read *The Turner Diaries*; she also believed that Waco was a big lie. But her older brother was clearly far beyond her now.

"I'm no longer in the propaganda stage," he told her. "I'm no longer passing out papers. Now I'm in the action stage."

He turned back to the word processor, and slowly his long fingers tapped out one more letter. This one was for the enemy.

"ATF Read" he began.

"ATF, all you tyrannical motherfuckers will swing in the wind one day for your treasonous actions against the Constitution and the United States. Remember the Nuremburg War Trials. But . . . but . . . but . . . I was only following orders. . . .

"Die, you spineless cowardice bastards!"

He kept that one in the word processor; who would he send it to, anyway? Let them find it, he decided. Let them come to his home and learn for themselves who Timothy McVeigh was.

Christmas would soon be here, but McVeigh did not stick around. Before leaving, he stopped over at the Burns Security office and visited with his old friends. Like others, Carl Lebron saw the drastic changes that had come over the man. McVeigh was talking about going to "Area 51," a Nevada location that he said stored alien space vehicles. Fifty-one was a magic number for him; the Waco siege lasted fifty-one days. He drew Lebron over to his Pontiac and showed him a baseball cap with a hole torn through it.

I was on a ridge one day, he said. "Some people" saw me and took a shot.

The cap was black and dirty, and McVeigh's parting words to Lebron, the friend with whom he had shared many of his first conservative leanings, were equally ominous.

"This is just a hobby for you, reading these books," McVeigh scolded. "You're stomping your feet and not doing anything about it."

Before he left Pendleton—for the last time—he stayed up late with Jennifer, six years younger, and warned her that a revolution was coming. She could be a part of the future. And since she believed in her older brother, she told others.

According to her friends, she became boastful at a Christmas party. "You'll see in either April or May something big is going to happen with my brother," she said. "I don't know what it is, but it's going to be big. There's going to be a revolution and you're either going to be with us or against us. I know I'm going to be ready."

Chapter Nine

From Intellectual to Animal

So began 1995. His last link to family, to the Pendleton of his youth, would be through Jennifer. On the final road trip of his life, he would write and telephone his sister, who became his sounding board. He did not let her in on what he was going to do, or when or where, and certainly not to whom; never did he mention Oklahoma City.

He began to unburden himself of his personal belongings. He mailed a box to Jennifer containing mementoes—his high school yearbook, his military records. Keep them, he said. They're yours now.

He included a letter again hinting that "something big is going to happen in the month of the bull"—a reference to Taurus, the astrological sun sign for the character with the trait he cherished above all others: dependability.

"Like a bull quietly grazing in a pasture, you're not looking to challenge anyone," warned the horoscope, a copy of which he mailed along. "But it would be a fatal mistake for anyone to challenge you." The month of the bull commenced on April 20—the day after his revolution would be launched.

He told his sister to burn the letter. She followed his instructions, she went out to the garage at the Pendleton home and set it afire. Other letters followed, some in code, but all written in his distinctive backslash handwriting. If she was going to write him, he

warned, she must disguise her penmanship. "They don't know anyone's handwriting," he told her. "Don't concentrate; just 'flow it.'
. . . If your hand screws up, flow with it. It will look like a natural
signature."

He told her of the Fortiers, and assured her she could trust them.
With thoughts of his own mortality, he sought to bring together the
people closest to him. He might not be around afterward, he might
have to go into deep hiding—and oh how he loved that idea, of bur-
rowing away somewhere, surviving on his own.

"In case of 'alert,' contact Mike Fortier," he wrote. "Let him
know who you are & why you called. . . . If you must call him,
Jenny, this is serious. No being lazy. Use a pay phone, and take a
roll of quarters with you! They will, w/out a doubt, be watching
you and tapping the phone—use a pay phone! . . . Note: Read back
cover of Turner Diaries before you begin."

In McVeigh's mind he at last was fighting the war, his war, and
acting out the greatest fantasy from his favorite book. Now it
would all come true.

"What will you do when they come to take your guns?"—that is
the question asked on the back cover.

"The patriots fight back with a campaign of sabotage and assas-
sination," is the answer. ". . . Turner and his comrades suffer terribly, but their ingenuity and boldness in devising and executing new
methods of guerrilla warfare lead to a victory of cataclysmic inten-
sity and worldwide scope."

He wrote again to Jennifer, this time rambling about his own
self-importance and, equally, his concerns that maybe the authorities were already on to his plan.

". . . Won't be back forever. . . . Keep an eye out for P.I. [private
investigators]—they will more likely be looking for me than cops—
and remember—they could be anybody, and they don't follow the
rules. Be especially careful at bars, etc., where they will try to get
you to talk. (A female friend was caught by one at a bar—another
female who 'confided' in her, and got a lot of info in return.)"

He signed the letter as though everything were normal: "Tell
Dad Hi," he wrote. "Seeya, Tim."

Drifting constantly now, McVeigh was communicating chiefly
by mail. On January 10, he sent a five-page letter to Roger Moore in
Arkansas. Moore still wanted help solving the gun robbery, but

McVeigh was more interested in talking about his own frightening experience in Michigan when he was rear-ended while transporting the blasting caps in the trunk of the Spectrum. He wrote that he was becoming "too paranoid" in worrying that the government was involved in both incidents.

"I'd be dead, plain and simple," he wrote of the accident. "I've been tossing around the possibilities since then, non-stop."

He added: "I'm on the edge. I'm vulnerable, and I don't like that one damn bit! I suspect everyone I see now—constantly looking over my shoulder. My situation more easily reflects direct intimidation—but don't be fooled. It won't deter me!"

McVeigh stopped by a gun show in Grand Rapids, Michigan, and then turned southwest and by early February he was back in Kingman, now driving the blue Pontiac wagon with Michigan plates. He took a motel room in the western outskirts of town and, once settled in, called the Fortiers and invited them over.

McVeigh was upset. He wanted to know why Michael had not sold any of the guns he had transported from Kansas. What was taking so long? he asked. Let's move it! The Fortiers stayed maybe twenty minutes; they left with yet another impression of their friend. This McVeigh seemed the darkest yet; he was wound so tight that it was impossible, Michael thought, to make small talk.

On February 10, he mailed a three-page letter to Gwenn Strider, the aunt of the woman married to Kevin Nicholas, the friend who had helped him when the Spectrum was wrecked. She lived in Caro, Michigan, and they had picked up a friendship during his stays up there. They occasionally wrote each other, and this time he was responding to a letter from her that she had mailed to his Kingman postal box. She was concerned about a local problem in Michigan, and he began his letter by advising her to write her congressman.

"They represent the people and they listen to them," he wrote. "Yea, right!"

But this was not going to be just a friendly letter. McVeigh was beyond being sociable to a female acquaintance two thousand miles away; idle chat did not do it for him any longer. If he was going to write, he was going to tell her something worth reading.

And yet he rambled again, even more confusingly than in his earlier letters to his sister. He explained that he was writing her from a spot out in the desert somewhere. He said that he understood the

need to distribute antigovernment literature if it would encourage
people to open their eyes to the evil that was the federal government. He had worked as an activist for the far right in the past, he
said, before it was fashionable to do so.

But his thoughts were incoherent, and, with breaks for describing the difficulty of writing outdoors, his words just seemed to
explode out of his pen in twists and bursts.

"I was in the educational/literature dissemination (desert wind
is wreaking havoc on my already scratchy writing) field for quite
some time. I was preaching and 'passing out' before anyone had
ever heard the words 'patriot' and 'militia.'

". . . Just got out of the wind—Onward and upward."

He said he was changing his thinking, that his days of passive
resistance were behind him now.

"I passed on that legacy about a 1/2 year ago. I believe the 'new
blood' needs to start somewhere; and I have certain other 'militant'
talents that are short in supply and greatly demanded. So I gave all
my informational paperwork to the 'new guys'; and no longer have
any to give. What I can send you is my own personal copies; ones
that are just gathering dust, and a newsletter I recently received."

He said it was risky to stand up to the government; he said the
government maintained the names of those it feared.

"If you are willing to write letters, I could pass your name on to
someone; but let there be no doubt, with the letters I have in mind,
the literature that would be forwarded to you for copying, etc., you
would probably make a list. (Currently there are over 300,000
names on the Cray Supercomputer in Brussels, Belgium, of 'possible and suspected subversives and terrorists' in the U.S., all ranked
in order of threat.) Letters would be of an 'on notice' nature, like the
ones many people (myself included) wrote to Lon Horiuchi (the FBI
sniper who blew Vicki Weaver's head off), saying, in effect: 'What
goes around comes around. . . .'

"Hey, that's just the truth, and if we're scared away from writing
the truth because we're afraid of winding up on a list; then we've
lost already."

He quoted the sixteenth president: "To sin by silence when they
should protest makes COWARDS of men—Abe L."

He compared himself to America's first revolutionaries: "If the
founding fathers had been scared of a 'list,' we'd still be under the

tyrannical rule of the crown. They KNEW, without a doubt, that by signing the Declaration of Independence, they would be sentenced to death, for HIGH TREASON against the crown. But they realized something was more important than their sole or collective lives—the cause of LIBERTY."

He turned the pen on himself, and described Timothy McVeigh the modern rebel: "Hell, you only live once, and I KNOW you know it's better to burn out, than . . . rot away in some nursing home. My philosophy is the same—in only a short 1-2 years, my body will slowly start giving away—first maybe knee pains, or back pains, or whatever, but I won't be 'peaked' anymore. Might as well do some good while I can be 100% effective!"

Then came his summation; here he sought to define his own essence.

"Sorry I can't be of more help, but most of the people sent my way these days are of the direct-action type, and my whole mindset has shifted, from intellectual to . . . ANIMAL. (Rip the bastards heads off and shit down their necks!, and I'll show you how with a simple pocket knife . . . etc.)"

And then again, abruptly, the boyish signature: "Seeya, The Desert Rat."

Thinking his own end was coming, McVeigh continued to give away his belongings. Even if he made it out of Oklahoma, if he could get to some desert hideout, he would have to travel light. Water, canned food, a flashlight—he knew the drill. So he again invited Fortier over to his motel room; he gave him his toolbox and some car-towing straps. He talked about a college paper he had been helping Jennifer write on the subject of gun control. There—guns. What is happening with the guns you were supposed to sell? he asked Fortier.

But Fortier was getting nowhere, so McVeigh arranged for a sales table at upcoming shows in Tucson, St. George in Utah, and Reno. For the St. George show that last weekend in February, he drove Fortier up to Utah and, at the Dixie Palm Motel, used his old ruse of checking in as a single guest. He gave his address as Fort Sill, Kansas—there is no such place, but there is a military reservation called Fort Sill in Oklahoma, an hour's drive southwest of Oklahoma City. Norma Phillips, the motel manager, recalled that she and housekeeper Ann Mitchell became suspicious when McVeigh and another man kept coming and going in his Pontiac wagon. Once the maid tried to enter his room, but McVeigh would not open the door. What was he hiding? she wondered.

The Reno show came next, and it was a two-day affair. One evening in their motel room, McVeigh suddenly announced that he had talked to Nichols and that Nichols wanted $2,000 for his share of the take from the stolen guns. "And then we can call it even," Nichols had promised. So Fortier took some of the proceeds from the shows and paid it back in two $1,000 installments.

McVeigh was pushing Fortier on other fronts, too. He wanted help getting a phony ID and credit card, so Fortier sent away to a mail-order company and obtained a kit for making a false identification card. McVeigh came to the Fortiers' trailer and borrowed Lori's typewriter. When he returned it, he asked if he could use her iron to laminate a fake South Dakota driver's license. No, she told him. Worried that he would ruin the iron, she laminated it herself.

"It was white," she recalled. "It had a blue strip across the top, and Tim had put his picture on there. And it was the false name of Robert Kling." He had taken the name from the Klingon creatures in *Star Trek*. For his new birthday, he chose April 19.

Everything seemed to be coming together. Terry Nichols by now had returned to the States. In March he bought a crackerbox of a house in Herington, Kansas, another small town in the center of the state not far from the Junction City–Fort Riley area. He moved in with Marife and their small daughter, having persuaded his wife to return.

But he had refused to sign any loan papers for the house, because he still did not believe in paper transactions. Instead he was supposed to pay cash into a special account set up at a local bank. He occasionally deposited money into the account, and the owner, Kenneth Siek from nearby Abilene, Kansas, had been desperate to sell. But Nichols did not really have a job, or so he told his local real estate agent, Georgia Rucker. He said he was going to set up a venture selling military-style cardboard food containers. Not the prepackaged food that goes inside them, just the containers. Like most everyone in Herington, Rucker thought him odd. Here comes this man trying to get away from his past, she remembered thinking.

Nichols was rarely seen around Herington. Sometimes he would drop by the local military surplus store, trying to set up a new account. Or he would stop in at the bank to put down his cash money. Marife, still speaking only a tortured bit of English, was not making friends. Nor did her husband; he had never been a joiner. He seemed not aloof but rather detached, vacant, disinterested, as though he was occupied in something beyond little Herington.

He would see McVeigh again soon enough.

On March 25, Jennifer received another letter from her brother in Kingman. He asked if his mail was getting through. "It's important to know if you received it, or if it was intercepted either by G-men or Dad," he wrote.

He gave her new instructions. "Send no more [letters] after 01Apr [he underlined that part], and then, even if it's an emergency—watch what you say, because I may not get it in time, and the G-men might get it out of my box, incriminating you."

This time he signed his letter without fanfare, simply "T."

In Kingman, Michael Fortier, nursing a sore back, was on a routine of daily walks. Sometimes McVeigh walked with him, and he told Fortier that Nichols was trying to weasel out of their plan. Again he asked if Fortier would be willing to accompany him back to Oklahoma.

"Never," Fortier said.

Well then, pleaded McVeigh, help me escape. "If I can make it to Las Vegas somehow, give me a ride out into the desert," he said.

"I won't do that either," Fortier said.

Fortier realized that McVeigh planned to hide out after the bombing. One day the two young men went four-wheeling in the desert and McVeigh stashed a duffel bag full of canned foods in the sand out near their old campsite. Always the survivalist, McVeigh would be prepared.

He was living with the Fortiers then, or at least until they started baby-sitting a niece in their small trailer home. McVeigh could no longer stand children; he moved out to another motel in Kingman. Tensions were boiling. Each day drew McVeigh closer to his goal; each day also brought more stress. The waiting was electric; he felt wired, hot-wired.

"Tim was starting to call me names and give me dirty looks," Fortier recalled. McVeigh's chief complaint was that Fortier was "domesticated."

"He said it like a curse word," Fortier said. "As if that was something that was bad. He was urging me to leave my wife and travel with him on the road, sort of like being desperadoes or something."

Fortier said he never would abandon his family. "I'm not going to help you do this," he told McVeigh.

And yet he again went out to see McVeigh at his motel room, and McVeigh lent him several books, one called *The Rise and Fall of Far-Right Extremists*, the other dealing with a white-supremacy movement called The Order. Fortier did not feel it safe to be unarmed around McVeigh; he began carrying a gun himself. "On the off chance he would do something," Fortier said. He and Lori also were using drugs heavily—marijuana and speed. It helped cut the tension.

McVeigh gave him one last book, this one about a group of white separatists living in Colorado. "We can't be friends any longer," he told Fortier. "I'm going to Colorado to find some real friends, some manly friends."

Fortier studied McVeigh's face; he could see the look of desperation. McVeigh was trying to insult him, to humiliate him into helping him carry out his bomb scheme. Fortier thought, It's all falling apart. Him and Terry aren't going to do it any longer.

Now it was April, and McVeigh was preparing to leave again.

But first he mailed a final letter to Carl Lebron in Buffalo, again accusing him of not being a true patriot. "All the reading you do is just a hobby," McVeigh complained again to his old friend. "You stomp your feet, but you're not doing anything."

On the 5th, now staying at the Imperial Motel on Andy Devine Avenue, the old Route 66 through Kingman, McVeigh made a series of phone calls—one to a religious compound called Elohim City in far-eastern Oklahoma, another to the National Alliance in Arizona, a white separatist organization.

He also telephoned a Ryder truck rental agency in Lake Havasu, Arizona. He inquired about prices, availability, and, of course, size.

On the 7th, Jennifer stayed up late in Pendleton, planning to leave the next morning for a vacation. As she packed, she separated many of the items her brother had sent in recent weeks. She placed his military records and personal items in one box, his letters to her, his political literature, and his Waco videotapes in another. She had

asked him several weeks ago if he wanted her to destroy the literature and tapes. No, he said; absolutely not. So she placed the box
with the military records and the personal items inside her closet;
the other box she gave to a friend, Rose Woods. In the morning, she
headed for Florida.

On the 11th, McVeigh made two telephone calls to Nichols in
Herington. He was reporting in, making sure that Nichols was still
with him; he wanted to know that everything was "code green"—
all clear.

On the 12th, Timothy McVeigh checked out of the Imperial
Motel.

Ten days later, FBI agents were standing in the motel's office
lobby, asking questions of Helmut Hofer, the owner and manager.
Hofer told them that McVeigh had been a good tenant, had paid his
rent in advance and always kept his room spotless.

The motel is a two-story brown structure, and Hofer a short,
balding man who favored white T-shirts to keep cool under the
broiling desert sun. Yes, he said in his thick German accent; he
would show them Room 212. He took them around outside and up
to that door, and the agents peeked inside; then they paid Hofer for
two nights so they could have the room to themselves.

"Tests. Yes, yes, yes, they were doing tests," Hofer recalled. "A
couple of fellows there were testing the fiber from the carpet and
the blankets and the walls and the mirror. It was a messy room
afterwards. Let's say that we had to do a lot more cleanup than
when Mr. McVeigh left."

Chapter Ten

Final Days

McVeigh's old Pontiac station wagon coughed into the Firestone parking lot on West 8th Street in downtown Junction City. The head gasket had blown; white smoke poured from the exhaust. The battered wagon that had carried him on a hard two-day drive out of the Southwest and back to the middle of Kansas was now a goner. He knew he needed something more reliable for what lay ahead.

Kansas was afloat this morning of April 14—Good Friday. Spring rains were falling, and the showers would continue through much of the weekend into Monday evening. Nearby Geary State Lake was already high, and so were the Republican and Smoky Hill rivers, which merge into the Kansas River, the state's great waterway, the one people from this state call the mighty Kaw.

This was a homecoming for McVeigh. At neighboring Fort Riley he had trained for the Gulf War, and he had returned there a celebrated soldier. It was here too that he had left the army a bitter man, and from this spot he would embark on his greatest mission. His sore feet had done him in with the Green Berets, so he knew better this time than to trust a worn-out car. He wanted dependability, something efficient—something to get him away.

The Junction City–Fort Riley area is home to many of the 23,000 soldiers and their families who live either on post or in the residential communities around the sprawling base. McVeigh knew the neighborhood well—the Junction City gun stores, the pawnshops, the motels, the restaurants, and the local Ryder rental shop where soldiers lease trucks to haul their life's belongings in and out of Fort Riley.

For the next five days, McVeigh would be a soldier again. What he set in motion here, his final steps, he thought would make him a revolutionary. He was convinced that when he acted, an angry nation would follow. His was an undeclared war, because it raged solely in his head. The enemy did not know he was coming; the enemy did not even know it was his enemy.

He tried to plan well; he should have planned better. He would lie about his name and his age, and he would shift in and out of town. Trying to be polite, he most of all hoped to be invisible. Just blend in, he told himself, be another army grunt going about the paces of life around town.

But people would remember his face—the harsh blue eyes, the young cheeks, the pleasant way he could carry himself around strangers. And he became so wrapped up in what he had to do that he occasionally let down his guard. Moments before renting the truck, he allowed himself to be captured on a restaurant surveillance camera—he, Timothy McVeigh, the stealth fighter who prided himself on eluding the turnpike tollbooths because as everybody knew the government spied on people.

Thomas Manning recognized McVeigh almost immediately. He remembered him from McVeigh's days at Fort Riley in the early nineties, just as he recalled many of the young soldiers whose cars he had serviced for years at the local Firestone. McVeigh pulled in sometime after nine in the morning. He did not have the money to have the car repaired, nor the time.

"I need a cheap car," he said. "I need a car to get me to Michigan."

Parked around back was a yellow 1977 Mercury Grand Marquis, a rusting relic from the era of the gas-guzzling highway cruiser. The odometer read 97,204 miles. As the Firestone manager, Manning had purchased the vehicle eight days ago from a used car dealer for $150. He was planning to break down the car for parts.

It was a four-door sedan with a burnished tan interior and a dark-colored primer spot on the rear quarter panel. A gray splotch of what appeared to be silicone putty had been rubbed into the hood to stop leaks. The ashtray was jammed with cigarette butts. The guys around the dealership had been ridiculing this car as the "roach motel." Mechanic Jim Fulgium had driven the Mercury on small errands, including one for gas to the Quick Sack near the McDonald's on 16th Street. He had to return to the Firestone to look for the key to the gas cap. He never found the key, and so he used a screwdriver to pry open the cap. In all, he probably pulled the car in and out of the shop three times.

"The transmission was slipping and the engine had a miss," Fulgium would recall. "The car was big and ugly."

It was a bitch of a car, but the bitch ran.

McVeigh and Manning agreed to swap vehicles. Manning would take McVeigh's exhausted Pontiac plus $300. Not a bad deal for Manning—he would pocket $150 in profit plus have the Pontiac to sell for parts.

But McVeigh always considered himself shrewd when it came to business, and he would not be totally outdone. He reached for his camouflage-colored wallet and counted out three $100 bills. Then he looked at Manning with those eyes of his. He said that now he did not have enough money to get to Michigan, and Manning, feeling some sympathy for McVeigh as he often did for these young soldiers, handed him $50 back.

Manning asked where he wanted the car titled, and McVeigh said it did not really matter. Mail the Firestone service form to 3616 North Van Dyke, he told him, the address for the Nichols family farm in Decker, Michigan. And send the bill of sale to 1711 Stockton Hill Road, #206, in Kingman, his old mail drop in Arizona.

Frankly, McVeigh was not at all interested in the paperwork. "It doesn't matter, because I'm going to junk the Mercury out when I get to Michigan," he told Manning.

On one of the sale forms, he listed his address as a post office box at Fort Riley, and he filled out a series of boxes:

Employer: "U.S. Army, Ft. Riley, Kan."

Years employed: "1."

Monthly salary/wages: "$900."

Occupation: "Active army."

Art Wells, a Firestone mechanic, began preparing the car for the new buyer. A young black-haired army veteran who like McVeigh had seen combat in the Gulf War, Wells had been working at Firestone for five months. This morning he was told to take the Mercury and "start changing it out."

"The right rear tire was bald, so I put a spare on and put stuff in the back of the trunk like oil, antifreeze . . . you know, your stuff for the road, to make it road-ready," Wells recalled.

McVeigh walked over, and Manning introduced him to Wells.

"I just shook his hand," Wells said. "I knowed he was military because of the haircut, because I was prior military. And then I started working on the car."

McVeigh hung around and watched. He was clearly in a hurry, itching to get in the front seat of that Mercury and move on. But now a second mechanic slung his head under the hood, checking the radiator hoses and the fan belts. The battery still had life. Then Wells drove it a few blocks to Jim's 66 and filled the tank; he had to pry open that cap again too.

McVeigh took a walk. As Manning recalled it, he leaned over to him in the shop and said, "I'll be back in a couple of minutes."

Manning guessed he was gone maybe ten to fifteen minutes. Where McVeigh actually went, Manning did not know. Across 8th Street and down a few doors sits the J and K Bus Depot; out front is a public telephone. From that phone and at that time, two calls were made by someone using the Spotlight credit card belonging to McVeigh and Nichols.

The first call was placed to Terry Nichols's home in Herington, just south of town down US 77. The call lasted under a minute.

The second was to Elliott's Body Shop, the Ryder truck rental agency in Junction City. It lasted well over seven minutes. Vicki Beemer, the office clerk and secretary, answered the phone. The man on the other end identified himself as Robert Kling.

"He asked about renting a Ryder truck," Beemer said. "I remember that he told me he was going to be going to Omaha, Nebraska. When I asked him the size of truck that he was interested in, he asked me, 'How many pounds does a fifteen-foot truck hold?' "

She had to get up from her desk and walk around to a chart hanging on the office wall. She ran her finger down the list and stopped; then she went back to the phone and told him that that size of truck could carry around 3,400 pounds.

That was not large enough, said Mr. Kling. "I need a truck that will hold five thousand pounds."

Again she stood up from her chair to consult the chart, then came back to the telephone. She told him he would need a twenty-foot truck.

McVeigh returned to the Firestone shop, and the Mercury Marquis was ready. McVeigh removed the Arizona license plate from the Pontiac wagon and put it on the Mercury. He transferred a one-gallon orange plastic hand cleaner bottle he kept to wash up with on the road, for all those mornings his eyes opened to some isolated backroad scene after he had slept in his car. He tossed in the olive drab canvas bag that held his clothing, along with a couple of quarts of transmission fluid. He slipped in behind the wheel around ten-thirty. Timothy McVeigh had a getaway car.

The next people to remember seeing the yellow Mercury this Friday were at the Dreamland Motel, located just off Interstate 70, the east-west thoroughfare through Fort Riley and Junction City. Eric McGown, whose mother runs the motel, would not forget this day. It was his seventeenth birthday.

A student at Junction City High, he lived with his mother, Lea, at the motel, handling general maintenance chores around the property, caring for the pool, trimming the yard, answering the telephone, and checking on the guests. Anything that needed to be fixed that she could not do, he learned how to get done.

His hobby was old cars; his passion old race cars. Today his own car was back in the shop, this time for another turbocharger, and so when the battered yellow Mercury pulled into the Dreamland parking lot, it immediately caught his eye.

Lea McGown would remember the driver well—his crew cut, his "smiling, friendly" face. He looked a little older but not that much different from her own boy, Eric. "He was a very neat person," she would say later of Timothy McVeigh, speaking in her clipped German accent.

Indeed, she found him so pleasant that she let him talk her down to $20 a night for a $28 room. Why not? she thought. It was Easter weekend.

For some reason he abandoned the Kling alias and wrote his real name on the motel registration card—"Tim McVeigh." But then he caught himself, and he listed his address as the Decker farm. Through the window he could see the Arizona license plate on the Mercury, and he included that number on the registration card. He paid cash for four nights: tonight, Saturday, Sunday, and Monday. The total with tax came to $88.95.

Always cash—don't leave a trail. And he would not be staying past Tuesday. By Tuesday night, he would be gone.

Lea McGown also glanced out the window at the big Mercury sedan. She noted that the rear license plate seemed to be hanging loose, perhaps attached with just one screw, she thought. She asked why he had a Michigan driver's license and an Arizona license plate; he told her, "I drive around a lot." She remembered he also said he would be bringing a "large van" to the motel.

Her son was drawn to McVeigh when he spotted him unloading the car. For McVeigh, the car was just another "Warrior"; for the kid, it was cool wheels.

"I was working on the pool doing something, and I walked past his car and he hit a button which buzzed and had an electric trunk and the trunk popped open," the boy recalled. "I thought that was interesting on a car that was that old. So I went over and talked to him for a few minutes."

Eric also noticed the Arizona plate, and they talked some about the desert heat. The youth was curious about this because the weather here was cool and the skies wet. He had seen so many men come through the Dreamland in the years that he and his mother, a German immigrant, had managed the small business. Truckers would stop on their red-eye routes, traveling salesmen too. Get to know them a bit, the boy told himself. Everyone had a story to tell.

McVeigh smiled at the kid's wonderment; he shut the trunk and carried his duffel bag into Room 25. Evening would fall but the clouds would not break.

The next morning, Saturday, Timothy McVeigh, pretending he was Robert Kling, walked into the Ryder truck rental agency in Junction City. Elliott's Body Shop, like the Dreamland, sits along the frontage road of Interstate 70, and it is clearly visible from the highway. The owner, Eldon Elliott, also runs a Montgomery Wards delivery service and a Rocky Mountain snowplowing business in Estes Park, Colorado. In Junction City, he owns a combination auto body repair shop and truck rental stop, a six-employee operation popular with his military customers from Fort Riley.

From the highway, looking north, the yellow Ryder vans loom up on a small ridge in the parking lot, next to the frontage road, Goldenbelt Boulevard. McVeigh could not miss them, for they stand out like golden bales of hay.

Elliott had been renting trucks for five years. On Saturdays, he was open from eight to ten to assist weekend customers.

This morning, April 15, the day before Easter, he was reviewing a written quote taken the day before by Vicki Beemer. It was a workup sheet for a one-way haul to Omaha for a young man who had called and said his name was Robert Kling. This Kling fellow was requesting a twenty-footer. Also quoted were two days extra rental given free because Kling had stated that he was "military"— a little freebie Elliott had established to pamper his Fort Riley customers. Kling also wanted to rent a hand truck for loading and unloading—$15. The truck deposit would be $80. Farther down the paperwork, Elliott could see that the customer had declined insurance. The truck was scheduled to be picked up on Monday, around four in the afternoon.

Elliott was at his desk in the rental office when McVeigh walked in. He looked up, and the man was standing just four feet from him in the tight little office lobby.

"Can I help you?" Elliott asked.

"Yes," the man said. "I got a quote yesterday and I want to make a reservation."

"Okay. I'll need your driver's license."

Elliott had done this hundreds of times, maybe more—just another soldier on the move. He swung around to the computer and began to type in a reservation, tapping the name off the man's driver's license, Robert Kling from someplace called Redfield, South Dakota.

He looked up at the man in the crew cut leaning slightly over the counter, and he reminded him about the $80 deposit.

The man did not appear nervous or hurried. He spoke again.

"Can I just pay the whole thing today while I got the money and I won't spend it?" he asked.

"Yes, you can," said Elliott.

The customer asked whether the truck could be ready around four on Monday; he stressed that time: four o'clock. This was very important, he said again. Four o'clock.

"Yes, it will," Elliott said.

What about insurance?

The man waved that off. "No," he said. "I don't want insurance."

That was not so odd. Elliott had been in business long enough to know that soldiers from the post don't always make a lot of money, particularly the young ones like this man Kling. Nevertheless, Elliott, ever the businessman, tried to change his mind.

"Well, at this time, I just . . . doesn't make any difference to me," he told his customer. "But I just have to tell you, if you don't take insurance, you're liable for the truck if there's any damage—"

The man stopped him. "I won't need any," he said. "I don't want insurance. I'm not going very far."

He gave Elliott another reason why he was turning down the insurance; he said he drove large trucks for the army. "I'm a good driver. I drive these deuce-and-a-halfs out at Fort Riley. I don't want no insurance."

He said again how he was just going up to Nebraska and maybe over to Iowa, and that was a short distance anyway, and while he would not need any extra miles, he would like a couple of free extra days on the rental.

Fine, Elliott said. He began computing the cost, and as he worked the numbers, his customer suddenly announced that he would be paying cash. So Elliott printed out the rental agreement, totaling the fee at $280.32, and spread the form across the counter. He turned it to face the young man and explained everything from top to bottom, the price of the truck, the discount, the hand truck, the sales tax. The customer ran his bright blue eyes up and down the form, sort of leaning a bit over the counter to get a good look.

It has to be ready on Monday, the young man reiterated. At four o'clock. Then he set down $281.

Elliott counted it out, and before he could finish, his customer had slapped down the thirty-two cents in change and pushed that across the counter too. Elliott scooped it up and handed the man a single dollar back.

The man who said he was Robert Kling left, the door banging behind him.

Across town that morning, Terry Nichols showed up at the Junction City Conoco. He had left home in Herington for a series of errands with his family—his wife, Marife, their infant daughter, Nicole, and his son, Josh, who was visiting from his mother's house in Las Vegas during the Easter school break. They drove up to Junction City, and he stopped for gas and spoke briefly with the Conoco assistant manager about the Easter holiday.

"I don't generally get into it," said the employee, Jamie Carroll Gilley.

"I don't care for it either," said Nichols.

Terry Nichols always seemed a darting, furtive figure—a shadow next to the taller, wandering McVeigh. Nichols would insist that he had returned to the middle of Kansas to start a new life, that he was "a devoted family man" with a young daughter at home, that he was looking to get out of the gun show business and find a spot to finally settle down. Too many false starts in his life, he would say, too many missed opportunities.

For a while he imagined himself someday owning an organic farm harvesting blueberries, or maybe something more exotic like kiwi. He asked around about speciality farming and even visited the Herington Chamber of Commerce. He wanted to grow his own food, and he preferred to be left alone. Nichols had a vision of complete self-sufficiency. He would say he chose Kansas for its rich soil and, after Michigan, its relatively short winters. Having already tried the outside world—the army, the real estate business—now he wanted to keep life simple.

So he would say he was going to build a small business selling military surplus items at gun shows close to home. His plan was to market prepackaged Meals Ready to Eat, known in the military as MREs. He was tired of the road, he told friends, worn out from traveling the gun show circuit, and he believed he was smart enough to see that the federal government was only going to make this kind of business worse with future restrictions on firearms. It was always there for Nichols, as it was for McVeigh—the hated federal government.

Nine days ago, on April 6, Nichols had obtained a new Kansas driver's license. He took out insurance on his pickup and ordered state license plates, which he would pick up later. He had labels and business cards printed up for his new venture selling MREs. He also purchased $3,250 worth of additional military surplus items he planned to sell. Mostly they were laser sights and blowguns, similar to air rifles, and they would arrive on Thursday, April 20. He planned to sell them soon, and he reserved and paid for two sales tables at an upcoming gun show in Hutchinson, Kansas.

Terry Nichols would say he was just going about the business of getting his life back on track now that Marife had returned from the Philippines. And sure, he knew McVeigh was around. Because (he would claim) he had written his friend in Kingman a month or so earlier and had asked if, during one of his road trips, as long as it was "convenient and possible," McVeigh could bring out a television set from Nichols's ex-wife Lana's home in Las Vegas for Josh to use in Herington.

That evening, "Robert Kling" ordered takeout Chinese food for dinner. China-born Yuhua Bai took the telephone call about five o'clock. She owned the Hunam Palace, a Chinese restaurant on the north side of Junction City, very close to Fort Riley. Eighty percent of her business was takeout delivery, mostly to active-duty soldiers, and the man on the other line wanted moo goo gai pan and egg rolls. The bill was $9.65. He asked that it be delivered to his room, No. 25 at the Dreamland Motel.

Bai's English was still rough, and she asked him to spell his last name. To her, it sounded like the Chinese name Ling. No, he told her. It's Kling. K-l-i-n-g.

She took the order, had the food prepared, and gave it to Jeff Davis, the deliveryman. But when an hour passed and no moo goo gai pan arrived, this man Kling called the Hunam Palace a second time. She apologized for the delay and assured him that Davis would be there promptly.

The rain was holding up the food. Twenty-two years old, Davis had worked for the restaurant for four years now, and he knew the routes well. That evening he had two orders, and he set out with both in his delivery car. The first was to a trailer park just four blocks away. The second, to the Dreamland, would take longer. The bridge on Flint Hills Boulevard was closed for construction, and that meant Davis had to skirt around town and pass through Fort Riley in order to reach the motel.

Finally he pulled into the motel lot and parked up close to Room 25. Almost immediately he noticed a man standing in the doorway. He handed him the bag with the moo goo gai pan and egg rolls; the

Timothy McVeigh holds court at Waco, warning reporter Michelle Rauch that the FBI siege on the Branch Davidians trampled on people's rights. (Photo by Lauren Aldinger/Gamma Liaison)

Two days before the bombing, McVeigh is captured on a McDonald's restaurant surveillance camera just before renting the truck he would drive to Oklahoma City. (Government exhibit photo used at his trial)

Smoke and fire cover downtown Oklahoma City at 9:02 a.m., April 19, 1995, when a truck laden with explosives is ignited at the front of the Alfred P. Murrah Federal Building. (Government exhibit photo)

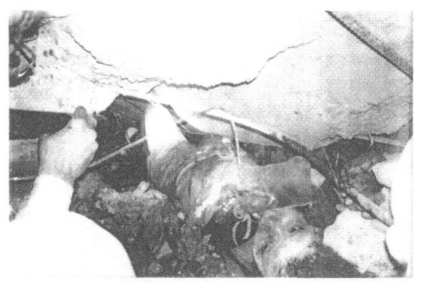

Daina Bradley lies trapped. Her leg had to be amputated to free her from the rubble. Her two children and mother were killed, and a sister badly injured. (Government exhibit photo)

In what became the FBI's first big break, the truck axle from McVeigh's rented Ryder truck was recovered after it hit a red Ford Festiva, nearly killing a family. (Government exhibit photo)

The aftermath of the worst terrorist strike in America shows a third of the building gone, with nine floors crashing down into a crater on 5th Street. (FBI photo)

Digging through the debris, rescue workers search for the living while federal agents begin the long process of putting together the nation's largest criminal case in history. (FBI photo)

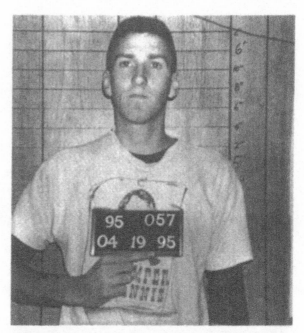

Just a few hours after the bombing, McVeigh posed for his prison mug shot. The drawing on his T-shirt denigrates Abraham Lincoln, and the card he holds in his hand bears his jailhouse ID number and the date he made famous—April 19, 1995. (Noble County Jail photo)

FBI Agent William Eppright opens an envelope of antigovernment propaganda McVeigh left behind in his getaway car. "Obey the Constitution of the United States and we won't shoot you," McVeigh wrote in his manifesto. (Government exhibit photo)

Hoping to soften their client's image after an ice-cold McVeigh was walked out of the Perry, Oklahoma, jail, his lawyers released photos of them conferring with McVeigh in prison. Stephen Jones is at right, Rob Nigh at left. (McVeigh defense team photo)

Defense lawyers for Terry Lynn Nichols also sought to show him in a softer light, insisting that he was "building a life, not a bomb." He is joined by his wife, Marife, and their daughter, Nicole. (Nichols defense team photo)

The wanted poster for John Doe No. 2, the man three employees of a Ryder agency in Kansas said accompanied McVeigh when he rented the bomb truck. (FBI sketch)

Private Todd Bunting, who had visited the Ryder truck agency the day after McVeigh, was for a time suspected of being John Doe No. 2 but was cleared by the FBI. (Government exhibit photo)

man gave him $11 and told him to keep the change. He remembered the man as tall, with blond hair that fell to the collar.

Certainly that was not McVeigh.

"I do not believe it was," Davis would insist.

Nor was it Nichols, shorter, with glasses and brown hair cropped tight like McVeigh's.

Whoever he was, he would be the first of many unexplained figures whom witnesses would insist they saw lurking next to McVeigh in the days and nights ahead.

On Sunday, April 16, Lenard and Diana White, a farm couple from Cheney, Kansas, were waking up in Room 29 at the Dreamland. They had driven to Junction City to visit his son, who had just been discharged from the army at Fort Riley, and his son's new child. They stopped at the Dreamland the night before, around eight o'clock, when "it was getting dark and there was a storm coming," Diana said. She awoke in the morning, "at about eight when the storm let up," and headed outside in search of hot coffee.

Along the way, she recalled, "I saw an old, faded yellow car." Hurrying under the motel awnings, she noticed the Arizona license tag on the rear.

The vehicle stuck in her memory. "I have an old car in the dead car pile, a small Ford, that is that color. That was a favorite color of 1977, and it just gave me nothing but trouble."

Back in her room with the coffee, she told her husband, "Can you believe that they drove that car from Arizona?"

Diana took him outside for a look. As he walked past, he also noticed the Arizona tag on the Mercury Marquis. "It was solid on that car," he said. "I don't know what it was fastened with, bolts or screws or what. But I know it was an Arizona tag and it was on there solid."

The Whites checked out around nine-thirty and headed home. The man in Room 25 was up too; McVeigh telephoned Nichols from his room about that same time.

Others at the Dreamland, including manager Lea McGown, would swear they saw the Ryder truck already there that day, which poses a difficulty, since McVeigh had not yet picked up the truck. Her teenage son Eric recalled seeing McVeigh with the truck on two occasions. Once, McVeigh was backing up the van next to the swimming pool. "I have a recollection of my mom telling me to go and tell him he can't park there because the person having Room 34 is a longtime resident and gets upset when someone parks back there. So I went out to the truck. He was starting to get out of the truck, and I asked him if he could move the truck up next to the motel sign because the person in 34 was kind of grouchy. He was really polite about it. He said yes and moved it right away."

Another time, he saw McVeigh near the back of the van. "He was trying to close the rear tailgate of the Ryder truck but he was having trouble closing it. He was leaning on it and trying to close it shut instead of lifting it up and letting it slam shut."

If the McGowns are right, then there was a second truck and McVeigh played some sort of role with that truck too. And perhaps with someone other than Nichols. But if the McGowns are mistaken, if they are innocently caught up in the rush of hysteria that came with the search for the Oklahoma City bombers, then their recollections were nothing more than fodder for conspiracy theorists and defense lawyers hoping to confuse a trial jury.

Correct or mistaken, there is no disputing one other fact in the younger McGown's mind. He was sure of this much: "Once I saw the Ryder truck, I never saw that Marquis again."

Visiting the Dreamland that Sunday was Herta King, a Junction City resident whose son David lived at the motel. "On Easter Sunday I called my son, and he was very depressed on the phone because his girlfriend broke off with him," she said. "I told him I would come by the motel and I would bring him an Easter basket."

She stopped by the Dreamland around twelve forty-five with a basket of German chocolate Easter eggs filled with liquor. Her son was in Room 24. As she pulled in, "I saw a yellow Ryder truck sitting right there, and I could not see my son's car because the Ryder truck blocked the view."

That night, between seven and eight, she returned to the motel to bring David some Easter-dinner leftovers. At that time, she said, the Ryder truck was gone. But had it been there at all? How could a truck rented Monday be there on Sunday?

One thing more—no one saw Nichols on Sunday anywhere near that motel, truck or no truck.

From his home in Herington, he was spending Sunday much as he had spent the day before, making another series of seemingly covert trips, dragging his family along perhaps to cover himself should he need an alibi. According to Marife, they were to attend Easter Sunday Mass. Nichols drove alone to the local Catholic church to check on the time, then returned and said there was no Mass today.

Where had he really gone? How could there be no Mass on Sunday, on Easter Sunday at a Catholic church?

No, he said. They would have to drive twenty-five miles up to St. Xavier's in Junction City.

And so they did, and after church services, they stopped at the McDonald's in Junction City, then returned home and had a second Easter meal at home in Herington. Shortly after three in the afternoon, the phone rang in the Nicholses' kitchen.

The Nicholses were nearing the end of their ham dinner. Terry took the call and spoke for no longer than five minutes. Then he abruptly announced that he was leaving for Omaha. Josh asked to go along. No, his father said.

Nichols drove off in his blue-and-white pickup. He would not return home until after midnight, long after Marife had gone to bed. Terry Nichols had not gone to Omaha at all. He had rendezvoused with McVeigh this Easter Sunday in downtown Oklahoma City.

Marife Nichols slept in. When she finally awoke around ten on Monday morning, April 17, her husband was already gone. The television set that had been at his ex-wife's house was indeed now sitting in their home in Herington, and Terry told her later that McVeigh had brought it because Josh wanted to watch TV during his visit. Later on Monday, the Nichols family went out and rented movies for the boy; one was a Disney animation film, *The Lion King.*

The television set was virtually unusable except for playing videos. It had no antenna, and without cable service the family could not pick up any programming, even the local news. But Marife remembered that later in the week, on Thursday, her husband arranged for cable TV service.

Terry Nichols stayed home Monday afternoon. He worked at odd tasks around their small house. He fidgeted with a fuel meter that he had bought for $65 and was hoping to resell. It had broken gears, and Nichols had been in contact with the manufacturer to see about replacement parts. He had placed an ad in the local paper a week ago.

Later in the day, they all drove out to dinner at the Sirloin Stockade. Then that night they drove to the Kansas City airport to put Josh on a late flight home to Las Vegas. Nichols used an airport pay phone to make two calls, both placed with that Spotlight calling card. One went to Lana's house to tell her Josh was on his way, the other to the Dreamland Motel to ask the man in Room 25 how his day had gone.

McVeigh had good news to report. He had left the Dreamland around three-thirty that afternoon and walked over to a pay phone at the nearby Plaza Stop gas station. He called for a cab.

David Ferris, a Bell Taxi driver, drove McVeigh the four or so miles to a McDonald's restaurant within walking distance of Elliott's Body Shop. The fare was just $3.65, and no tip, a short trip, but Ferris would be haunted by its memory nonetheless.

When questioned by FBI agents, he broke down and, tears covering his face, he lied. "I never picked up McVeigh," he said.

Ferris was emotionally wrung out, and a diabetic too, and he was not feeling well. In a subsequent interview with the bureau, he changed his story and said he had indeed driven a young man from the Plaza Stop to the McDonald's in south Junction City. Ferris thought the man was a soldier because of his crew cut and generally polite demeanor. He also recalled the man was wearing Levi's and a white T-shirt.

Was it McVeigh? the agents asked again.

"In all probability, yes," Ferris said.

There was no doubt McVeigh was at the McDonald's. He was breaking his own cardinal rule about staying out from under Big Brother's ever-watchful eye: he was captured on the security camera buying a hot fruit pie. The black-and-white stills show him walking through the restaurant, past the Uncle Sam "I Want You" army poster, up front to the counter, and then out again. He had slipped a long-sleeved shirt over the T-shirt. He lingered inside less than ten minutes and, before leaving, he checked his watch. It was 3:57 in the afternoon.

The walk from McDonald's to the Ryder agency along the highway frontage road is no more than a mile and a quarter, and at a fast clip should take no longer than fifteen minutes. The highway frontage road winds past the Comfort Inn motel, the Country Kitchen, a Sirloin Stockade, and an apartment complex. When McVeigh left the McDonald's, the American flag was not flying out front, because it was raining. But when McVeigh, again as Robert Kling, stepped into the Ryder agency, he did not strike others as being particularly wet. Keenly mindful of the time, he had hurried over.

Some at the Ryder rental agency would insist that a second man came in too—a man with a baseball cap, a lantern jaw, and a tattoo on his upper arm. Whether he was real or imaginary, at this moment was born the legend of John Doe No. 2.

The owner, Eldon Elliott, asked McVeigh to join him outside for a "walk-around" to inspect the truck. But McVeigh preferred to stay inside. Elliott recalled: "There was another gentleman standing there in the corner. I just barely glanced at him as I walked by."

Vicki Beemer remembered that other man too. "I don't know who he was," she said. "It was just another man. They just came straight to the counter. They were both in the office."

McVeigh handed her the South Dakota driver's license; she saw the name Robert Kling and the birthday—April 19. That made her smile. She always smiled at the young soldiers. "I've been married longer than you've been alive," she told him.

Tom Kessinger, the shop mechanic, was eating popcorn, and from his chair he may have gotten the best look at this second individual. He would remember the square jaw and the blue-and-white baseball cap and the tattoo. But Kessinger would have problems identifying McVeigh. He remembered him with beady eyes and a "peculiar" chin—both of which fit—but also that he was wearing "military camo" and khaki pants—which McVeigh was not.

Outside, Elliott noted a few scratches on the truck, plus a mark on the front bumper. A light mist was falling as he circled the vehicle. Inside, McVeigh was getting nervous; he was anxious to get a time stamp on the rental contract. When Elliott stepped back inside, McVeigh swept up a pen, leaned over the counter, and signed the paper.

Elliott handed him the keys. "Thank you very much," Elliott said. "And have a safe trip."

Everything had gone down with military precision. Timothy McVeigh drove off in his truck and with the rental contract stamped just exactly the way he wanted it, on the dot at 4:19 p.m.

4:19 as in April 19.

Lea McGown stirred awake about four in the morning. She peered out her window, and in the Dreamland parking lot she could see McVeigh in the driver's seat of the Ryder truck. The dome light reflected across his lap, and he appeared to be slightly hunched over, as if he was studying a road map.

She looked outside an hour later, and the truck and McVeigh were gone.

That morning, Tuesday, April 18, according to the government, McVeigh and Nichols met at Geary State Lake in east-central Kansas, not far from the Dreamland, and not far from Herington either, and there, having unloaded the contents of the storage lockers, they assembled, blended, and built the bomb they had dreamed about this past half year. The government would say, but during McVeigh's trial never prove, that the two army veterans rolled large plastic barrels into the back of the truck, took knives and slit open the bags of ammonium nitrate, and poured the fertilizer into the barrels. Then they mixed in the racing fuel, turning the white ammonium nitrate pellets into bright pink balls. In less than ten minutes the fuel and fertilizer would blend together—94 percent ammonium nitrate, 6 percent racing fuel, a deadly mixture that would be ignited by the blasting caps and dynamite that they next wrapped around one or more of the barrels.

The government could never convincingly put McVeigh and Nichols together at the lake, a low-lying area near the highway connecting Nichols's hometown of Herington with Junction City, where McVeigh was staying. But they did locate a man who spotted the Ryder and a pickup on the bank of the lake. Another witness, Richard Wahl, an army sergeant from Fort Riley, had taken his son fishing that morning. It was cold and windy, a miserable morning, and their fishing boat was tossing about in the water. He too saw the yellow Ryder and the blue pickup parked side by side near the boat ramp, and though he never made out anyone near the vehicles, Wahl did see activity, remembering that once the side door on the Ryder was open, then later closed.

Other witnesses would say they never saw the trucks there. Even more confusing, others would say they had seen the Ryder out there the week before, long before it was rented, raising again the confusion about one truck or two.

But this much is certain: when McVeigh drove the Ryder back to the Dreamland, he had in the back of his truck a twenty-foot, four-thousand-pound bomb. Packed into those barrels was enough explosive to blow a hole into the breast of America. Tomorrow was Waco remembrance day; and in *The Turner Diaries*, the bomb was exploded in the morning.

When they were done at the lake, they needed only to wait. Nichols attended a military surplus auction at Fort Riley. He picked up address labels and business cards for his new business, and he swung by the Chamber of Commerce to get his Kansas license plate. Then he went home, and he stayed home.

At the Dreamland that evening, the guest in Room 25 checked out of the motel. His Ryder truck cleared the parking lot, and he turned the steering wheel hard with his big hands, heading south.

In Kingman, Arizona, the Fortiers were having another party in their trailer home; Michael stayed up all night smoking crystal meth and playing video games. In Florida, Jennifer McVeigh was still away on spring vacation. In Pendleton, Bill McVeigh, after another night on the late shift, came home to an empty house.

On Interstate 35, at the Cimarron Travel Plaza truck stop, attendant Fred Skrdla watched a large Ryder truck pull up to the gas pumps. The station is next to a town called Billings, just south of the Kansas state line. In a few hours, the sun would come up on April 19.

Timothy McVeigh was in Oklahoma.

Chapter Eleven

Patriots' Day

Deputy Fire Chief Jon Hansen was one of the first to arrive. The center of downtown Oklahoma City was like a scene from Dresden, like a page from a Berlin diary. Thick black smoke mushroomed skyward, flames filled the corner of 5th and Harvey streets, and pieces of automobiles were scattered everywhere. The bleeding and the dying lay on the scorched pavement, some people holding together their torn faces and broken heads as they waited for help.

Hansen, a career firefighter, stepped up to a small knot of television cameras and radio mikes. The front of the nine-story Alfred P. Murrah Federal Building had been ripped off, the top stories had crashed down to the ground below, and everyone was suddenly aware that there had been a children's day care center on the second floor.

"This isn't supposed to happen in the heartland," Hansen said.

The bomb had exploded at 9:02 a.m., and 168 people were dead or dying. Among the victims was a nurse who hadn't been in the building at all. Rebecca Anderson, rushing to the Murrah building to save others, was struck on the head by a piece of falling debris. For four days she lingered near death; when she was gone, her heart and kidneys went immediately to others waiting transplants.

The oldest victim was seventy-three. Charles E. Hurlburt had worked as a medical missionary overseas. He had gone to the building's first-floor Social Security office with his wife of forty-five years, Jean. She was sixty-seven years old, and a nurse. She died too.

The youngest was four months, Gabreon Bruce, who was in the Social Security office with his mother, who had come to pick up a Social Security card.

Florence Rogers, chief executive of the federal credit union, was holding a staff meeting when suddenly the third floor gave way and all of the eight employees sitting around her desk disappeared.

"I just turned around from my computer screen, reading the next agenda item, and then was covering some items on a sheet of paper," she said. "And I had leaned back in my chair to kind of relax while one of them started talking when, literally, the whole building started to blow up. I was thrown against the floor in kind of a tornadolike rush. And when I was able to stand up, all the girls that were in my office with me had totally disappeared with the six floors from above us on top of them. I never saw them again."

She was left perched on less than eighteen inches of flooring, and her desk was sliding away. "It was about to fall off into the hole that had been made from the blast," she said. Then she looked up. "I could see the blue sky." In all, she lost eighteen staff members killed in the explosion.

Nineteen of the dead were children. One of the most searing images of that morning, and there were many, was the photograph of firefighter Chris Fields cradling the lifeless body of Baylee Almon, just one day past her first birthday.

More than five hundred were injured, some suffering severe wounds, losing a limb or an eye or coming away from the Murrah building with their faces and bodies so scarred that their lives would never seem normal again. Others, though lucky to get by with only a cut or a bruise, would grapple with demons of a darker sort, the psychological trauma that wells up when they hear a car backfire or awake sweating in their bedsheets.

And so many orphans. Ten children lost both parents that morning. Others, the children of split families, endured the death of the only parent in their lives. More than 150 people under the age of twenty-three lost a parent in the bombing.

Nearly 40 percent of local residents at least knew someone killed or injured in the blast. Everyone else surely saw or heard it, and no one truly escaped its impact, not even Stephen Jones, a lawyer from Enid, Oklahoma, eventually appointed to defend Timothy McVeigh. At the trial two years later, Jones recited the names of those lost, his words resounding in the courtroom like an honor roll as he read backward by age from Mr. Hurlburt to the baby Gabreon.

"For those of us from Oklahoma," he said, "the bombing of the Alfred P. Murrah building is the event by which we measure time. It is to my generation in Oklahoma what Pearl Harbor was to my mother and father's generation."

The common theme in the survivors' accounts is the ordinariness of how this day began.

Michael Weaver had taken his wife's car to work, stopping off at the Goodyear station to have it serviced. His wife, Donna, could only pray later that he had been detained and was late reporting to work at the Murrah building, where he worked as a HUD attorney on the eighth floor.

Susan Gail Hunt, a HUD supervisor, a forty-seven-year-old mother of two who had moved to Oklahoma from Texas and brought her Texas twang, arrived at work about seven-thirty that morning. Tom Ward and Freida Bean were there, and they chatted. She began to look at paperwork from the day before, then went in search of a cup of coffee. She helped Ward assemble his supplies, since he had only recently been transferred to this HUD office as the department's new inspector general. "He was getting ready for a case and didn't have paper or pencils and some index cards he needed," Hunt said.

Otherwise, the day was starting out as any typical middle-of-the-week morning. She talked for a while to Paul Broxterman, then returned to the coffeepot. The coffee grounds had slipped down into the pot. She walked into the ladies' room, poured some more water, and walked back through the HUD office. "That was my kind of thing," she said. "I usually kind of checked things as I walked through. I turned the corner, and the first person I saw was Tony Reyes."

"Would you like some candy for breakfast?" Reyes asked. She laughed. They all knew she was notorious for not eating breakfast. Reyes's phone rang, and he picked it up. She continued walking to her office in the far corner of the room. She glanced at Ruth Hill and Lanny Scroggins and Don Burns. They were working on a construction file. She said good morning. "Part of my job was being Miss Congeniality." She passed George Howard, a new employee still in the process of switching his health insurance policy from California. She reached her office door.

"After taking some phone calls, it dawned on me that we were trying to expand our space," Hunt said. "HUD had a significant amount of employees crammed in a small area." She walked back out of the office. There was Mike Weaver, standing by the coffeepot. Susan Ferrell walked past her and up to Weaver, and they began to chat. She saw Lee Sells, a secretary in the legal department. She talked to Kim Clark, who soon was to be married. Hunt was arranging the wedding bouquets.

"Do you have the flowers yet?" Clark asked.

"This weekend," Hunt promised.

She turned to head back to her office. She moved past the front of the Fair Housing and Equal Opportunity section. There was Reyes in the doorway leaning into the office of Peter Avillanoza, the section director. She kept walking. She stopped at David Burkett's desk. He showed her some pictures from his recent trip. Now her secretary, Freida Bean, called her to the phone. She spoke, hung up, and next chatted with Larry Cook and Rita Cruz in the single-family-housing unit. She glanced at the clock. It was nine o'clock. Freida would be taking her morning smoke break.

"Her break partner was sitting there waiting," Hunt recalled. "And I was standing in front of Freida's desk talking to her when the explosion happened."

Among the dead in the HUD office alone: Paul Broxterman, Tony Reyes, Don Burns, Lanny Scroggins, George Howard, Susan Ferrell, Lee Sells, Peter Avillanoza, David Burkett, Kim Clark. And Mike Weaver, too. He was not still at the Goodyear station.

Richard Williams was on the first floor. This morning he arrived at work about six-thirty and headed to his building maintenance office on the far-west end. He sat at his desk reviewing paperwork and yesterday's mail. Robert Dennis, the clerk of the federal court for the Western District of Oklahoma across the street, had come over for a meeting. They adjourned around five minutes of nine. Dennis left to return to the courthouse. One of Williams's aides, Tom Hall, came up, and they were talking near his office door. "That's the last thing that I remember," Williams said.

Helena Garrett had dropped off her sixteen-month-old son, Tevin, at the day care center. She simply loved its bright colors and warm interior and—especially—the nine-foot-high plate-glass windows where the children could press their hands and flash a good-bye to their parents outside.

Garrett awoke that morning around six-fifteen. Also at home were Tevin and his sister, five-year-old Sharonda. "He came to the bathroom with me, and he would always reach up and pull the curling irons down, but he would never get burned," Garrett said. "He would pull them down and run out, and I would get them and put them back up."

"Go wake up Sissy," she told him.

Tevin had a little plastic vase, and he would go into his sister's room and pop her gently on the head. He woke her that way every morning. She never got mad. Their mother was twenty-six years old. She was from Peoria, Illinois, and now worked at the *Journal Record* building in downtown Oklahoma City, across the street from the Murrah. She had to be at work at eight. She dressed Tevin and tossed him awhile on her bed and they played "airplane." Then they had to go. She drove Sharonda to school, and then Tevin to the day care center. She was running a little late, and did not get him there until around seven forty-five. She greeted some of the other children. Elijah and Aaron. Chase and Colton. Zachary.

When she turned to leave, Tevin began crying. The other kids consoled him. "Elijah and Aaron came and sat him down and they patted him," she said. Then she went off to work, leaving the day care center and the Murrah building and her baby Tevin, and because she was running late, she did not have a chance to look over her shoulder one more time on 5th Street, as she had done in the past, to see if the children were at the windows.

Marine Corps officer Michael Norfleet was on the sixth floor of the Murrah building, in the Recruiting Station and Command Center. He had woken early—about four-thirty—at his home in Stillwater, a good hour and fifteen minutes from Oklahoma City. A tall, clean-cut young man, Norfleet worked as a Marine recruiter on the Oklahoma State University campus. He had been trained as a fighter pilot, and had been stationed in Bahrain during the Gulf War. He flew thirty-five combat missions during Desert Shield and Desert Storm, and later some NATO exercises and antidrug interdictions in South America. He came home with the prestigious Air Medal; his wife, Jamie, decided it was time he stayed home. He had

graduated from Oklahoma Baptist University, so it made sense for
Michael and Jamie to return to Oklahoma. They were raising three
children.

He drove in early that morning to attend a prayer breakfast at
Oklahoma City's Myriad Convention Center. The governor, Frank
Keating, was there, as were many of the city's leaders. Afterward
Norfleet decided to stop by the Marine Corps office at the Murrah.
He parked out front, hit the parking meter, stepped in the lobby,
and caught the elevator up to six. "I went into our operations section," he recalled. "It was a big day for Sergeant Benjamin Davis,
who wanted me to call headquarters to find out if he had been
selected to become an officer. So I sat down at the desk in our operations room, which is right at the very front of the building, and I
placed a call to headquarters. But the phone was busy."

He hung up. He looked over at Davis.

"I'll be back in five minutes," Norfleet said.

He walked over to the other side of the floor and toward two supply sergeants. It was just such a normal early-spring morning in
Oklahoma. The sky was blue, the sun up, the wind a bit chilly.

Norfleet was thinking, as he moved about the recruiting office,
of what he had seen outside the building. It was there right in front
of the building, a Ryder rental truck parked on 5th Street next to
the little circle drive. He had seen the truck, and he had thought it
odd that it was there at all. Usually commercial vehicles would go
around to the side and into a parking lot and down to the loading
docks underneath the Murrah building. But this Ryder truck was
out front. Norfleet had even parked his black Ford Ranger in front
of the Ryder. That is why he remembered it—its color. A Ryder
rental truck with the large yellow cargo shell as big and bright as
the sun.

Norfleet stepped up to the two supply sergeants. "Just about the
time I got hello and good morning out of my mouth," he said, "the
bomb hit."

Sergeant Davis never heard about his promotion; he died in the
blast.

Cynthia Lou Klaver caught it on tape. She lived in the center of
town and worked as a lawyer for the state Water Resources Board.
The water board building was just north of the Murrah, on the
northwest corner of 5th and Harvey. She was from Kansas origi-

nally, and now as an attorney she had the job of settling disagreements between Oklahoma residents, mostly farmers, who had applied for new water rights and their neighbors, who were worried about diminishment of local groundwater. This morning she was mediating a neighborhood dispute involving a case from down around Ardmore. A farmer, Roy Weikel, wanted to operate a bottled water company using his groundwater. He and his family had gathered at the water board. So had four or five of his neighbors. "They had come wanting to protest that application," she said, "and we were getting ready to open it up at nine that morning."

Klaver assembled the group in the boardroom on the third floor. State funds were limited, and the water board could not afford an official reporter to transcribe the proceedings. So she turned on a small tape recorder, and opened the hearing. She had begun to describe how the proceeding would run when suddenly the whole room erupted into a roar—a long, overpowering blast followed by shoulder-snapping thuds as pieces of the ceiling and bookshelves came crashing down. Next was the sound of what seemed to be rushing water.

It is her voice screaming on the tape. "Everybody get out! . . . *out!* . . . Watch the electricity lines. Watch the lines! . . . Out the back door. All the way to the right. . . . Let's get out of *here!* . . ."

The tape would become the first piece of information presented to the jury in McVeigh's trial, and Klaver would become the government's first witness.

"I thought the whole building was coming down on us," she remembered. "I didn't see any way we were going to make it out. The building shook and the whole ceiling fell down. And lights continued to fall even after the original cave-in. There was debris, lights, wires, lines hanging down all over. Electricity was still running, so the lights were on, and everyone was bewildered."

She and Connie Siegel Goober, a recording secretary, tried to help some elderly people out of the room. She thought at first it was just this room, the boardroom, but then they could not get out the front door. Too much rubble blocking the exit. So they forced open a back door and ran down a hallway, and she was one of the last out. She joined a small group walking down the middle of the street, dazed. The smoke was thick outside, and debris and papers and glass were still filling the air; they still did not know where the explosion was centered. She walked over to the St. Joseph parking lot. "I turned this way to look for water board people. I found a few. There were some people sitting on curbs cut up. It seemed very desolate and quiet and smoke everywhere."

She bumped into Mike Mathis, a coworker. He had a deep gash across his forehead and was going to drive himself to the Southside Clinic. She helped him into his pickup truck, but she drove. Then she called her sister, and she went home, spending the rest of the day frantically phoning around the city for other water board employees. Later, when they were allowed inside to recover belongings, she noticed the tape recorder, and she saved the tape for the FBI.

They also found another piece of evidence.

"We had one of those school clocks, and it had stopped," she said. "It had fallen off the wall and stopped at 9:02 exactly."

The explosion was so powerful that people living in towns thirty or forty miles distant, like Guthrie and Chandler, mistook the noise for a sonic boom. Some were confused about why lightning had just struck on a clear sunny day. Some were sure a gas main had erupted.

Authorities would estimate the first wave of superhot gas flashed at a speed of eight thousand feet per second. Those standing out front were slammed with a force equal to thirty-seven tons. In a half second, the gas dissipated and the air was suddenly whipped by an equally violent vacuum. Oxygen was sucked out of the air. The ground shook as if it were being tossed by a full-scale earthquake. The north face of the building buckled, the structure rose up, and the beams swung back and forth. The front of the Alfred P. Murrah Federal Building then fell into itself, with huge sections of the concrete and mortar and glass and plyboard thundering down into a thirty-foot-wide, eight-and-a-half-foot-deep crater.

Luke Franey, a federal ATF agent on the ninth floor, the kind of law enforcement official that McVeigh hated so much, found himself suddenly trapped in the skeletal remains of the Murrah building. He is an expert on explosives, but he could not immediately recognize what had blown up the building. He found a small tape recorder in the rubble and began dictating into the mike. He was trying to preserve his impressions, not just for history but also to aid the criminal case he was sure was coming.

"It's April 19," he said, breathing hard into the tape machine. "I'm making this tape for evidence purposes. . . . I was sitting at my desk on the ATF office on the ninth floor talking about obtaining an arrest warrant. . . . During that conversation, a loud explosion occurred, blowing me from my desk across the hall into the opposite office. It took me a minute to figure out what happened. But once I regained my senses I heard people screaming for help. I looked. I got out of my office. The building is basically destroyed. The DEA office is gone. There's a sheer dropoff outside of my office. . . . The building has been ripped apart and there's a straight dropoff approximately nine floors straight down."

Franey continued to describe his surroundings, and all the while muffled screams could be heard in the background, mixed in with the noise of emergency sirens below. He searched for his colleagues but found none. "I can't get any verbal responses. I'm just holding tight. I'm not hurt. A little bit disoriented, I guess."

He noted that the phone lines were dead. "Hell, I don't know what else to say. I've never seen anything quite like this before."

It was three minutes after the blast. He turned off the recorder. Fifteen minutes later, he was speaking into the machine again. "I want to put this down too before I forget," he said. "Right after it detonated, I got up and looked out the part of the building that wasn't there. I could see where the Greek restaurant across the street was gone and there was a huge orange-colored flame with black smoke. I don't know if it was a natural gas explosion that did this. I have no idea. I don't know whether it was a bomb or a gas explosion or whatever. I'm not sure. But hell, who knows, it might be important."

Waiting for rescue, he found an evidence poster board that had been used in a recent trial, and he flipped it over and wrote on the back. He put the sign in the window jamb: "ATF Trapped, 9th Floor."

Down below in the Marine Corps officer, Norfleet lost 40 to 50 percent of his blood, and his right eye. He would never fly again; his Marine Corps pilot days were over. He is out of the service with a 50 percent disability; today he sells digital test equipment.

"The explosion, the force of the blast, threw me into the west wall, breaking my nose, fracturing my skull, and leaving me lying there on the ground. I took a piece of glass from the top of my head, and it flayed open my right eye. It essentially just expunged and burst the whole eye, and in the process, it cut an artery in my fore-head. It cut an artery here in my cheek, and at the same time, it cut an artery on my wrist."

He began to rise. The two supply sergeants seemed fairly okay. They had been sitting in high-backed chairs with their backs to the wall and so, except for minor shrapnel punctures, were relatively unscathed.

"How bad am I hurt?" Norfleet asked.

"Sir, you look really bad."

He felt in good hands. One of the sergeants had also served in Desert Storm. "He immediately went into combat mode and started taking care of me. He laid me on a table and he started to look for bandages to administer first aid. And while I was laying on that table, I could feel the life ebb out of my veins. I just knew that I was losing strength and that if I stayed in the building, I would die."

He lifted himself up. He took the sergeant's shirt and wrapped it around his own head and face to stop the bleeding. They guided him to the back, way up there on the sixth floor, where the north face of the structure had been blown off, and now they could feel the harsh rush of the wind and see with sudden awe the brilliant blue sky. They climbed over waist-high rubble to the stairs and began slowly, ever so carefully, to make their way down. "I was amazed that the stairs were even there, because the building was gone, and the only thing I could see, because of my limited vision, was fol-lowing a blood trail of somebody that had gone down the steps before me. And that was just kind of like the yarn leading me out of the maze, that blood trail, and I followed it out of the building."

He walked into the arms of an Oklahoma Highway Patrol trooper, and he was put in an ambulance. Also inside was an army sergeant with a broken leg, yelling and pounding his fists. The driver turned the ignition, the engine roared, and the siren wailed. They turned into the street and headed to St. Anthony's. "I felt myself losing consciousness," Norfleet said, "and I regurgitated there in the ambulance because I was almost completely in shock."

Up and down 5th Street, on Harvey and Robinson too, within and around the large downtown commercial district, automobiles and mailboxes and parking meters, light poles and trees and street signs, were shattered or burning or exploding with the sound of live ammunition.

Donna Weaver, having rushed out of her phone company office several blocks to the north, came running toward the Murrah building in search of her husband, Mike—still hoping he had not yet made it to his eighth-floor HUD office. They had two sons, and Mike coached high school sports. He had just attended a coaches' meeting last night. They were in the middle of their lives together—a normal family in the heart of America.

Running down the street now, through the smoke and past the burning cars, she remembered the windows, the plate-glass windows on the Murrah building, and how sometimes she could see Mike at his desk way up on the eighth floor, and she was thinking, hoping, praying, Dear God, let me see him in the window, let me see him wave.

"I could see the building and see that the big chunk was out of it and I knew that was Mike's side," she said. "There was glass on the street. There was more and more glass and debris and bricks and rocks. And we saw people coming out of buildings in all directions at that point. There were some things falling, it seems. Paper, and, I don't remember anything really hard, but, kind of paper fluttering, fluttering down.

"There was wire and debris, and people were hollering about being careful. And of course we were down in front of the building and looking up at the big gaping hole, and the roofing material was kind of waving in the wind and smoke everywhere.

"That is what I saw, right down there looking up at the big hole where I knew Mike's office had been. I knew that if he'd been in that office, he wasn't there."

She just stared at the building, the tan-and-black structure, the place the kids when they were younger called "Dad's work."

She could not see Mike.

She heard him.

"A voice kind of talked to me in my head and told me that I had to be careful. I couldn't get hurt. That I had to take care of those boys. And I think it was Mike telling me to go back, to get away from there. Not to go any further."

Inside the HUD offices on the eighth floor, as throughout the building, death was indiscriminate: Mike Weaver was dead and Susan Hunt was left among the living.

"I did not hear the blast," Hunt said. "I heard what I thought was the floors falling, but I did not hear the explosion itself. Just the debris hitting us."

She was standing with her back to the southwest windows that overlooked the building's south plaza. Freida Bean's desk was right in front of her. "The last face I remember seeing was Freida's face as she fell." Hunt came to on the floor. She unhooked twisted wire from around Marla Hornberger, a secretary, wires that were so twisted that they were even wrapped around her earrings. A mailroom clerk was yelling that they had to get out of the building. Dianne McDonald was lying on the floor. They helped her up.

"It was really odd because we were pelted with glass and debris from the front and from above," Hunt recalled. "And then the glass in the windows behind us hit us in the back. It sucked the glass back in, which was probably good because it would have blown us out the windows."

Bean was trapped under a desk, pinned down by a filing cabinet; her leg appeared broken. "I know I couldn't have done it by myself— Freida obviously had to help me. Because I pushed the filing cabinet off of the desk and pulled her up over the desk and helped her to her feet. We helped each other. The copy machine—we had a huge copy machine in my office that had blown over. We tried to get out the door, but we had to climb over the copy machine."

Bean's face was marked with glass. Hunt reached up and pulled the shards out of her secretary's cheeks. They remembered the fire drills that had been run by Richard Williams and the crew down below in the GSA unit. And that was the thing to do now. Just moments earlier, Hunt had been walking through the HUD offices, coffee cup in hand, wishing good morning to her staff, starting the workday rolling. "I had just seen these people. And I was going after them. After all, my job was to take care of them. So I was going to take care of them."

They made it to a stairwell. The doors and the windows had been blown out, and the stairs seemed to sway; it was like walking a wire without a net. On the seventh floor, Hunt ran into a woman she knew only as Regina. She was holding up Larry Cook. His forehead was gashed, his arm cut, his foot broken. "Regina is a little person, although she was pretty mighty that day," Hunt said.

Hunt, who is six feet tall, took Cook, and Regina said to her, "I'm going to go back in and see if I can find anyone else that's hurt."

Hunt would learn later that Regina Bonny was a policewoman from nearby Midwest City, working on loan with the federal Drug Enforcement Adminstration. Bonny remembered that when the bomb hit, the world went silent; she looked around and "there were no walls or ceilings or doors."

As a police officer, she knew what to do. She began looking for survivors and helping them to their feet and toward the stairwells. She found Jim Staggs, an ATF employee. "He was bleeding bad from the head," she said. "I took off his shirt and I stuck part of the shirt down to the hole on his head, and I wrapped the rest of the shirt around his head."

Hunt was still helping Cook maneuver down the stairs. She counted out each step, and then each floor. "And as we reached each floor, people like us with blood on them in varying degrees of injury were coming out of the doors into the stairwell. The stairwell at that point appeared to be the only exit route. So I counted the floors all the way down."

She stepped outside into the confusion. Cook was trembling and about to go into shock. A policeman appeared with a blanket. She started to return to the building to search for others, but at the second floor she spotted a body under the rubble. She put her hands to her face and went back outside, to the Murrah plaza just south of the building. More HUD employees began to stagger out, collecting on the plaza. She spoke to Ruth Heald who lay there on the pavement, her neck bleeding profusely.

"I know that's you," Heald told Hunt. "But I can't see you. Do I have an eye?"

The woman raised her head toward Hunt. "I have five kids," she said. "And I'm alive."

The small group of HUD employees worried about others. A man appeared from somewhere with a piece of paper and a pen. They wrote down names, what they hoped would be the names of the living, those who seemed okay, those who would need to go to a hospital, those who might still be trapped inside, those whose status was unknown. They were a broken, battered bunch, trying to make sense of things, trying to carry on with their lives in the whirl of chaos around them. And everything seemed so cold. Hunt's lips tasted like ice. Her hands were trembling. And still she tried to calm her nerves long enough to add another name to the list. "Fran? . . . Ted? . . . Dave?"

She heard the screams and the awful wail of mothers pleading with police officers to let them inside the Murrah building, begging them for any word about their children. Then she saw Helena Garrett.

Garrett had been working at the *Journal Record* building. She had heard what she thought was a "thunder boom"; it shook her and she screamed. She ran outside with others, and it occurred to her to check on Tevin next door.

She saw the parking lot on 5th Street. "Then I looked up and I saw the federal building."

She ran for the Murrah, but a policeman ordered her away. "You can't go there," he said.

She ran around the *Journal Record* building and found a friend, and they hurried back to the policeman.

"You have to let her through there," pleaded the friend. "Her baby's in there."

"I told this lady I cannot let her through here," the officer said. He was adamant. "I'm not going to let her through."

Garrett ran up to 6th Street and down Harvey and finally to the west side of the Murrah. She closed her eyes, trying to imagine the building as it had been, picturing Tevin safe inside.

She began to count out loud.

"One."

"Two."

Two—the second floor—the day care center. That was where Tevin should be. "And I started climbing the debris."

The rubble was higher than her head, and she did not get far. A man pulled her back down. Not safe, he said. She looked away and spotted two women lying on stretchers. She bent down and pleaded into the face of one of the ladies, "Do you know where the babies are?"

The woman did not know, so Garrett ran again, around the side of the building, until she came up to the back plaza, where Susan Hunt and the group from HUD were listing names on the sheet of paper. Now other mothers were arriving too, and shouting, and Garrett joined them, making one plaintive cry: "Where are the babies?"

Two men stood nearby, and it was Garrett's voice they heard above the others.

"My baby's in there!" she screamed.

"What?" asked one of the men. "What do you mean?"

"There's a day care center in there! My baby's in there!"

Both men hurried inside. And then, after several minutes that seemed to last forever, began the procession of dead and dying infants carried outside. In her hysteria Garrett mistook one girl for her son. "Her head looked as if it was gashed," she remembered. "It was kind of smashed, and she was unconscious."

A man inside the building yelled for help. "I need two stretchers! I can put four on two stretchers!"

There was a bench in the Murrah plaza, and they placed two-year-old Colton Smith there. A doctor came up, and examined him briefly. "There's nothing I can do," he said.

Garrett remained with the dying boy. "He was bleeding from the mouth," she said. "His stomach looked like it had been busted open. And I didn't want to leave Colton, but I had, had . . . I didn't leave Colton. And I was still looking for my own baby. But I didn't leave him."

They brought out more children, and they laid the infants on the ground, covering them with white sheets taken from the beds in the day care center. They made a line from Colton down through the plaza, a windrow of dead babies shrouded in white.

Garrett did not move. "I didn't want to leave our babies," she said. "And I didn't see Tevin. And I started crying up there, and I . . . and I was crying and I was screaming. . . ."

The plaza was covered with thick shards of broken glass. "Please don't lay our babies on the glass!" she screamed. "We don't want our babies on the glass!"

A man she did not know came up with a broom, a large broom, and he started to sweep the glass. He swept it this way, and he swept it that way, and Garrett could see he was crying as he strained against the handle, as if it were the most important thing in the world to do—sweeping the glass away from the dead children.

A nurse arrived—they knew she was a nurse because of her uniform—and she began tagging the babies, placing numbers by the bodies. "And right then I realized they were dead," Garrett said. Soon she became convinced that one of the dead was her child.

"No, no," a man told her. "That isn't your baby."

"Are you sure?" she asked.

"That's a white baby," the man said.

"Tevin is really light. Are you sure that's not my baby?"

"No, ma'am. I'm positive that's not your baby."

She continued to stare up at the Murrah structure, imploring the building to unburden itself, to give back her child. But by the afternoon, the winds brought rain and Helena Garrett went home without her baby. The police came later to her house and lifted prints from his high chair and the glass on her stereo and a Mickey Mouse picture that hung over his crib. It was to help identify him when he was found. On Saturday she went to a local church where people went to learn of their missing loved ones, and it was then that she was told that Tevin's body had been recovered.

At the funeral home two days later, they did not want her to see her son's face; the injury to Tevin's head was deep and crushing, and they feared it would be too much for her to bear. But they did agree to lift the bottom part of his small casket. "I kissed his feet and I kissed his legs," she said, "and I couldn't go up higher."

Police Sergeant John Avera, forty-seven, not far from retirement, with glasses and a mustache, an old farm boy from out near Washita, Oklahoma, west of the big city, was that morning doing some very routine police work—moving equipment around in a storage room in a downtown precinct building. He had been a cop for twenty-five years, had worked the airport detail and communications and patrol. He handled permit applications and IDs, and he did police recruiting for a while too. He had just sat down with his commander, Lieutenant Bob Bowman, when the station house seemed to explode. Ceiling tiles fell, walls buckled. The lieutenant ordered the building evacuated. Outside, Avera realized it was not his building that had been hit.

"As I scanned the sky, I could see debris going up into the air," he said. "And so I started towards the black smoke and debris. And as I was running towards the building, the closer I got, the debris started falling down on us. I stopped and grabbed some of the paperwork that was falling and looked at it. One of them was an application for a visa. I continued running towards the federal building."

He reached the St. Joseph's parking lot, and only then realized the magnitude of the blast. "The extremely dense black smoke was going up in the air. You couldn't see what was there, and I thought that was ground zero where the building had blown up." He rounded a corner and spotted a man in the middle of the street, rolling around in a fetal position. "As I got to him, I realized that he was hurt worse than anything. I couldn't do anything for him. And the closer I got to him and was looking at him, the more he was trying to roll around and get away from me. And he was laying in a bunch of glass. I thought it would be best to leave him alone. So I backed off."

Another man approached. "There is a day care center in there," he told Avera. "We need to go get the kids out."

Avera did not hesitate. "I immediately went over to the closest window and crawled inside." He ran across another police sergeant carrying a badly injured man. Avera hollered that he was going to hurt himself trying to save that man. "He didn't stop. He just carried him out." Avera dug deeper inside, past upturned desks and tabletops. Slabs of wallboard and cinder blocks littered the route. Piping and electrical cables blocked the way. He stumbled into a large room. "I found two women laying down in the back of that room. Both of them were conscious and both of them were talking." He met a man in a suit. The two of them carried the first woman outside and laid her down in the middle of the intersection, first brushing off as much of the glass as they could. The woman groaned, and said that fourteen workers were still trapped in that large room. Again Avera did not hesitate. "I turned around and went directly back in."

He crawled back through the same window, digging his way. At first he heard no one, saw no one. Then he reached the back of the room, and a dark hallway. Down the hallway, toward the end, he could hear people screaming for help. "This particular area was extremely dark, very, very dusty, had a real bad odor. I hadn't ever smelled it before." But he made it back there, along with another man, and they found several women trapped inside. He said more help would be coming and told them to be patient, and he marked them in his mind as he continued farther, deeper into the blackness.

Just north of where the elevators should have been, he found a young woman whose foot was sticking out of the debris. "That's all I could see at that point, or feel," he said. "And I heard a baby choking." Avera and two others dug back toward the elevators again, and then began digging downward. "The rock that we were moving took—there were three of us digging in that hole—it took two of us to lift the rock off these babies, it was so heavy."

They picked up one child, and another police sergeant cradled the infant in his arms and worked his way back to that broken window. Avera began to feel around in the hole, and he found another child.

"I picked this baby up. It was not making any noise, and I knew it was unconscious. I couldn't feel any life." He stuck his hand down the baby's throat, trying to clear it for breath. But the throat was hard, and very, very dry.

"I knew I couldn't hold the baby. The baby was broke up pretty bad, and I knew it was hurt real bad. And I knew I couldn't crawl out the way I came. Because you'd have to crawl over debris and I couldn't crawl and hold the baby at the same time." He searched for another exit. He went south by the elevators and waded through water that swirled over the tops of his boots. Suddenly he was in the parking garage, and it was darker still down there. He sloshed through the water, heading for a dot of light far up ahead, until at last the light grew brighter and he burst into the sunshine and the fire and the smoke outside. He was on Robinson Street, still running, running north now. He spied a concrete fence, and people lying on the ground, and others bending over them. He saw firemen standing in the street, near 5th Street, and they were pointing to an ambulance, and now Avera, his uniform black, his pants ripped, his boots wet and scraped, ran up to them to offer them the baby, the child in his arms.

And that is when he met Chris Fields, a fireman who stepped out from behind the ambulance.

Avera was shouting, "I think the baby is critical. Please take it. I've got to get back in the building."

And Fields took the child. It was a girl. Her name was Baylee Almon. She had just turned a year old yesterday. Now she was dead.

Five miles away, the child's mother was at work at her desk. She had heard and felt the bomb's terrible blast. Someone turned on the television. Aren Almon saw what had been done to the Murrah building and, she said, "my heart sank."

For Sergeant Avera, there would be one more trip inside the Murrah, this time not for a child but for a young mother, the woman whose leg he had seen jutting from the debris. He had marked her in his mind and he would return. He had promised that to himself, and to her. "I started trying to dig in the area where the leg was sticking out," he said. "And I could talk with the lady that was in there. She was very calm. She didn't . . . I don't think she knew where she was or how she got there. But she was talking to me."

She mentioned her husband and two children. He asked her what she had eaten for breakfast, where the kids went to school. He talked and he dug and then he realized that honestly he could not move all of the bricks and the large concrete blocks that pinned her below. "So I just stayed there and visited with her."

He was able to scratch out a small hole closer to where she was trapped, and he thought he could see her hand. Which hand, though? He did not know. Nor could he touch her hand. But he could see it. In his pocket he found a piece of paper. He took it out, and a pencil too. Overhead they were beginning to train spotlights on the wreckage, and Avera could see a little better now. The smoke was clearing some. He asked her name; she told him and he wrote it down. He asked her husband's name, and he wrote that down too. "I thought, that's what I'll do. As soon as I get out of the building, I've got to call him and tell him she was alive. I thought that's what I'd do."

But then other men were hollering from behind him, warning that they believed the rest of the building was going to crash down upon them. He was ordered out, ordered out now, but he would not go. More help came. They brought in some heavy equipment, and bolt cutters, and took turns trying to break up the rebar, to set her free. But it was making too much noise, and the area around them was beginning to sway. The generators were vibrating and a lot of loose material was crackling above them. The exhaust fumes from the generators were making them sick.

And then: panic.

A rumor swept the Murrah wreckage that a second bomb was about to go off. Rescue workers were ordered to evacuate. Avera worked another five minutes, maybe ten. Then someone placed a firm hand on his shoulder.

"I don't think you understand," the man said.

Now the order was clear: everyone had to get out.

The woman trapped below was frantic.

"Please don't leave me," she begged. "Don't leave me in here. Don't go."

But Avera left. He had no choice; they all left.

Out on the street he fished around in his pocket for the note, but it was gone. He thinks that her name might have been Terry. Terry something . . . Terry what? He does not recall; he cannot remember. He has been told that the woman survived, but even that he can't know for sure.

The possibility of a second bomb, a false alarm as it turned out, was all the more terrifying because of what so many people had already been through. For Luke Franey, the trapped ATF agent on the ninth floor, "it was just like someone reaches in and grabs your heart and squishes it. Because I had nowhere to go if there was another one. And at that point I just made a decision that I'd rather die falling off the building than go through something like that again."

Priscilla Salyers, a U.S. Customs employee on the fifth floor and the mother of two, lay trapped somewhere near the child care center that had been on the second floor. She could hear someone yell, "We have a live one here!" She saw rescue workers and felt a man clasp her hand. Both her legs and the other arm were pinned down by a pile of rebar.

"We have to leave," the man told her. He was crying. "We have to go get a tool. I'm so sorry."

She made it easier for him; she let go of his hand.

He left; they all left, and, she recalled, it was very, very silent in there. For two hours she waited until they returned, and it was another two hours before they pried her free.

The firemen, the police, the entire rescue apparatus of Oklahoma City and throughout the state, from around the nation too, would work tirelessly for weeks. From the outset, officials insisted they were conducting a rescue effort, not a recovery of bodies, and they promised never to pause in their search for anyone still possibly alive inside. It was good stubborn Midwestern determination. But the odds against further survivors were far too high. By the evening of the first day, all of the survivors had been found.

But the rescuers could not know that, and so they toiled on, aided by rescue groups from around the country, with specially trained dogs, with cranes overhead, with helicopter spotters in the air and giant spotlights at night. Into the second day and night, and the third, too, they continued, carefully removing what pieces they could, carrying on undaunted when only bodies—and pieces of bodies—were coming out of the building debris. On the first day, in the afternoon, it rained. On the fourth day, Saturday, it rained again, then poured. And still they kept at it. And on Sunday, when the president of the United States and other high officials from Washington and around the United States, religious leaders too, assembled for a prayer service at the State Fair Arena, a mere mile from the site of the wreckage, even then the rescue workers pushed on.

The arena was filled to capacity. Survivors and their families and the relatives of the dead and still missing wore giant ribbons. Parents cradled teddy bears in memory of their lost children.

President Clinton promised the nation's support. "We pledge to do all we can to help you heal the injured, to rebuild this city, and to bring to justice those who did this evil."

The Reverend Billy Graham, looking old and tired, spoke with particular eloquence. "That blast was like a violent explosion ripping at the heart of America," he said. "And long after the rubble is cleared and the rebuilding begins, the scars of this senseless and evil outrage will remain."

Those in the arena joined hands and sang "God Bless America." At 5th and Harvey streets, the jackhammers and the cranes played their own mournful music as the men and women continued to dig through the wreckage. Hospitals were filled to overflowing. Blood banks were lined with volunteers. At the First Christian Church, the downtown church turned into a family notification center, crowds crushed in to learn the grimmest of news. Lists were posted on a bulletin board, and families waited to be called. Throughout the city, funeral directors planned multiple services. Still the rescue work went on.

Patrolling the scene of the Murrah rubble, police covered their badges with black bands in a tribute to the eight federal law enforcement agents killed in the explosion. One officer took a bar of soap and scrawled a message on the rear window of his patrol car: "We will never forget." A new billboard went up: "God Bless Oklahoma City." A chain-link fence around the perimeter of the site was blanketed with flowers and ribbons and more teddy bears. "Pins, $5," advertised a cardboard sign. "Proceeds to YMCA kids." In a newspaper cartoon, two rescue workers stood in front of the blown-out building. "How many hurt?" asked one. "260 million Americans," said the other.

They put down their shovels a little over a month after the bombing. On the morning of May 23, 150 pounds of dynamite, placed at strategic spots around the building's shell, imploded the old structure. The men and the women who had worked so hard to save the lives of their neighbors went home. But even then, their work truly was not finished. Still buried in the thirty-foot heap of metal and concrete were human remains never recovered. Safety concerns—and exhaustion—had put an end to the all-day, all-night madness of digging for a miracle.

With the Murrah building leveled, all that was left was a flattened city block. Nearby stood a scalded brick wall from a smaller office structure that had been badly damaged. Painted on that wall in dark, red, angry words was a warning from members of Rescue Team 5. It said:

> 4-19-95.
> We Search for the Truth.
> We Seek Justice.
> The Courts Require it.
> The Victims Cry for it.
> And GOD Demands it!

Chapter Twelve

Patriots and Tyrants

Little gets by Oklahoma State Highway Patrol Trooper Charlie Hanger. He patrols his patch of Interstate 35 and the Cimarron Turnpike like a bird of prey. So what fool would this be coming up his highway in broad daylight driving a bright yellow sedan with no license plate?

In his hurry, Hanger might have missed the car altogether. Less than an hour earlier, he had been working in eastern Noble County when the state patrol first learned about "some type of explosion in Oklahoma City," and he was ordered south to assist other officers converging on the capital city. He ran for his car and soon was racing down I-35. He had just reached Perry, the county seat, when he received this message: "Need to cancel units coming to OK City. Just be aware of the situation/OK."

Suddenly, the big chance was over. A twenty-year cop, Hanger did not like missing out on the action, but he obeys orders. He is a short man, with his brown hair slicked to the side and little beady eyes; his eyes are his most dangerous weapon. He has been a state trooper so long, and is so sharp behind the wheel of his patrol car, that by his own count he has booked at least eight hundred violators into the Noble County Jail alone, most of them after what started as routine traffic stops.

Which is exactly how this one with the yellow sedan began too, at 10:22 that morning, Wednesday, April 19—a Mercury Marquis

with no license plate headed north. Not speeding; not driving reck-
lessly either. Just no license plate.

Hanger was going nearly a hundred miles an hour as he barreled
back toward troop headquarters. Just moments earlier he had
stopped to help a motorist in a broken van—an incident not nearly
as exciting as what his imagination was telling him must be going
on in Oklahoma City. He noticed the plateless Mercury almost too
late, after he overshot it; then he slowed down, slipped in behind
the car, and pulled it over.

He stepped out of his patrol car. He was wearing his brown uniform; spring had come and he sported short sleeves. The day was
still cool, the wind light for Oklahoma. He noticed the large ugly
primer spot on the rear quarter panel of the car. Then he saw the
driver's door open and the combat boots drop to the pavement.

Hanger waited a moment behind his own open car door, using it
briefly as a shield. He did not know what he was walking into here.
Just two weeks ago, a fellow trooper, John Kugel, had been fired at
by a motorist with a 9mm semiautomatic pistol. The man missed.
Officer Kugel did not miss. He shot the man three times—after
stopping him for a routine traffic infraction. This had occurred just
fifteen miles up the road from where Hanger was about to question
this man with the lace-up black boots.

The important thing was to be very careful, to go slow. "There
was a slight pause," Hanger recalled, "a couple of seconds, and then
the driver stood up. I was able to see both his hands, and he started
walking toward me."

They approached each other, meeting halfway between the
patrol car and the Mercury. In his haste, Hanger had forgotten to
activate the camera mounted on his dashboard—a bad turn of luck
that meant the arrest would be forever lost to video history.

The first words came from Hanger. "I stopped you because you
weren't displaying a tag," the trooper said.

The young man—tall, pale-complected, wearing a light black
windbreaker and faded black jeans—looked back at his car, at the
rear bumper where the license plate should have been. He said he
had not had the car long and that was why there was no tag. He said
he had recently purchased the vehicle. Hanger asked to see the bill
of sale.

Can't, the man said. The paperwork was still being drawn up.

"Well, how long does it take to fill out a bill of sale?" Hanger asked.

"I don't have one with me," the man said.

Hanger asked to see his driver's license. The man reached into his right rear pocket and pulled out a camouflage-colored billfold. He started to slide out his driver's license, but Hanger was not paying any attention to the man's hands. He eyes were riveted on a bulge under the man's left arm, beneath the windbreaker. The man held up his driver's license, this one from Michigan, with the name Timothy James McVeigh.

Still the trooper was ignoring the license. He told the man to take both hands and slowly pull back his jacket. The windbreaker was zipped partway up. So the man started to unzip it and slide the jacket open.

"I have a gun," McVeigh said.

Hanger shouted, "Get your hands up and turn around."

He unholstered his own gun and, as McVeigh spun around, stuck it to the back of McVeigh's head. "Walk to the back of your car."

"My weapon is loaded," McVeigh advised.

Hanger, still pointing at the back of McVeigh's head, said, "So is mine."

At the rear of the Mercury, he ordered McVeigh to place his hands on the trunk and spread his legs. McVeigh complied. Hanger reached around—still with his own gun up against the back of McVeigh's head—and felt the shoulder holster under McVeigh's arm and pulled out the pistol. He tossed it onto the shoulder of the highway, out of McVeigh's reach. It was the one thing McVeigh cherished most in the world, a coal-black .45-caliber Glock military assault pistol, Model 21. In the chamber was a special Black Talon "cop-killer" bullet, designed to mushroom inside a person's body. In the clip were thirteen standard rounds of hard-ball, high-velocity ammunition.

McVeigh did not seem nervous, or angry. He told the officer he had a second ammunition clip on his belt. Hanger removed that clip, noticed that it was fully loaded, and tossed it to the ground.

"I also have a knife," McVeigh said.

Hanger removed the fixed blade from a brown leather sheath and threw it to the roadway. He handcuffed McVeigh behind his back.

"Why the loaded firearm?" Hanger asked.

"I have a right to carry it, for protection," McVeigh said.

The trooper walked him back to the squad car and put him in the front passenger seat, belting him in. Hanger went back and picked up the gun, the clip, and the knife. He broke down the gun, detached the clip, then tossed both clips and the knife into the trunk of his patrol car. He came around and slid behind the wheel, with McVeigh's pistol still in his hand. Calling his dispatcher, he asked for a wants-or-warrants search on Timothy James McVeigh, birthdate 04-23-68. He asked for a weapons check on the Glock. And he wanted a computer run on the vehicle identification number he took off the Mercury.

He held the Glock up in the air and turned it around in his hand, searching for the serial number.

"VM769," McVeigh said.

"Well, you're close," Hanger replied. "It's VW769."

"Well, I knew it was an M or a W."

"Most wouldn't know the serial number on their weapon."

"I do," McVeigh snapped.

He asked the cop what he was carrying. "A Sig Model 228," Hanger said.

"Oh," McVeigh said. "A 9mm."

Now the dispatcher called back. McVeigh was not wanted on any outstanding charges, had no criminal history. Hanger asked the dispatcher to double-check the Mercury. He read McVeigh a Miranda warning, then began to interview him in the car. "I didn't take any notes," Hanger would later say. "It was just friendly chitchat."

He asked him again about the missing plate. McVeigh said he had recently purchased the car from a Firestone dealership in Junction City, Kansas. He said the salesman's name was Tom. Hanger again called his dispatcher and asked for someone to check with the Firestone.

McVeigh said he had paid about $250 for the car and had traded in an older car that had broken down. He said he had the tag from the old car, but thought it best to drive without a plate rather than place the old one on the Mercury.

The truth would never be known. Those at the Firestone dealership saw him put the Arizona plate on the Mercury; those at the Dreamland saw the plate too. Had he later removed it himself to avoid suspicion? Or had someone stolen the plate, or taken it purposely to entrap him?

Hanger asked if he could search the car, and McVeigh consented. The trooper nosed around inside the vehicle. He found no other weapons or contraband, just a baseball cap, a short handwritten note, and a sealed envelope. Nothing in the glove box; nothing in the trunk. Walking back to the patrol car, he noticed McVeigh fidgeting in his seat.

McVeigh said he was in the process of moving to Arkansas, had just taken some belongings there and now was going back to Junction City for another load. When the dispatcher called back (on a cell phone, because there was so much radio traffic relating to the explosion in Oklahoma City), Hanger learned that the previous owners of the Mercury were a couple from Fayetteville, Arkansas.

Hanger asked McVeigh if he wanted the car towed, at his own expense, or if they should leave it on the roadside. He could retrieve it when he made bond on charges of carrying and transporting a loaded firearm, plus driving without a license plate.

Leaving it would be at his own risk, the officer said.

"Leave it," McVeigh said.

"What about the envelope that's sealed up on the front seat?"

"Leave it there."

Hanger locked the Mercury, then drove McVeigh to downtown Perry and the Noble County Courthouse. The jail sits on the fourth floor of the old building. Along the way, they talked a bit more. But Hanger messed up with the video camera again; he hit the wrong button and blew the chance to record their conversation.

He did remember some of what they talked about. McVeigh said he had purchased the Glock in New York, where he had lived some years ago. He claimed the weapon was worth $800. (He actually had bought the pistol in 1991 for $600 from Pat's Pawn and Gun Shop in Ogden, Kansas, just outside of Fort Riley.)

Over and over, McVeigh asked Hanger when he would get his gun back. Having his hands cuffed behind him was bad, but not feeling his gun under his arm or along his belt was much more unsettling. It made him feel naked; made him feel unprotected.

McVeigh was booked into the county jail shortly after eleven in the morning, just two hours after rescue workers in downtown Oklahoma City began rushing to the scene of a tremendous building explosion. He was assigned a prisoner number, 95-057. They took his jailhouse mug shot, McVeigh standing in front of a measuring chart, his bearing erect, his jaw tight, his lips clamped. The windbreaker gone, he was wearing two T-shirts, the top one emblazoned on the front with a drawing of Abraham Lincoln and underneath it the Latin phrase *Sic Semper Tyrannis*—"Thus Ever to Tyrants." On the back was a drawing of a tree with blood-red droplets and another quotation, this one from Thomas Jefferson: "THE TREE OF LIBERTY must be refreshed from time to time with the blood of patriots and tyrants."

For the photo, he held in his hand a little black card with white lettering listing his prisoner number and the date, 04-19-95.

But what stood out in the picture was not the date or the T-shirt. Rather it was his eyes, full and round and yet expressionless, now more black than blue, to some showing a nervous uncertainty, to others a dark defiance. It was that stare again, practiced and learned and drilled into him on hundreds of afternoons on the army parade ground. The eyes seemed totally focused, but on what? Not on surrender, because surely the game was not yet up. On what then? Something much larger: think it can be done, and it will be done; believe in the revolution, and it will happen.

"When do I go to court?" he snapped at booking clerk Marsha Moritz. "When do I go to court?"

Except for that brief outburst, she remembered that he was well behaved. "He was so polite and just so relaxed," she said later. "He was not nervous like a lot of the prisoners when they're fingerprinted." And that was different, because most people, particularly first-time offenders, can be difficult. "It's weird to be polite and calm and easy to book," she said. "And he was easy to book."

McVeigh hesitated when she asked him for the name of a relative to put on the booking card. On a large counter in the booking room, a television set was on, showing some of the first video from the carnage in Oklahoma City. At times he was looking at the TV, at other times looking away.

Moritz pressed him again for a next of kin, and he gave James Nichols and the farm in Decker. "But he didn't say he was a relative," Moritz remembered. "He just claimed that's someone to call in case of an emergency."

"Is that your present address?" she asked.

"Yes," he said.

"Want to make a phone call?"

"Don't need to."

McVeigh emptied his pockets—four rounds of .45-caliber ammunition, his billfold, some keys, yellow coins, Rolaids, and—most significantly—a set of earplugs.

Hanger escorted him into a storage room across the hall. He asked him to undress, drop his clothes into a brown paper Best Yet grocery bag, and slip on a bright orange jumpsuit. McVeigh began to disrobe, and off came his white T-shirt with the Lincoln drawing.

And then McVeigh was taken to the jail atop the county courthouse, stashed away in a small cell in a tiny prairie town, his past unknown to the local drunks and the other town miscreants incarcerated with him, his face shielded from the eyes of an angry nation that would soon be demanding to know his name.

Even Hanger did not put it together. He did not see McVeigh again for two days, when he watched on television as his arrestee was taken from the jail. And the day after that, on Saturday, he made a discovery while inspecting his patrol car. Feeling underneath the front bucket seat, he found a pocket-size business card and remembered how McVeigh had fidgeted with his handcuffs.

Hanger studied the card. It belonged to Paulsen's Military Supply in Antigo, Wisconsin. On the flip side, McVeigh had written a hasty note: "TNT at $5 a stick. Need more. Call after May 1." To federal investigators, it was a sign McVeigh was planning more destruction to follow Oklahoma City.

The highway patrolman also discovered a private security guard badge he had taken from McVeigh. The trooper had placed it in his shirt pocket and forgotten about it. He would turn both items over to the FBI, the card and the badge, but he would keep his own self-doubts. How? he asked himself. Why had he not seen it? Why hadn't he at least noticed the FBI's composite drawing of John Doe No. 1—the sketch of McVeigh with the long nose and the long ears? The man he had arrested with a loaded Glock pistol under his arm just outside of Oklahoma City . . . what could be more obvious?

But April 19 had been just another day on the beat for Trooper Hanger. He left McVeigh at the jail booking counter. It was nearly noon then, and Hanger took his wife to lunch, McVeigh's pistol and the clips and the knife still in the trunk of his patrol car. After lunch, he returned and inventoried the weapons and filled out a probable cause affidavit against McVeigh on the gun and traffic charges. When his shift ended at three, Hanger went home, unaware of the significance of the arrest he had made that morning. When he sat in his living room and watched television, he was stunned, hurt and angry, reacting like any good and decent Oklahoman, like any loyal American, at what he saw still unfolding just eighty minutes down the freeway.

Up in the jail, McVeigh was served lunch—a bologna sandwich, potato chips, and tea. He ate rather nonchalantly, as if he was not in trouble—real trouble. Dinner his first night behind bars was goulash and cornbread. Breakfast the next morning was oatmeal and raisins. Showers were on Thursday evenings. When night jailer Jack Branson passed out fresh toiletries, McVeigh asked only for a toothbrush and toothpaste.

Another inmate, John Seward, a local in for burglary, remembered that McVeigh talked easily about the army and Desert Storm. He offered the inmates stories about "being over there in the sand."

What about your family? they asked.

"I burned them bridges before I got out of the service," McVeigh said.

Your mother? they asked. Inmates always talk about their mothers. Their mothers are the only ones who understand them.

"She is still alive, but I don't know where she is," McVeigh said.

Jailer Farrell Stanley remembered McVeigh asking about getting a lawyer. But Stanley told him to save his money, said that a bail hearing was rather routine, and that he would be out of jail in no time. "I could tell it was his first time," the jailer said.

McVeigh slept restlessly, if he slept at all. It was not television that kept him awake; there was no TV in the Perry jail, only radio. And the radio sitting on the jailhouse shelf was locked onto one station, and that station was broadcasting just one story—live coverage of human chaos at the Alfred P. Murrah Federal Building.

In Washington, Merrick Garland, a Harvard Law graduate now running the criminal division at the Department of Justice, was sitting at his desk in his fourth-floor office when an "Urgent" report flashed on his computer screen. Garland clicked up the report. Much of the information was sketchy, some of it inaccurate; all of it was chilling. It had been written hastily in the administrative office of the U.S. attorney for the Western District of Oklahoma.

". . . An explosion was heard. Black smoke billowed from a few blocks north. . . . The explosion rocked the private leased space which houses the U.S. attorneys' office three blocks from the federal courthouse."

Federal safety officials were sent to investigate. "Along the three-block walk, they found massive glass in the streets from several of the high-rise buildings. Along the way, walking wounded were everywhere, along with emergency rescue vehicles.

"It appears, and has been speculated, that a massive bomb exploded in the area of ATF, DEA or Secret Service offices in the Murrah Federal Building. Employers from HUD indicated there were a few suspected deaths, and a couple of critically injured."

Garland scrolled down the page. "Damage to the Murrah building included the front of the building being blown off, several floors seem to be missing, and you can see right through the building in the area of the 7th, 8th and 9th floors."

He read more: safety officials had inspected the nearby federal courthouse and found extensive damage there too. More still: "It appeared some small explosions were continuing, perhaps gas lines."

Garland stepped into the office of Deputy Attorney General Jamie Gorelick, who then telephoned her boss, Attorney General Janet Reno. Reno asked the two of them to report again soon with additional information. Garland returned to his office, flipped on the television, and searched for any pictures from the scene. But there were none, and now a second "Urgent" came across his computer.

This one, again from the U.S. attorney's office in the Western District of Oklahoma, provided fresh details.

"Information was received by the district that it was a bomb.

"Information was received by the district that there was a second bomb and it was NOT detonated.

"The northeast side of the Alfred P. Murrah Federal Building was blown out.

"The 9th floor of the federal building is gone.

"All grand jurors have been evacuated.

"One WDOK [Western District of Oklahoma] employee has a child in the day care center in the Federal Building.

"Unconfirmed reports from the district were six children in the day care center killed, although CNN is reporting that all of the children are safe.

"The district reported that there was a bomb threat at a church located north of Oklahoma City.

"In reviewing cases, the U.S. attorney's office initially reports that a defendant in a methamphetamine case had apparently made threats against the government."

Garland turned back to the television. Now there were pictures on CNN, and he immediately thought, This is not a gas main break. This is like the scene of the Marine barracks in Beirut. This is a bomb.

His office was filling up; groups of stunned prosecutors were hovering around the television. He met again with Gorelick, and they hurried to see Reno. Their first priority was to seize control of the situation. They alerted the Federal Emergency Management Administration, which responds to large catastrophes, whether acts of God or man.

The White House quickly announced that the FBI would be the lead investigative agency, despite feelings among some in federal law enforcement that the ATF, with its expertise in handling explosives, should take charge. But the White House wanted to avoid the infighting and turf battles that had followed Waco. And besides, since Waco, the FBI had been holding training sessions at its Quantico, Virginia, academy on how best to respond to such a major event.

The FBI got the call, but the ATF would still be involved in the case, and there would still be some internal bickering. But from the outset, it was Reno, the person who gave the go-ahead on the final deadly assault on Waco, the incident that had so transformed McVeigh, who was responsible now for finding him. And yet someone like McVeigh—an American, a veteran no less—was far from the minds of those seeking the bomber.

Urgent Report No. 3 landed in Washington:

"A Channel 4 [local Oklahoma City television station] reporter reported the Nation of Islam has claimed responsibility for the bombing of the Alfred Murrah Federal Building in Oklahoma City.

Dahlia Lehman, the victim witness coordinator in the Western District of Oklahoma, has a daughter employed at the DEA office in the Alfred Murrah Federal Building."

Garland left Justice and scooted across Pennsylvania Avenue to FBI headquarters. He stepped inside the bureau's Statistical Information Operations Center and was amazed at the number of tips already pouring in. Here he stayed much of the day, helping to coordinate and assimilate leads and possible theories as they tumbled into the large room with its phone banks and computer screens. A large lead board was posting new details, and FBI Director Louis Freeh and members of his top staff were in an adjacent command room. Every hour, senior supervisory agents collated the most recent information and passed it on to Garland, Freeh, and the others.

Their best hunch continued to be international terrorism. Waco was mentioned as a possibility—maybe the bombing was intended to teach the federal government a lesson for its past mistakes—but that theory was relegated to a secondary position. This seemed too professional, too well done. No amateur here, they decided. This had to be the work of outside, foreign interests; no way was this one of ours.

Their best initial lead was a man seen running from the scene in a black jogging outfit. The U.S. intelligence apparatus abroad was tapped, and the CIA and other relevant networks were checking contacts in the Middle East and Europe, trying to gauge what person or group might claim responsibility.

Then their second lead fell right into their laps. And it looked perfect.

Abraham Abdullah Hassan Ahmad was a Palestinian-American, living in Oklahoma City, and he had a background in computer science. He had left that morning to fly to Jordan. In his five suitcases were multiple car radios, large amounts of electrical wires, solder, a VCR, and a small tool kit. Better yet, he also had packed a blue jogging suit and an extra pair of black sweatpants. An affidavit naming him as a material witness in the bombing was made out by federal officials in Oklahoma City and approved by a U.S. magistrate there. In their rush, they spelled his name wrong.

For Ahmad, his journey was a nightmare; he never made it to Jordan. He was stopped and questioned by U.S. immigration officials in Chicago. He was later stopped, detained, and questioned again in London, Washington, and back in Oklahoma City. In London, he was strip-searched and paraded in handcuffs through the crowded airport. He was photographed and fingerprinted, and his name was leaked to the news media. Within the hour, television crews and reporters descended upon his family at their modest home in Oklahoma City, and there they were joined by a large crowd of angry residents who spat at the house and threw trash on the lawn.

Ahmad's trip was completely innocent; he was traveling to Jordan to visit relatives because of a family emergency. A naturalized American citizen, he was thirty-two years old and had lived in Oklahoma City since 1982. Ahmad later attended memorial services for the bombing victims and called for community healing. He also filed a $1.9 million lawsuit against the federal government.

But who could really fault the government? Faced with a crime beyond any they had tackled before, the federal investigators had to run down every lead. They could not overlook any trail, and if that meant detaining someone—or everyone—better to err on the side of caution.

So there went the prime suspect, and still the best guess in Washington was that the bombing was the work of outsiders. Even after a tip about two men who were upset over drug charges filed against them in Oklahoma City, even after an erroneous confirmation from the U.S. attorney's office in Oklahoma City that a pickup truck had carried the explosives to the Murrah building, federal law enforcement was still looking abroad for a terrorist.

Here at home, it seemed as though the whole nation were under attack. Urgent updates continued to pour into Washington computers from every region of the country.

Oklahoma: "John Raley, U.S. Attorney for the Eastern District of Oklahoma, received notice from the chief U.S. marshal to evacuate the building due to information that was apparently related to a retired Muskogee police officer several days ago that there would be bombs in the Muskogee and Oklahoma City courthouses. The office has been evacuated."

Delaware: "John Polk, the first assistant U.S. Attorney, reports that the federal building received a bomb threat. The federal building has been evacuated."

Nebraska: "U.S. Attorney Thomas Monaghan notifies that the Federal Courthouse in Omaha received a threat this morning, advising that a bomb would go off in the courthouse at 2:00. The building was evacuated by the U.S. marshals."

Alabama: "China Davidson, administrative officer from the Northern District of Alabama, reports that a bomb threat to the federal building was received at approximately 3:00. The federal building has been evacuated and the U.S. marshals were bringing in dogs to do a search of the building. The bomb is supposed to go off between 3:15 and 3:30."

Similar reports involving courthouses and federal buildings came in from Michigan, Florida, and Idaho.

To Garland and other officials working the FBI command center, the questions were popping up as fast as leads on their massive charts. Could this be war? Was it the handiwork of religious fanatics? Of Middle Eastern terrorists? But why in the world Oklahoma? The failed attempt at bringing down New York's World Trade Center two years earlier, yes. The plan to blow out the Holland and Lincoln tunnels and the conspiracy to take down the United Nations building . . . it was understandable that terrorists might want to hit a recognizable national landmark. But the middle of the country?

President Clinton addressed the nation in a live television news conference from the White House press room. His tone was both somber and angry. He spoke deliberately: "I will not allow the people of this country to be intimidated. Let there be no room for doubt: we will find the people who did this. When we do, justice will be swift, certain and severe. . . . These people are killers and must be treated like killers."

Later that day his chief law enforcement officer, Janet Reno, speaking to reporters in another White House briefing, was equally stern. She vowed that the ultimate punishment lay at the government's disposal.

"The death penalty is available," she said, "and we will seek it."

Then the unbelievable happened. A truck axle that had fallen out of the sky at 9:02 in the morning was traced to a white American male.

Richard Nichols (no relation to the Terry Nichols family) saw it first. Thirty-eight years old, married, and helping to raise a nephew, he worked as a building maintenance man at the Regency Tower Apartments, just catty-corner from the Murrah building. The 273-unit apartment structure had been home to some of those killed in the blast across the street, including youngsters Aaron and Elijah Coverdale.

Indeed, the security camera in the Regency Tower lobby had just moments before the blast captured a Ryder truck heading east on 5th Street.

Nichols was walking out onto 5th Street because his wife, Bertha, had pulled up in their 1990 red Ford Festiva with their young nephew Chad in the backseat. They were going to take him to the doctor, and Nichols could see his wife getting out of the car.

"I took approximately two steps when there was a horrific explosion," he said. "We felt heat and pressure, and it kind of spun us around a little."

He grabbed Bertha. "What's going on?" he screamed.

First he thought the boilers in the Regency Tower had blown. Then he thought the *Journal Record* building had exploded. Then he remembered Chad. "I made a lunge for the car, 'cause my little nephew was still in there."

Glass and debris were filling the air. They both ran for the car, husband and wife, and they hurriedly opened doors. Bertha found him first and bent down to unbuckle his seat belt.

"All this stuff was coming down," he recalled. "We were getting showered with glass. It was just everywhere. I knew the doors behind us exploded. And so she was trying to get him out of the car, 'cause like I said, we was thinking that our building was coming down.

"And I heard something from the left of me, which would have been in the direction of the Murrah Federal Building. And it was up high, and I turned and I looked. And I seen this humongous object coming toward us out of the air. And it was spinning like a boomerang. And you could hear this woo-woo-woo-woo noise. And I looked and I seen it."

As he remembered it, "This object was coming straight at us." He yelled to his wife, "Get down!"

He pushed his wife to the floorboard, and the object hit the front of the car and smashed off the windshield. The tremendous blow drove the rear of the Festiva into the air, and then Nichols could no longer even touch the vehicle as it spun back about ten feet.

The object was a Ryder truck axle; it came to rest in the center of 5th Street, and it was the government's first big break.

FBI Special Agent James Elliott was the one who matched the axle to the Junction City Ryder shop. He was at work at the bureau's office in McAlester, Oklahoma, when the bomb went off. Fifty-five years old, an agent since he was twenty-three, and a new member of the bureau's Evidence Response Team, he was the kind of veteran who is always looking for new challenges; just six weeks ago he had received special evidence training. In the past he had worked civil rights cases, bank robberies, kidnappings, white-collar crimes, bank embezzlements, and public corruption. He was about to get the assignment of his career.

Learning of the blast in Oklahoma City, he drove home and packed his clothes and other gear as part of the Evidence Response Team. He brought boots, a battle-dress uniform, a camera, and a crime scene kit. In the kit were packaging materials, fingerprinting equipment, and special tools to dislodge pieces of evidence—all emergency tools he kept at the ready.

Elliott reached Oklahoma City about twelve-thirty that afternoon and passed through a number of security checkpoints before arriving at the temporary command post in a mobile home, at 8th and Harvey streets.

He was told to stand by. So he stepped briefly outside and met Special Agent James L. Norman, Jr. Norman had just located a vehicle identification number on what appeared to be a large piece of a truck blown apart by the bomb. Could the bomb have been inside a truck? Could it have been much like the one at the World Trade Center?

Elliott telephoned the National Insurance Crime Bureau in Dallas, read off the VIN, and asked for a match. The NICB maintains a nationwide registry of vehicle numbers and their owners, gleaned from stamps on millions of cars and trucks and their component parts. Too impatient for a call back, he walked to the corner of 5th and Harvey streets and stopped in front of the Regency Tower. There it still lay, in all its mangled glory, a jet-black, 250-pound truck rear axle blown 575 feet from the front of the Murrah building.

He bent down and studied the truck part. He read the VIN number for himself: PVA26077. His pager beeped; call Dallas. The veteran agent returned to the command post, dialed the crime bureau, and over the telephone discovered that the true VIN was actually much longer—1FDNF72J4PVA26077. But that was a trivial detail.

Much more significant was the fact that the vehicle was registered to Ryder Rental Inc., in Miami, Florida, and it currently was being rented under number 137328. In other words, the driver—whoever he might be—seemed eminently traceable.

Clark Anderson was working at Ryder headquarters in Miami

when the call came in. He is a senior administrative official, having slugged his way up from the rental counter to managing the company's consumer truck line. In 1995, the line operated a fleet of some 33,000 consumer rental vehicles. On the phone was the Federal Bureau of Investigation, which had questions about just one truck.

A quick check showed it was a 1993 Ford with a twenty-foot body, rented from an agency in Junction City, Kansas. VIN 1FDNF72J4PVA26077 carried a Florida license plate, a decal number of 10806440, and a unit number of 137328. It had been leased two days ago for a one-way haul to Omaha, Nebraska.

The man you want, Anderson told the FBI, is named Robert Kling.

And to be sure the FBI investigators knew what they were dealing with here, Anderson apprised them of the load capacity of this particular Ryder truck. It stood twelve feet tall, was eight feet wide, weighed 11,500 pounds empty, and could handle a load of many tons. It was a gas-powered vehicle, with a fifty-gallon gas tank, and it averaged no more than seven miles per gallon.

In Oklahoma City, agents came across yet another prize. Two county sheriff's deputies had been scouring through the bomb debris along the corner near the Athenia, an old Greek restaurant across 5th Street from the Murrah. They uncovered another piece of metal, part of a truck rear bumper. Still attached to the bumper—strangely enough—was Florida license plate NEE26R, and it too was traced back to the Ryder agency.

The next step for the FBI was elementary: get somebody out to Junction City.

Shortly after three-thirty in the afternoon, Eldon Elliott answered the phone at his Elliott's Body Shop, the Ryder agency in Junction City. Company officials in Florida asked him to pull the Kling paperwork and to keep everything in a safe spot. The Ryder people were coming out; in forty-five minutes the FBI was at his door.

Agent Scott Crabtree was the first FBI agent that Eldon Elliott had ever met. In the days ahead, he would meet dozens. Crabtree was the resident agent in nearby Salina, Kansas, and he had been alerted by the FBI's Miami field office to visit the Junction City shop and "pick up the documents and get them forwarded to headquarters."

He drove east on Interstate 70 to Junction City, and he too immediately noticed the large yellow trucks parked just off the freeway.

He stepped inside and began interviewing Eldon Elliott and Vicki Beemer, and Tom Kessinger too, and they told him about the man named Robert Kling who last had been there on Monday.

Eldon Elliott was stunned. His agency? The guilt was almost immediate, followed by confusion. For years he had built his business around providing good service to the soldiers out at Fort Riley. Sometimes he saw himself as sort of a father figure to them, helping them move into and out of this part of east-central Kansas. He always offered them special discounts, and had even given Kling a couple of extra days free.

"I just couldn't quite get in my mind placing him exactly," he said. "It was just real hazy. So much stuff had happened and so much excitement there that I just couldn't think right then."

There was indeed considerable confusion over Kling's description. Elliott and Beemer and Kessinger could not agree on aspects of his height and weight, the look of his face, his chin, his eyes. They also had different recollections about a second man with Kling— but they were sure nonetheless that there was a second man.

On another point they all agreed. Kling most definitely came from a military background.

For the FBI, and Garland and others in Justice back in Washington, the investigation now was turning quickly toward domestic terrorism. More agents were summoned to Junction City and the Fort Riley area. Some of them would be there for months. The investigation in Kansas moved on two fronts. The goals were to obtain solid composite FBI sketches of the Kling character and his friend, and then to fan out in the local community and on the army base and see if motel owners, restaurant managers, gas station attendants, soldiers, anyone, anywhere, could identify these two faces.

Weldon Kennedy, an FBI supervisor, was attending a regional drug enforcement conference in El Paso when his beeper went off. He is a big man, with large hands and a round, deeply lined face. A Texan by birth, he chose the FBI for a career after a stint in the early 1960s as a navy intelligence officer. He served as an FBI field agent and, later, in supervisory positions from Atlanta and Boston to his current position in Phoenix. In fact, he had been planning to retire soon. But his work on the Oklahoma City bombing would intervene; he would be given overall command of the on-site investigation, and his work there would catapult him to the number two spot as the FBI's deputy director in Washington.

When Weldon Kennedy answered his page, he had no idea of the impact it would have on his life. He is a man who reasons simply: catch the criminal. So, knowing he would be gone awhile and wanting to pack fresh clothes, he rushed home to Phoenix. He then flew to Dallas, but the storm front that was dropping rain buckets on Oklahoma City was also causing travel delays in Dallas, so Kennedy did not arrive in Oklahoma City until the wee hours of Thursday, April 20.

He would replace Bob Ricks, the FBI's special agent in charge in Oklahoma City, who had worked the Waco siege two years earlier. Director Freeh wanted Kennedy to run things in Oklahoma because of a bureau restructuring after Waco that called for beefing up group responses to major crime scenes. Kennedy had recently been training others in the new system of crisis management. He also had experience managing the FBI's response to prison riots in Atlanta. And there was another advantage in Kennedy—he was not from Oklahoma City, had not worked there, and therefore he did not know the dead or injured.

But he would be touched deeply, in another way, as a member of what tens of thousands across the nation call the federal government family. These were his colleagues, his fellow workers, and he could not help but share their deep sense of loss. " 'Angry' is not the right word for how I felt," he would say later. "It was more like an awesome feeling, like, my God, how could anybody do this?"

Right off the plane in Oklahoma City, one of his first briefings concerned Ahmad, the local resident who had tried to go to Jordan. It still seemed like a promising lead. When dawn broke he made his first visit to the site, and was humbled by the vastness of open wreckage, with the cranes and rescue workers still busy searching for signs of life, and the constant sound of glass crunching underfoot.

"I was awestruck," he said. "You can't imagine the scope of the damage until you stand in front of the building and see the rubble and realize a third of the building is gone."

He ruined a pair of dress shoes. "You couldn't put your foot down without shards of glass cutting up your shoes."

He was brought up to date on the trail that had led to Junction City, and told how probably one hundred agents now were swarm-

ing through that Kansas town, flashing copies of composite drawings of John Doe No. 1, identified also as Robert Kling, and his partner, known only as John Doe No. 2. Kennedy released copies of the
sketches to the press camped in Oklahoma City, holding the drawings up high for the cameras, asking the nation to help find these
two men.

The faces in the sketches were jarring; there were no bandannas,
no hidden eyes, no strange-sounding names. These were Americans; this, the public realized, was made-in-America terrorism.
Suddenly the FBI hotline switchboard lit up; now everyone, it
seemed, had something to say about this pair.

Jon Hersley, a twenty-year FBI agent in the Oklahoma City
office, recalled the rush to find the suspects, believing it imperative
to work fast to "prohibit another bomb from going off." For the
next several days, he and other agents were evaluating eyewitness
reports.

A motorist said he had seen a man dashing across the street near
where the Ryder truck had parked in front of the Murrah building.
"He had to slow down to keep from hitting him," Hersley said. A
woman said she saw an individual "strongly resembling" the Kling
sketch at the federal building a week before the bombing, and "possibly again" earlier this week.

A meter maid told how she nearly crashed into the bomb truck.
"The Ryder was approaching her," Hersley said. "It was going at a
very low rate of speed. She thought the person in the Ryder truck
was going to stop and ask her some questions." A man recalled seeing "two individuals" in the Ryder a full twenty minutes before the
blast, and thought one of them closely resembled the Kling character. Another witness saw a car "speeding away" from the scene,
"obviously in an effort to avoid the bomb blast." And the witness
was sure there were two people in that car.

The stories were not confined to downtown Oklahoma City. As
it became known that the truck had been rented in Junction City,
the stories grew fantastically. The manager of a Texaco mini-mart
in Junction City said the man in the drawing resembling McVeigh
and another fellow had been regular customers for four months.
They visited twice a week, she said, and always bought Cokes by
the bottle and Kools Filter Kings and Marlboros by the carton. At
the Silverado Bar and Grill in Herington, a bartender said McVeigh

and another man (Terry Nichols, he later would insist) had stopped in the last four weekends, shooting pool and drinking Budweiser and Coors Light.

People said the suspects were polite and nondescript, although certainly a bit odd, and that this McVeigh character sometimes looked "funny" at them. They also happened to recall that the men smelled bad, as though they had just come from a pig farm—perhaps this memory was an effect of the news that the bomb had been made with fertilizer.

Although the vast majority of the tips were implausible, agents tried hard not to dismiss any. When Kennedy remarked how the investigation was developing rapidly now that things had narrowed to the Junction City area, a fellow investigator stated the obvious. "Well," he said, "God doesn't like baby killers."

Some sort of higher power was definitely on their side. Because on Thursday night, they met Lea McGown, manager of the Dreamland Motel. She instantly recognized the sketch as her former guest. It was not Kling at all, she said; he had registered under his real name, Timothy McVeigh. Agents converged on the little strip motel off Interstate 70, sealing off Room 25 and reviewing her records. He also had given the Nichols farm address in Decker. Suddenly a new focus emerged in Michigan, and the Detroit field office for the FBI was asked for a background on the Nichols family. Soon an FBI SWAT team was forming to raid the Decker farm.

Who was this Timothy McVeigh? Another phony name, perhaps? Or the real thing? More important, where was he?

Then came yet another break. Carl Lebron, McVeigh's old friend and coworker at the Buffalo security guard company, was watching the late news on ABC television Thursday night and recognized his buddy's face in the first composite drawing. In the morning, he visited the FBI field office in Buffalo and told Special Agent Eric Kruss that he knew McVeigh. Kruss thanked Lebron and sent him home.

But as Lebron walked in his door, the phone was ringing; it was the FBI again, and Kruss was coming out right now to bring him back to the field office.

Lebron told them the story of McVeigh's fanatical views about the government. He described him as an army veteran who was "particularly agitated" about the conduct of the federal government at Waco. Why, Lebron said, McVeigh had even visited Waco during the siege and he afterward expressed "extreme anger." Lebron told the FBI that McVeigh had raged that "the government should never have done what it did."

He gave the FBI one more piece of extremely critical information: McVeigh's last known mailing address was a mail drop in Kingman, Arizona. Now the investigation widened further, spreading from Oklahoma to Kansas, then into Michigan, and now to the desert Southwest in Arizona.

The sense of urgency crackled across the country. As Lebron was driven home after the interview, he asked the agent what precautions he should take if McVeigh suddenly showed up back in town.

The agent smiled. "Don't worry," she said. "We've already got him."

Indeed they had.

He was still in the Perry jail, and that is where they found him after a national crime computer check alerted federal agents about McVeigh's arrest on the gun and traffic charges in northern Oklahoma. A federal agent had called the sheriff just shortly before McVeigh would have been released on bail.

So the FBI came to Perry and escorted McVeigh out of the jail in that bright orange jumpsuit, and the crowds yelled and cussed at him, but he looked away as though he were no longer of their world at all. The agents placed him, shackled hand and foot, into a sheriff's van and drove him to a helicopter. He was flown to the Will Rogers Airport in Oklahoma City, then put into another Suburban and taken out to Tinker Air Force Base. It was perhaps the most secure spot in the entire state, with military SWAT teams and Special Forces personnel—yes, Green Beret types, waiting with camouflage outfits and automatic weapons drawn. The regular air force workers, along with their families, were gathering around an office building when the van pulled up, and they too stared at the suspect, shouting their own epithets as he was taken from the vehicle and marched past the barbed concertina-like wire and the sounds of the SWAT crews racheting their weapons. Then McVeigh disappeared inside the building.

Weldon Kennedy had his man.

Earlier that day, Merrick Garland and a fellow prosecutor who had worked the World Trade Center case drove to an FBI airfield in

Manassas, Virginia. They were being sent to Oklahoma City to assist in the manhunt. As they were boarding the prop plane, an agent ran out on the tarmac with a cell phone.

Garland took the call from headquarters. "We've got the guy identified as McVeigh," he was told.

The plane took off. But it had to stop for refueling in Indianapolis. While on the ground, Garland took a second call. This time his instructions were to handle the court hearing at Tinker. They flew off again, and finally landed in Oklahoma City, where they were met by more bureau agents. Then they were driven to the FBI command post, past the National Guard roadblocks, and then to Tinker, where they could see the military Humvees and the police dogs. The sun was fading, and Garland noticed the glint of drawn bayonets.

Everything seemed cold, and somehow sterile. Something important was missing. Garland realized what that was—there was no press, and no public, inside the building. He thought to himself, This is not like America. Hearings are held in public, in open view. He asked the agents to draw a dozen names out of a hat, or do something like it, and get some reporters in there.

Nolan Clay was one of the lucky ones. He had been waiting for what seemed like hours outside the building. He heard the jeers as McVeigh was brought through, heard the guns being cocked. A veteran reporter for the *Daily Oklahoman*, the state's largest newspaper, Clay had long covered cops and the courts, but nothing had prepared him for this evening.

On the morning of the bombing, he had seen the trail of smoke from his car as he drove to work. He was one of the paper's big-play guys, and so he spent Wednesday and Thursday chasing down leads, beating his source bushes, looking for leads to tell his readers, all of them gravely affected by the tragedy of the Murrah explosion. On Friday morning, he had been chasing sightings of the character in the Robert Kling sketch, and he had even driven out to a trucking business just off the downtown corridor where employees swore they recognized that long nose and prominent chin. The ceiling tiles from their shop had been blown down by the force of the blast, and they were telling Clay who they thought was responsible.

But then the news broke about Timothy McVeigh and the Perry jail, and Clay was back at the office, telephoning truck stops up and down Interstate 35, hunting for anyone who had seen a yellow

Ryder truck or an equally yellow Mercury Marquis sedan. At rush hour he was dispatched to Tinker, one in a gaggle of twenty or so reporters and camera crews to get inside to await the arrival of the biggest news story they would ever cover.

They were ushered inside, searched and patted down, and then taken upstairs to a second-floor room. Clay was not sure where he was; it appeared to be a courtroom setting, though, and there were benches in the rear. He and the other reporters were seated in the back row.

Through a side door, at last, came the defendant, still in the orange suit, with socks and no shoes. McVeigh sat at a table and studied the document in front of him. It was the criminal complaint, an affidavit, signed by an agent of the Federal Bureau of Investigation, and it laid out in fourteen pararaphs over just six pages of type what the United States of America so far had gathered to justify holding Timothy James McVeigh for the worst act of terorrism in the history of this nation. There it was in black and white, and McVeigh picked up the paper and glanced at its pages— the massive explosion detonated by a Ryder truck bomb, the phony Robert Kling rental agreement, the recollections of Lea McGown and Carl Lebron. And there too, on page 5, paragraph 12, the word "Waco."

Garland studied McVeigh's face. He was amazed at the young man's stoic demeanor.

Federal Magistrate Ronald L. Howland, tall, thin, kindly-looking, an Oklahoma judge whose office was just across the street from the Murrah building, entered, and everyone rose. The hearing lasted just minutes. The magistrate advised McVeigh of his rights, a prosecutor summarized the charge, and two local defense attorneys stood to either side of their new client.

McVeigh stood too, ramrod-straight, in front of the judge to give a perfunctory "yes" or "yes, sir" to a few routine questions, mostly about whether Timothy James McVeigh was indeed his "true and correct name." Asked how old he was, he said twenty-six.

Nolan Clay was not watching the lawyers or the judge; his neck was straining to see McVeigh, and the first thought that struck him was the Waco connection. Now it all clicked; now it all made sense.

"He seemed like such a kid," Clay recalled. "I've covered courts for years and I've seen hundreds of killers and usually they have an aura around them of being a killer. That look in their eyes. You can tell in their eyes they're killers, and they are scary. But he looked like the kid next door. It's true, that image about him. I was very surprised by that."

Clay noticed one thing more. Before McVeigh was led out of the room, he tossed the affidavit onto the tabletop; he threw it with what first seemed like disdain but was more likely dejection. It had been three days now, and the revolution had not happened.

Chapter Thirteen

Betrayal

For the past few days Terry Nichols had been making sure that he could be seen. He had not heard from his friend McVeigh since Tuesday and here it was Friday and God knew any number of things could have gone wrong. McVeigh had not called or shown up in town, had not even sent so much as a postcard. Where was he?

Arrested? That was possible. Since the bombing the press had been focusing on the FBI manhunt for two men, and one of the composite sketches was a ringer for McVeigh. But if McVeigh had been captured, surely the feds would have paraded him out like a circus prize for the whole world to see. So no, it was not likely that McVeigh had been caught.

Or maybe he was arrested and was cooperating with authorities and telling them about him too. But that was not likely either. If McVeigh was anything, he was a patriot, a true believer. He would not talk. And if he did open his mouth, he would never give up a brother.

So then he must be dead, Nichols reasoned. Blown up with that truck full of ammonium nitrate and fuel oil. Maybe it was suicide. Or he had not gotten away fast enough, just hadn't had time to clear the front of the building and make it safely to that ugly yellow Mercury parked in the alley.

Terry Nichols was better off with Timothy McVeigh dead.

Nichols had spent a lifetime shifting from job to job, moving

around the country, working on the family farm in Michigan, selling real estate in Colorado, sleeping in the desert in Arizona. Now
he was living in small Herington, Kansas, in a little house off Broadway, the center strip. He was tucked away in the middle of nowhere.

He realized that he might be called upon to explain his recent
activities, such as why on Sunday he had driven McVeigh back from
Oklahoma City, where the yellow getaway car had been stashed.

On Wednesday, the day of the bombing, he followed the news
from Oklahoma City on radio and in the papers. Thursday he went
to the local television cable company to sign up for service, and
there the clerk was showing him how the controller worked. She
was flipping through the channels when suddenly Nichols stopped
her with a shout. It was a news bulletin on Oklahoma City.

"What's that?" he asked, feigning ignorance.

At home, he made certain that he was noticed. He spread so
much ammonium nitrate on his front lawn that neighbors watched
it accumulate like snow, and then they saw weeds sprout up and die
from too much fertilizer. He also dallied around the front porch. He
cleared out one of the storage lockers, taking McVeigh's rifle and
sleeping bag and placing them in his garage. He was so busy around
the house and in town that neighbors would later remark how surprised they were to see so much of Mr. Nichols.

But Nichols was being overtaken by events beyond his control.

McVeigh had registered at the Dreamland Motel under the
Decker farm address, and the FBI called the local sheriff in Michigan, asking for information about the Nichols family. They interviewed James Nichols's ex-wife, and she told them that Terry had
been married to her sister, Lana.

The FBI contacted Lana in Las Vegas, and teams of agents began
interviewing her and her son, Josh, on Friday morning. Yes, she told
them, Terry Nichols was her former husband, and in fact she had
just gotten off the phone with him. Then she gave the FBI his
address: 109 South 2nd Street, Herington, Kansas.

Terry Nichols left for an errand to the lumberyard around two in
the afternoon. The radio in his pickup was broadcasting the flurry
of activity, both in Perry, Oklahoma, where McVeigh had been
found, and in Decker, where the FBI was moving in on the farm.
Then he heard that he and his brother, James, were suspects.

He returned home and told Marife, and they turned on the television. They saw that McVeigh was indeed being arrested, and they heard Attorney General Janet Reno declare at a Washington press conference that the death penalty would be sought.

Nichols noticed a large fuel meter in his garage and said, "I need to do something about that." He handed his wife $200 in cash and then loaded his family into the pickup. They drove off—but they were not alone. An FBI car was already on their tail.

Indeed, several FBI agents had been sent down from the bureau's mobile command post at Fort Riley to learn what they could about James Nichols's brother. It was James, the older one, whom they really wanted at that time. McVeigh not only had left the Decker address, but had given the Perry jail the name of James Nichols as the person to call in case of an emergency. To the bureau, the hot pursuit was in Michigan; this check in Herington on Friday afternoon was just for gathering background on James Nichols.

FBI Agent Stephen Smith, just five years with the bureau, was working out of the Fort Riley command post that morning when the Las Vegas field office notified the post that Lana had provided Terry Nichols's address. She had described Terry simply as an "associate of Tim McVeigh." Smith was told to go to Herington and learn what he could from Terry Nichols about his brother James and Timothy McVeigh.

Smith drove alone the twenty miles or so south to Herington. He reached town around two o'clock, the first agent to arrive. His initial plan was to visit the police station and see what the police knew about Terry Nichols.

Chief Dale Kuhn said he had never heard of Nichols, but he did verify the home address.

Smith next met two other agents who had just arrived in town, and they drove in separate cars to Nichols's house on Second Street. It was then they saw him leaving, and they slid in behind the pickup.

Nichols was driving his family out Broadway, heading away from town. But he could still see one FBI car in his rearview mirror, and another turning around and falling in behind. He waved at them, trying to stay calm. Then he turned into the driveway at the local Surplus City store, which he had visited often to set up his business selling military supplies. He stepped out of the pickup, paused, then hastily climbed back in.

Marife, holding their not-quite-two-year-old daughter, Nicole, tight to her chest, also saw the black cars with the strange men inside. She turned to her husband but did not get a response.

He drove on, this time straight to the Herington police station. He parked the pickup and told his wife that if the agents asked, she must tell them that last Sunday, when he had suddenly disappeared during their Easter dinner, he had told her he was going to Oklahoma City. To Oklahoma City, he stressed; not Omaha, as he had told her at the time.

Then he took Nicole in his arms and carried the child into the station. The agents, by now also pulling into the parking lot, assumed he was using the girl to shield himself from their guns.

Marife bolted from her side of the pickup, and she hurried in fast behind her husband. "He was scared," she would recall. "He was pale and just anxious to know what's going on."

Inside the police building, Nichols felt secure in the hands of local authorities. Always trust the town sheriff over the federal agent, he believed.

He walked up to Chief Kuhn, demanding to know why media reports on television and the radio were connecting him to the Oklahoma City bombing.

"I just heard my name," he said.

Kuhn was stunned. So this was Terry Nichols?

And Nichols was pacing about the front of the chief's office, repeating the same question. "Why did I just hear my name?" he asked.

Nichols took a step back. "I'm supposed to be armed and dangerous," he said, mocking the news bulletins he had heard. "Search me," he demanded.

Marife took the baby, and her husband began to remove his green jacket. Kuhn tried to calm him down. Outside, Smith and the other agents huddled in the parking lot. Their first concern was that Nichols had taken hostages—his wife and his daughter, maybe the police inside the station too.

The agents called FBI supervisors in Kansas City, and the supervisors phoned the police station, receiving assurances from Chief Kuhn that everything was secure inside. Then, around three in the afternoon, Smith and the other agents walked inside to confront this man who was acting so very strangely.

Nichols turned to them with his same question.

"Why was my name on radio and television?" he demanded.

"I don't know," Smith said. "but we'd like to talk to you. We believe you are an associate of Timothy McVeigh."

They took him down to the basement, and there, through the afternoon and far into the night, in a series of stop-and-start interviews, was held the proverbial bare-light-bulb interrogation session. The agents never let up; Nichols strove mightily to save his soul.

Where McVeigh had stood silent all day, Nichols tried to barter with the devil. He talked.

The basement was dark and cool. It was primarily used as a locker room, with two stalls to store evidence, and near the stairs was a large water heater that kept clicking on and off. Smith and fellow agent Scott Crabtree did most of the questioning, occasionally taking breaks to run upstairs for coffee and a chance to write up their notes; the FBI, incredibly, does not use tape recorders. Their spiral notebook pages were turning fast, and it was difficult to keep up. Best to get it all down, and at the same time keep this guy talking. Because slowly they were coming to realize that Nichols had played a much larger role in this case than anyone first suspected.

He was not yet under arrest, and authorities would insist later that Nichols was indeed free to go. In fact, they gave him that impression. But had he risen to leave, had he made a move for the stairs and the front door, they would have slapped a federal hold on him, and they would have charged him immediately in the bombing. Even as the agents were talking to him at the police station, other agents and federal prosecutors were preparing an arrest warrant for him in Oklahoma City.

Terry Nichols was going nowhere. Even in Washington, a thousand miles away, FBI headquarters was closely monitoring the events unfolding in the basement of the Herington police station. Howard Shapiro, the FBI's lead counsel, was advising the agents by telephone on legal strategy. Their top priority? Keep his lips moving. And don't tell him yet about the arrest warrant.

They were speaking to Marife, too. She was frightened, suddenly feeling alone in this strange country. Why had she not stayed in the Philippines? Why had she come back with Terry? She did not know it then, but she was already pregnant with their next child, a son they would name Christian.

Once, when Nicole needed a diaper change, agents would not let
Marife go out to the pickup to get a fresh diaper. They insisted it
was not safe. They still worried that maybe the truck was wired
with explosives. Better to stay inside for her own safety, they said.
What they also wanted was to keep the pickup untouched until FBI
lab technicians could arrive to sweep it for evidence. So an agent
went for diapers at a local grocery. No one was going to touch that
pickup just yet.

Marife waited upstairs. Downstairs, they talked.

The first session began at three-fifteen. Asked for his Social Security number, Nichols said he believed it was 371-68-4869, but said
that he did not use it any longer, did not believe in having a federal
government number. He preferred his Kansas driver's license number. At least that, he said, was "randomly generated." He also said
he did not pay federal taxes.

They asked him where he worked, and he said he was self-
employed, that he bought and sold surplus military items. He dealt
in ammo cans and hand shovels, and he sold his merchandise at gun
shows.

Enough of the preliminaries. When did you hear of your possible
involvement in the bombing? the agents asked.

Just today, he said. He was driving to the lumberyard when a
radio station in Manhattan, Kansas, broadcast his name. Actually,
he heard the words "Terry and James Nichols" from Michigan, and
that two people were in the process of being arrested, one of whom
he understood to be McVeigh.

How do you know McVeigh?

Army training, he said. They met during basic in 1988 in Georgia and later served together at Fort Riley.

Go on, they said.

Nichols told how he had come home after hearing the broadcast
and asked Marife if she had seen anything on television. "This is
serious," he told her. They switched on the television news and he
saw one of the composite drawings, but it did not look like
McVeigh.

He said he thought it best to go to the local police before the feds
arrived. He looked directly at the agents. "I didn't want another
Waco," he said.

He had left home with his family, planning to trade some tools for shingles at the Surplus City. When he got out of his pickup there, he said, he noticed the agents' cars. "I had a feeling I was being followed."

So he came here to the police station, never trying first to leave town. "You won't find any clothes in my truck," he told the agents.

Tell us about your brother, they said.

He described the large, two-story farmhouse in Decker, and said that he and Marife had lived there for a while. He told them about the little boy Jason, who had suffocated to death, and added that McVeigh had been living with them then.

It was three-thirty. The agents handed him a form titled "Interrogation: Advice of Rights." He was asked to read it aloud.

"I understand my rights," Nichols said.

He agreed to continue talking, but refused to sign the form. He pointed to the word "Interrogation" at the top. "That reminds me of the Nazis," he said. "I don't like that word."

He did sign a separate form, titled "Consent to Search," that allowed agents to go through his home and pickup.

He asked if he could be present during the searches. The agents said it was possible, but in fact they never allowed him to watch. And he said, repeatedly, that he hoped anyone doing the search could tell the difference between cleaning solvents and bomb components.

"There is nothing in my house or truck that could be construed as bomb-making materials," he told the agents.

Tell us some more about McVeigh, they said. When was your last contact with him?

Two months ago he had sent McVeigh a letter to a place where he was staying near Kingman. He asked him if, the next time he was in Las Vegas, he could pick up the extra television set at Lana's house. He wanted it here in Herington for when their son, Josh, visited.

Go on, they said.

Nichols told them that McVeigh had called his house about three in the afternoon on Easter Sunday, just as they were finishing dinner. He said he was in Oklahoma City, and was having car problems.

McVeigh told him he was on his way to see relatives in New York. "I'm pressed for time to get back East," Nichols said McVeigh told him. "If you want your television, you'll have to come to Oklahoma City and get me."

Nichols told the agents that McVeigh instructed him to lie to Marife and say he was going to Omaha instead of Oklahoma City. "Just keep this between the two of us," McVeigh had said.

Nichols tried to explain McVeigh's behavior.

"He has a private nature," Nichols said. "He has told me that no one is to know his business. Some of the things he wanted kept private were trivial matters. He just doesn't want people to know what he is doing. That is just his nature."

The agents took a breath. Everyone paused. Then Agent Smith spoke. Tell us your most recent contact with McVeigh before Easter, he said.

Last November, Nichols said. Or maybe this past January.

Then he looked directly at them. "In my eyes, I did not do anything wrong," he said. "But I can see how lawyers can turn stuff around."

Again it was quiet.

"I did not know anything," Nichols repeated.

He did not want to say anything further. "Lawyers can turn stuff around," he said.

Another pause. The agents were not responding; Nichols could sense that they did not believe him.

So he told them he had already heard McVeigh was in custody. But he said he had never seen McVeigh at any motel in Junction City, nor had he ever seen him with a rented Ryder truck. McVeigh had not asked him to buy anything related to the bomb, he said.

The agents took him back to the Easter Sunday phone call. Nichols said McVeigh provided specific roads and exit ramps for him to follow. He recalled that McVeigh told him to drive around several downtown city blocks. "Make sure you come down 8th Street," McVeigh had said.

He drove the five hours to Oklahoma City, exiting Interstate 35 at one of the downtown ramps. He cruised around looking for McVeigh.

"I went past that building a couple of times," he said, meaning the Murrah.

He guessed he drove around for half an hour. "I kept passing all these big buildings," he said. He finally spotted McVeigh at the end of a downtown alley. He was wearing a T-shirt, jeans, and tennis shoes—odd for his old friend, who always wore combat boots.

McVeigh put the television into the pickup, along with his green mil-itary-style laundry bag. A light rain was beginning to fall. McVeigh told him how to get out of Oklahoma City, and they headed north.

Nichols said he never did see McVeigh's car. "The way Tim talked it sounded like it was a large model," he said. "And Tim was leaving it in Oklahoma City."

It rained all the way to Kansas. They did not reach Junction City until nearly one-thirty in the morning.

So what did you two talk about? the agents asked.

"McVeigh talked in code," Nichols said.

Only when he thought about it later could he understand what his friend meant. They talked some about Waco and several articles that had recently appeared in the *Spotlight* newsletter.

"He seemed hyper, or nervous," Nichols told the agents.

Nichols said he told McVeigh about his plans for selling surplus military items. Then McVeigh jumped into the conversation.

"I'm doing fine," he suddenly told Nichols. "I should get some-thing going here shortly. You will see something big in the future."

"What?" Nichols asked.

"You will see something big in the future."

"What are you going to do, rob a bank?" Nichols asked.

"Oh, no. I got something in the works."

The talk turned back to Waco. McVeigh mentioned an upcoming protest rally in Washington to mark the Waco incident. Nichols said he thought the rally was going to be some kind of remem-brance gathering.

"Waco was a year or two ago," Nichols said.

"Yes," McVeigh said. "It was two years ago."

Okay, the agents said. Why was McVeigh going to Junction City?

Nichols said he did not know. Maybe to pick up another car. They reached Junction City and stopped at the McDonald's, but it was closed. McVeigh said Nichols could drop him off anyway; he would call someone. He was hungry. Nichols spotted a Denny's restaurant up the street that was open and pulled over that way. McVeigh grabbed his clothes bag and hopped out.

"I'll catch you on the way back," McVeigh said.

He always used that phrase, whenever he was leaving town, and Nichols did not hear from McVeigh again until around Tuesday morning, at six, when McVeigh called him at home.

"I'd like to use your pickup a little bit," he told Nichols. "I need to pick up a few things and look at a few vehicles."

Nichols said he drove up to Junction City. He visited a military surplus auction at Fort Riley while McVeigh used his truck. When they met, again all that McVeigh had with him was the green bag.

"Tim lives and travels light," Nichols told the agents.

The agents were not buying it. So Nichols told them McVeigh was always trading in old cars. He told them about the car that had been rear-ended in Michigan, and how McVeigh later bought another one from his brother, James, for $400 or $500. "Then he went west," Nichols said.

He said the last time he saw McVeigh, his old army friend told him he had other belongings in a local storage shed.

"If I don't pick them up, pick them up for me," McVeigh said.

Nichols did just that. Yesterday, he'd removed McVeigh's sleeping bag, rucksack, and rifle from the storage facility and put them in his garage. The agents would find the rifle there now, on a box next to the fuel meter in the garage, he said.

This morning, he said, he'd spoken on the phone with Lana, and that upset Marife. His new wife did not like him talking to Lana, and Marife suddenly announced that she wanted to return to the Philippines again.

"I've got friends there," she told him. "I don't have friends here. You got friends like Tim."

Nichols said Marife did not like McVeigh, that she complained that he lived his life on the edge, that he drove too fast. This morning, Nichols came home from his trip to the lumberyard, and he told her he had just heard his name on the radio. They turned on the television news and watched for about fifteen minutes.

"I then heard Tim's name on the TV for the first time," Nichols told the agents. "I thought and swore that I could not believe it was him because he was heading back to see his family! And he was back there in Oklahoma City?

"When I heard his name on TV, that is when I figured out why my name was on the radio, because I was his friend."

Nichols was talking real fast now, spitting out his words. "I was feeling shock, because I heard my name. How am I involved? How am I connected to it? I must not have known him that well for him to do that."

The agents leaned in. So what was your relationship with McVeigh?

They had split up recently because McVeigh did not like Nichols's penchant for practical jokes. McVeigh had even complained to Marife about that.

But the agents were not interested in that. Get to the heart of the matter, they said. Did McVeigh do it? they asked. Did you help?

Nichols again answered quickly, talking faster than he was thinking. The agents could see that his responses did not stack up.

"I feel upset that I am involved, in a sense, because of him, and knowing that I am not."

But then he said, "I feel I cannot trust anyone any more than Tim. I would be shocked if he implicated me. Tim takes responsibility for his actions, and he lives up to his arrangements."

And then, "I cannot see why he would do it."

The agents sensed it was time to slow things down. Take the focus off McVeigh; turn the spotlight on this man.

Nichols said yes, he had purchased two fifty-pound bags of ammonium nitrate about a month ago at a Manhattan, Kansas, elevator. They could check that; the receipts were at home. He had read up on ammonium nitrate and he planned to sell one-pound bags for $5 to $10 at gun shows. He wanted to beat the price of a vendor at a recent Tulsa show, who was selling bags for $35. He was going to sell it as fertilizer, because ammonium nitrate contains nitrogen and, when diluted with water, makes "plant food."

In fact, he said, he had already sold some at a few weekend gun shows. "If I sell any more at these shows, they will question me," he said. He had put what he had left over on his own lawn this morning.

Why didn't you mention this earlier? the agents asked.

Anyone with ammonium nitrate would be a potential suspect, he said, any farmer or homeowner. "It would make me look guilty to a jury," he said.

Okay, fine, the agents said. Tell us more about you.

He told them about his year in the army and his honorable discharge in 1989. At one time he'd thought he might get an assignment in Germany, but his sergeant told him he must remain behind at Fort Riley. He was given the ignoble job of driving visiting German officers around the fort. After two weeks he quit the army because his wife had left him, and he needed to care for Josh.

He described Michigan and the family farm, and how after he split up with Lana, he too moved to Las Vegas, so they both could raise their son. But he could not find a good job. Then he moved out here, to the middle of Kansas, and found work as a farmhand on a large family spread at Marion. There they lived last summer, he and his new wife, Marife, and the baby, Nicole. This past February or March, he couldn't remember which, they'd moved to Herington.

He'd come out here to start up the military supply business. In the past, McVeigh had wanted to work with him at the gun shows. But Nichols said he no longer wanted a life on the road; he preferred now to stay closer to home.

But sometimes the pair did work the gun show circuit, including events in Colorado, Nevada, and Arizona. They would pool their funds, deduct their expenses, and share the profits. They only dealt in cash; Nichols said he did not have a checking or savings account, and that he did not believe in credit cards.

He said he and McVeigh would sit at their sales booth at the gun shows, but did not know the other vendors. They kept to themselves. Nor did they associate with militia members, although Nichols said he'd recently sold thirty cases of Meals Ready to Eat to a group connected with the Michigan Militia.

At the shows he would often hear talk about Waco and claims that the FBI and the ATF had murdered the Branch Davidians. Something should be done about it, the people said. Nichols said he would listen; sometimes he would respond, "Possibly."

"The government is getting out of hand," some people would say.

What do you think? the agents asked.

"I feel that way also on occasion," he said. Some guys got "hyped" and wanted to take action.

Now the agents took it back to McVeigh.

Was there anything he said on the ride from Oklahoma City to Kansas that would make you think he might be behind this bombing?

"Yes," Nichols said. "He was much more hyped about Waco."

Both he and McVeigh had read the literature. There were articles by Colonel Bo Gritz, a former Green Beret commander who turned against the government after Vietnam, and Officer Jack McLamb, a former Phoenix police officer who travels the country warning that law enforcement and the military are being trained for martial law in America. Their writings, and those of others in the far-right community, would "open eyes," Nichols said, to what was beyond the mainstream media. He too believed in these alternative views. Anyone, he said, could go to a gun show and find books on how to make bombs, cannons, silencers, whatever. He had bought some himself.

The agents listened awhile, and then brought him back to McVeigh. Nichols said McVeigh had been more "hyper" or "nervous" recently. McVeigh had served in Desert Storm, and a lot of the change seemed to come after that. After the war, McVeigh tried out for Special Forces. But on a training walk or a run, something like that, he decided to drop out. A short time later, he left the army altogether.

"He was pissed off," Nichols said.

So McVeigh traveled a lot, seldom staying put at any one spot. For a while he lived out West, and Nichols joined him for a week last fall and they camped together out in the desert near Kingman.

"He's a loner," Nichols said.

Yes? the agents said.

Yes. It was possible McVeigh could make a device to blow up a building. "He could be capable of doing it," Nichols said. But the agents shouldn't assume that Nichols would necessarily know about it.

McVeigh knew guns well. "But he is no sharpshooter," Nichols said. He could break down weapons quickly, down to their "bare parts." He knew the makes and models of firearms, and he knew their round capability, the speed of bullets, their different calibers. Nichols said he looked at guns as a way of making money. "I have too many," he said. For McVeigh, "guns are a way to talk to people."

He named some of their common acquaintances, mentioning friends in Michigan and Kansas, and Arizona too. He recalled the name Fortier, but not his first name. He just described him as a white male; he did not mention that Michael Fortier had soldiered with him and McVeigh.

All right, the agents said. You've talked about guns. What about explosives?

Nichols had recently attended a gun show in Tulsa, where he'd met a man selling bomb-related items. They chatted quite a bit. He learned about the various chemicals that can go into making a bomb, such as ammonium nitrate, potassium, and "something else." But he said the man became rude when Nichols asked for more specifics.

He read the articles about explosives that came across the tables at gun shows. So had McVeigh. They would talk about bombs, and whether the instruction books sounded logical. Would it make sense to make this bomb over the next one?

Nichols looked directly at the agents. "McVeigh knows as much as I do about bombs," he said. McVeigh had a lot of free time.

How much do you guys know? the agents asked.

From talking to different people at gun shows, Nichols said, he knew you had to use certain types of fertilizer, and it must be nitrogen-based. A liquid fertilizer, he said, could not have done Oklahoma City. But a 28 percent nitrogen mixture could cause an explosion. Some people said urea could lead to an explosion, others said no. All Nichols knew, he said, was that urea is a granular solid, and people put that kind of fertilizer on their lawns.

Another kind is ammonium nitrate. "I imagine you have to put a blasting cap on it to explode," he said.

He recalled a farmer stopping by his table at a gun show and talking about blowing up tree stumps. You take ammonium nitrate and fuel oil, the farmer said, and you mix it. Drill a hole down below the tree stump and put the mixture down. Detonate it, and the stump is gone.

You got any firsthand knowledge? the agents asked.

"No," Nichols said. "I have not made any. I don't know if the mixture stays granular or becomes liquid."

But you can find the ratios in the books; it's all right there. And for a triggering mechanism, "I would assume electricity could start it." He said he guessed they had electrical blasting caps these days; you probably could purchase them just about anywhere, such as up at the grain elevator in Junction City.

Now it made sense to ask him about storage facilities. He had one in Las Vegas, and others in Kansas, here in Herington and in Council Grove. But he just used them for household effects, along with some guns and ammunition. The agents found that interesting, because already their colleagues were reporting back from the search of Nichols's home, where they had found numerous large drums in his garage. He said he bought those at a dump in Marion, and used them to haul trash. Well, then what about that fuel meter in the garage? He said that came from a sale at Fort Riley.

This first session, the longest, was winding down. All three men were tiring; Agent Smith wanted to get upstairs to unload his notes. But still the first objective was to keep Nichols talking. So they began tossing out names of other men who had served in the army with McVeigh and Nichols. He knew them. But he did not think they were involved in Oklahoma City.

"What about McVeigh?" Smith asked. "What was his role?"

Nichols fidgeted in his chair, but only briefly.

"I suspect it now," he said.

And so they took a break. It was ten minutes after six; everyone needed to cool off. The agents brought Nichols a glass of water and two slices of pizza. But he was not allowed to see or visit Marife.

Special Agent John F. Foley sat with him for a while. Nichols talked idly some more about fertilizer and an old fire truck he had owned in 1986, which he had used to make deliveries of liquid fertilizer. He brought up that fuel meter again too, said he had purchased it just two weeks ago. He seemed proud that he paid only $65 when the man wanted $147. Now he planned to resell the meter, and had offered it for sale for as high as $900 in a local newspaper ad. But then he realized the gears were bad, and he had taken it apart in his garage.

A little after seven in the evening, Agents Smith and Crabtree came back downstairs. The search was proceeding at Nichols's home. The agents wanted assurances there were no "booby traps" on the property. Nichols said there were only electronic intrusion alarms on the front and back doors. At one point he drew them a map of the interior of his house.

They talked some more about the events on Tuesday, and Nichols stuck to his story about McVeigh's borrowing his truck. And he did not budge from his claim that he had gone off to a Fort Riley auction. He added that McVeigh was late in returning with the pickup.

He had ordered business cards and mailing labels for his new sales venture. He was trying to distance himself from his old lifestyle with McVeigh. He recalled again the change in McVeigh's attitude after he could not complete the Special Forces training. McVeigh was very upset, increasingly so, with the federal government. He would mention Waco, and he did not like the way the government had handled Randy Weaver at Ruby Ridge.

It was growing late. By now the agents upstairs had obtained an arrest warrant naming Nichols as a material witness in the bombing; it had been faxed from the command post at Oklahoma City. Nichols was tired of talking, and the agents were growing restless, both upstairs and down. It was time to ratchet up the tension.

At eleven-fifteen they played for him a taped message from Lana and Josh, urging him to cooperate. He listened to the tape twice, but he was confused. "I caught everything except what my son said," he told the agents. What his son had said, several times as he cried, was "We love you, Dad. I love you."

About an hour later, at 12:03 a.m., they handed him copies of the letters he had left at Lana's house, including the "Go for it!" message for McVeigh. He read all four pages. "I wrote it because I did not have a will," he said.

At that time he was going to the Philippines, an unsafe area for foreigners, and these letters were instructions to those closest to him on what to do should he not return. "The Filipinos do not like Americans," he said. "I might even get run over by a car."

The conversation was winding down. They had their warrant, and more agents came down to place him under arrest. He was asked to take a lie detector test, to weigh the truth of what he had told them over the last nine hours. No, he said. "Not reliable." He also refused to sign a form saying he had been advised of his Miranda rights. Then he flat-out denied any personal involvement in the bombing.

But they arrested Terry Nichols anyway. They had not believed him, because their search of his house and garage turned up not only the barrels, but, later, a safe deposit key and other belongings that had been taken from Roger Moore's farm home in Arkansas. And they certainly did not believe his story about picking up McVeigh in Oklahoma City on Easter. A surveillance camera at the Regency Tower—the same one that captured the Ryder truck on Wednesday—also caught Nichols's blue truck circling the downtown area on Sunday. He was there, all right, but not to pick up McVeigh. The government decided they had both gone down there to leave McVeigh's yellow Mercury Marquis.

Nor did they care for Nichols's story about going to the Fort

Riley auction on Tuesday while McVeigh used his pickup. No, they were convinced that the two of them had spent that morning mixing the bomb and packing it into McVeigh's rented Ryder truck.

So they had Nichols now too. It was after midnight when they drove him west to the county jail in Abilene, Kansas. The next afternoon, they drove him south to Wichita for his initial court appearance. Agents Smith and Crabtree rode with him. Incredibly, he agreed to talk some more.

He said he often used aliases—Ken Parker and Jim Kyle. He said McVeigh too used phony names, like Shawn Rivers and Tim Tuttle. It was McVeigh who insisted they use secret names.

"But we parted ways last fall," Nichols said. "The way we both live did not jive."

McVeigh always liked to be "careful" when talking on the telephone. He liked to keep things "low-key."

But as for his brother, James, and McVeigh, "They got along well," he said.

Nichols remained in Wichita until he was sent to Oklahoma. There, a federal grand jury was gearing up for the summer-long process of deciding whether to indict McVeigh and Nichols in the Murrah building explosion. Before he left Kansas on May 10, he was watched closely in the county jail in Wichita.

And still he talked.

On the afternoon of April 26, just a few days after his arrest, he and a deputy struck up a conversation about farming. They talked about planting, livestock, soils . . . also fertilizers and chemicals. Nichols described the problems that pop up when siblings live together on a farm.

"My brother has a certain way of doing things and it's either his way or not at all," he said. "That's why I got out of farming."

Later the guard asked him if he would like a book to read. "I would really like to go home," Nichols joked.

That was his problem, he said, cutting up like that, making light of difficult situations. "I made a joking comment once to someone, and that was the start of all my problems."

He talked some about the FBI search of his home. "I gave them permission to search and they even confiscated three cases of MREs. I can't understand why they would want three cases of MREs."

The guard listened quietly and at one point peered at him through the bars. Nichols seemed near tears.

Four days later, another deputy was watching the cell and Nichols appeared distraught. He looked at the deputy and said he wished he had another book to read.

"I can't handle this book," he told the jailer. "It's a little too much."

"What do you mean?" the deputy asked.

"It's a book of short stories or novels and one of the stories is about an innocent man who is charged with murder, two counts, and it took him fourteen years to get out of prison."

"Is that right?" the guard asked.

Nichols looked up at the deputy; he again appeared on the verge of tears. "I guess you really don't know what your friends will do," he said.

Who? the deputy asked.

"I'm talking about some of my friends, my friends," he said. "We were good friends. For five years . . . but it looks like . . . maybe he did it. And I think I may have . . . I may have accidentally helped him in doing it."

The deputy said he would try to find something lighter for Nichols to read. And like the FBI agents, he also filed a report about what Nichols had said.

"His last few words appeared to have been very hard for him to say," the deputy wrote. "I believe he wiped a tear from his right eye."

Chapter Fourteen

The Why

The yellow Mercury Marquis arrived on a flatbed trailer late in the afternoon, hauled down Interstate 35 to the FBI warehouse near downtown Oklahoma City. Agent William Eppright watched them truck it in. Twenty years ago this might have been a fashionable sedan; today it was a wreck. He peered through the windows; the tan bucket seats in the front were worn raw.

The car had been built in 1977, just one year before Eppright joined the FBI. Assigned out of the Dallas field office, he worked primarily as part of the bureau's Evidence Response Team, which gathers forensics and other materials that can be used to assemble a federal case for prosecution. Like so many other agents, he had come up here the day of the bombing, and he would be around for quite some time. Now, as the Mercury was off-loaded in the warehouse and rolled to the back of the building, he walked up and took another long look.

The doors were still locked. He ordered everyone to stay back. "Nobody goes near that car," he said.

He allowed some agents to step forward long enough to photograph the exterior, the front and back, and the side panels, and to take a few shots through the windows. That is when he spotted the object on the front seat.

The agents vacuumed the door handles to collect particles that might still contain some traces of explosive material, and a few minutes later, using a Slim Jim to pop open the door locks, the FBI entered the vehicle. At that time, McVeigh had already been walked out of the Perry jail; Nichols was still sweating under a crossfire of questions in the basement of the Herington police station. The FBI had the "who" of their investigation. When they opened the envelope that McVeigh had nonchalantly left behind, they found the "why": a thick wad of antigovernment materials . . . Timothy McVeigh's manifesto.

Agent Eppright watched as Supervisory Special Agent Steven Burmeister, assigned to the crime lab's Chemistry and Toxicology Unit, was the first to go inside the Mercury. He wore a Tyvek suit with protective footgear and a double pair of gloves. He took swabs and other samples of the interior of the car.

He handed out a small sign that McVeigh had originally placed on the dashboard after stashing the car in the alley nearly a week ago.

"Not abandoned," he had written on the sign. "Please do not tow. Will move by April 23."

He added: "Needs battery and cable."

A check by the agents showed that the car's battery and cable were fine.

Burmeister handed the envelope to Eppright. They photographed it first, on both sides, and then Eppright, also wearing cotton gloves, opened it by tearing along one end. Inside were two stacks with each pile folded neatly into thirds. A small note lay on top.

McVeigh had written: "Obey the Constitution of the United States and we won't shoot you."

Puzzled, Eppright set the note aside on the table where he was working. Then he decided to finish processing the car before continuing his way through the envelope. So he gathered up the note and the envelope and placed them in a plastic container. He and the other agents turned back to the Mercury. For the next two hours, they vaccuumed, swabbed, and isolated various samples from both the interior and exterior of the car. They marked the samples for shipment to the crime lab in Washington.

Now Eppright was back at his table. He cleaned off the tabletop and spread large sheets of white paper on the surface. Again he slipped on the white gloves, and he directed a photographer to lean over his shoulder and record each step.

From inside the envelope he pulled several pieces of paper: typewritten pages, and some pages from books and magazines, many of the passages highlighted in yellow marker. It was all virulent antigovernment literature.

He examined pages 61 and 62 from *The Turner Diaries*. Some of the lines McVeigh had highlighted with a yellow marker; some he had highlighted twice.

"The real value of our attacks today lies in the psychological impact, not in the immediate casualties," read the marked passages. "More important, though, is what we taught the politicians and the bureaucrats. They learned this afternoon that not one of them is beyond our reach. They can huddle behind barbed wire and tanks in the city, or they can hide behind concrete walls and alarm systems at their country estate."

Eppright tagged the pages with FBI evidentiary stickers and set them aside. He pulled more papers from the envelope, and out came a series of clippings that had been cut and pasted together, including one document that had been photocopied and pasted in the middle.

One clipping recounted a scene from the Revolutionary War, and where the date April 29, 1775, had been mistakenly printed, McVeigh had scratched it out and corrected it with the proper date, April 19. It described the Battle of Lexington and the tremendous risks that American patriots took in defying the British. McVeigh had highlighted a portion of the narrative that described a coiled rattlesnake, "which when left to exist peaceably threatens no one, but when trodden upon strikes as viciously and with as deadly an effort as any creature on earth."

Some of the clippings railed against high taxes; some complained about overzealous government agents. One urged states' rights over a concentrated national government at Washington. Another clipping was carried under the banner headline "U.S. Government Initiates Open Warfare Against American People."

And of course, there was Waco. An article about the Waco siege and raid that he had clipped from a copy of *Soldier of Fortune* magazine posed the question "Executions or Mercy Killings?" McVeigh had highlighted the word "Executions."

Indeed McVeigh had highlighted almost all of this page.

"They deployed in a military manner against American citizens. They slaughtered 80-plus people, committed acts of treason, murder and conspiracy."

"If the heat gets a little high they'll throw us some yellow-livered piece-of-shit bureaucrat to quiet us down, but all in all, they'll get away with it."

He had slashed streaks of yellow across bits of sentences or small turns of phrase. "The foul ashes of Waco" . . . "power gone mad" . . . "the Bureau of Alcohol, Tobacco and Firearms, the Gestapo of G-men" . . . "they backed Lady Liberty into a corner and shot her in the head."

"This country's in trouble, guys, bad trouble, and it isn't coming from any street criminal."

The final passage—also highlighted—had particular meaning for McVeigh. "Army spokesmen confirmed involvement of Green Berets in training some 80 ATF agents, as part of final preparations for the bloody raid on the Branch Davidians' religious compound."

It all began to run together. The Green Berets. Waco. April 19. The federal government. And there was more. A copy of the Declaration of Independence. A warning about the "mania" to outlaw handguns. The clips were sliding out of the envelope, spreading across Eppright's tabletop, the photographer behind him click-clicking as each new document appeared in view. Everything was coming into focus; everything made sense.

Eppright pushed his chair back from the table. The smallest clipping carried the darkest message, a quotation from American revolutionary Samuel Adams, printed in big letters: "When The Government Fears The People, THERE IS LIBERTY. When The People Fear The Government, THERE IS TYRANNY."

Underneath it, McVeigh had written six small words in his distinctive backslash style. These words, he assumed, would be found and read and interpreted as his call for the Americans of today to rebel against their government.

"Maybe now, there will be liberty!"

Eppright took his own pen. Next to McVeigh's words, Eppright signed his initials, "W.E. III," and the date, "4/21/95," and he replaced the envelope and its contents in a plastic container. He marked it too for transfer to Washington. McVeigh had spoken, and the government would use his words against him.

FBI Supervisor Weldon Kennedy and Merrick Garland from the Department of Justice would oversee the on-the-ground investigation in Oklahoma City. They worked out of a command post near the scene of the bombing, agents taking phone calls and writing reports, on the wall a list growing daily of the people—mostly army buddies—whom McVeigh had known. Next on the wall were two drawings of the still-not-found John Doe No. 2, and next to that, black-and-white still photos from the Regency Tower surveillance camera that had captured the slow march of the Ryder truck up 5th Street just moments before the bomb went off. For weeks the command post was crowded and noisy, a buzz of activity, sworn law enforcement officers and local volunteers, all trying to help. Garland was amazed at all the energy, the sheer human drive. People came in offering to do anything, even if it was just answering the telephone. Others came in to do the laundry for the out-of-towners. The command post took on the look of a small city, self-sufficient and organized.

Kennedy would manage the bureau's resources, watching as grid searches of ten square blocks of downtown Oklahoma City were carried out, making sure that every gas stop along the highway was checked. He would see to it that every promising phone lead was followed up.

Garland would spend three months in Oklahoma, helping to shape the federal prosecution until his boss, Reno, set up a team of U.S. attorneys from around the country to take the case. When he was not going over legal strategy, he would step outside, maybe wander up to the bomb site when the rescue effort was still underway in those early days. Here he could see the huge crater and hear the cranes moving overhead; here too he saw the men, big, muscular construction workers in hard hats, their faces a mix of tears and sweat.

From the bomb scene, agents hauled 129 dump truck loads of debris to a sifting site at the county sheriff's gun range ten miles away. The twisted steel and broken concrete, the ash and soot and dirt and powder, were piled in three different areas on the thousand-acre range; altogether, 1,035 tons of debris was sifted, much of it by hand from yellow plastic buckets, as federal agents searched for any possible clues tying McVeigh to the blast.

To Louis Michalko, a special agent assigned to Oklahoma City, fell the tedious task of going through the last fifteen months of sales receipts from the Mid-Kansas Co-op grain elevator in McPher-

son, where the four thousand pounds of ammonium nitrate had
been purchased. He went to the company headquarters in
Moundridge, Kansas, and the staff brought out boxes of yellow,
pink, and white copies of sales receipts. He sat down at a table in a
back room and reviewed them one by one, culling through 132,000
tickets to find what he was after.

He discovered that for all that time, only the man using the alias
Mike Havens had paid cash for more than a thousand pounds of
ammonium nitrate. Only two other customers ever bought more
than a thousand pounds during that same time period.

By the time McVeigh went to trial, the government had compiled more than 25,000 witness statements; the index alone
exceeded 580 pages. They assembled several sets of some 2,000 document files, 350 audiocassette tapes, and 500 videotapes of potential evidence.

Reconstucting the phone records was a monumental task. FBI
Agent Fred Dexter spent more than fifteen hundred hours, or nine
months of forty-hour work weeks, sorting through the telephone
data. His colleague Special Agent Jay Matthews invested another
thousand hours by his side. In all, 156 million phone records were
scoured over a fourteen-month period.

Tables were set up at the Fort Riley command post, and there
agents hunched over nearly 600,000 registration cards taken from
selected motels in the Midwest. The cards were hauled to the command post on two tractor-trailer trucks, and then hundreds of
white-gloved agents sat along tables inside the fort's gymnasium
flipping through them.

At the FBI Crime Laboratory in Washington, scientists pored
over more than fifteen thousand entries. They produced more than
ten thousand pages of lab notes. The focus here was on McVeigh's
personal effects.

No high-explosive materials were detected on McVeigh's black
windbreaker or combat boots. Nor were any found on his blanket
or cloth bag recovered from the car. But traces were picked up on
the pockets of his jeans and both T-shirts.

Most incriminating of all were the earplugs. They held traces of
chemical components consistent with the ammonium nitrate and
fuel oil in the bomb used to blow up the Murrah building. The gov-

ernment would hold up those earplugs as the most damaging of all pieces of evidence against McVeigh.

McVeigh spent the next year in Oklahoma, locked up in a federal penitentiary in El Reno, less than an hour's drive from the state capital. He would attend initial court hearings in a prison cafeteria adapted as a courtroom with a judge's bench and attorneys' tables and, later, in a federal courtroom in the United States courthouse across Fourth Street from where the Murrah building had once stood.

The first preliminary hearing was held on April 27, just eight days after the bombing, again before Magistrate Howland, in the El Reno prison cafeteria. Howland was asked to weigh whether there was ample evidence at that time to continue to hold McVeigh in confinement. In the back of the room could be heard the click-clacking of a soda pop machine. Outside the window on this warm, blustery spring day, robins were calling.

Only two witnesses testified. Garland called FBI Case Agent Jon Hersley of Oklahoma City to the stand and asked him to describe not only the ties that already connected McVeigh to the Murrah building, but also the still-expanding federal investigation. Too many questions remained unanswered; for each name run to ground, a half-dozen more surfaced. Jennifer McVeigh was being questioned and requestioned. Marife Nichols was under intense review. The government still held James Nichols in custody in Michigan. Another mobile FBI command post was setting up shop at the National Guard armory in Kingman as agents in Arizona sought to wrap their fingers around Michael and Lori Fortier.

"Our primary focus right now," Hersley told the judge, "is to try to determine the identity and the location of the other subjects so that we can prohibit another bomb from going off."

The second witness, called by the defense, was Trooper Hanger. He retold the story of McVeigh's arrest on the traffic and gun charges, how McVeigh had been polite and had given him the yessir-no-sir routine and had allowed him to check the Mercury. At one point, Hanger looked across the room and identified McVeigh, now wearing the tan uniform of a federal prison inmate. The buttons were plastic, not brass; the uniform was pressed, but not starched.

McVeigh never spoke. He sat expressionless, looking cold and, some said, heartless. His stoicism would infuriate victims; they could never get past those eyes that were the color of robin's eggs, could find no way inside his thoughts.

"He will stand mute, your honor," said McVeigh's lead attorney, John W. Coyle III. So the lawyers did all the talking. Coyle noted the forty guards crowded into the room and asked the judge whether the marshals could not undo his client's handcuffs.

No, the judge said. "If the marshals indicated that he should be cuffed, he should stay cuffed. That will be it."

Susan Otto, his federal public defender, also addressed the court, asking if she and Coyle could be removed from the case. They were Oklahoma residents. They too had heard the bomb and seen the pulsing red lights. "I have found no case in the history of this country that is of such magnitude as the one we are involved in right now," she said.

She recited the names of many victims and victims' relatives whom she and Coyle had personally known, including several of the federal agents assigned to the Murrah building. "I know these people," she said. "I have done business with these people." She cited the intense local and national publicity of the last week, and spoke of the "tenable position to take and the tenable position to maintain" if local lawyers are expected to represent the man that their neighbors had come to hate so much.

"We don't really have to rely on all this media coverage," she said. "We don't have to rely on the video pictures and on television and Connie Chung standing there with a bombed-out building in the background. We know what it looks like because we were all there and we all saw it. We heard it. We smelled it. We lived through it."

Otto would be removed from the case, and Coyle too. He had made it clear in meetings with reporters in those first days that he also felt the sharp conflict between personal pain and professional duty. When the TV cameras appeared in his office, he hid the family pictures on his desk and bookshelves; he did not want those watching to see the faces of his family. There might be people eager to seek revenge, and the telephones in his law office and at home were already ringing with threats.

Coyle, after a lifetime of work as a criminal defense attorney, understood the greatest maxim of the law: that everyone deserves competent legal representation.

"If ever anyone needed a lawyer, it is this young man," Coyle told the reporters. "And it should not be me."

So the case shifted to Stephen Jones, an oil and gas attorney and Republican politico from Enid. That seemed far enough removed. But Jones too recognized the impossibility of defending the indefensible. One of his first moves was to remake his client's image, and for that he brought a crew from *Newsweek* magazine into the prison.

The cover spread ran the day before the Fourth of July. The prison interview was headlined "The Suspect Speaks," but McVeigh said nothing of the charges against him.

Did you do it?

"We are going to plead not guilty."

Any reaction—even in hindsight—to the large number of children among the victims?

"For two days, in the [Perry jail] cell, we could hear news reports, and of course everyone, including myself, was horrified at the deaths of the children. . . . It's a very tragic thing."

Does the government make mistakes?

"Most definitely."

Have you experimented with bombs before?

"It would amount to firecrackers."

You were just having fun?

"It was like popping a paper bag."

McVeigh chose *Newsweek* because of his respect for its military affairs consultant, the highly decorated Colonel David H. Hackworth. And Hackworth was impressed in return.

"Looking into Tim McVeigh's eyes in the El Reno prison, I realized my gut feeling was right," he wrote. "He has what a lot of soldiers, good and bad, have: fire in the belly. When we talked about the military, a change came over him: McVeigh suddenly sat straight in his chair."

Hackworth continued: "The Timothy McVeigh I talked with didn't seem like a baby killer. He was in high combat form, fully aware that his performance in the interview was almost a matter of life and death. If he'd been in combat, he'd have a medal for his coolness under fire. He might also be the most devious con man to come down the pike."

Then, eerily, Hackworth summed up the two faces of McVeigh—the excitable boy running barefoot across the lawns of Pendleton, rushing unannounced into his neighbors' homes, contrasting with his image on the day of his arrest. "At times, McVeigh came across as the boy next door," Hackworth wrote. "But you might never want to let him into your house."

Chapter Fifteen

Playing Rough

With her husband locked away in the long, narrow box of a federal jail cell, Marife Nichols was alone in America. In the weeks that followed his surrender, she was always surrounded by FBI agents hurrying her into and out of motel rooms in Kansas and Oklahoma. Repeatedly, she was escorted back to her home in Herington to pick up another item or two—and to allow the agents one more search of the little house and the detached garage in back. She was shielded from the news media, from the public, and from lawyers; she was kept virtually incognito. She was afraid for her baby, unsure of her husband, frightened for her own safety. Each day the government tried something new to draw her closer into their confidence. They wanted more from Marife about her husband, hoping that what she knew would also give them more on McVeigh.

She is a small woman, a foreigner in a land she does not understand. She wanted to take the money she had hidden in her home and return to her family in the Philippines.

"All the time, I want to be in my house," she recalled. "But they won't let me. I did ask, but they won't let me because the media is going to be around there. There's going to be a lot of bills, too, is what they told me."

She tried again and again to figure out a way to pass unnoticed back into her home, to sneak into the bedroom and slide her hand under the mattress where she kept the $5,000 in cash and the handful of precious coins that Terry had saved for just this kind of emergency.

The FBI sought permission to search and re-search the property. Agent Sheila Dobson asked about the vacuum cleaner, because they wanted to comb through the vacuum bag and see if any hair or fibers or other minute particles might reveal something about her husband and McVeigh.

"I don't know," a flustered and confused Marife told Agent Dobson. "I haven't seen any."

Dobson presented her with FBI forms to sign. They were going to get that vacuum cleaner. And the tableware too.

"They want to get the dishes in the house to see if there's any fingerprints from Tim McVeigh," Marife recalled.

They took apart the television set that her husband said McVeigh had brought out to Kansas for Josh. What could they want with that old television? "They were talking about it, if there's any . . . anything in that TV that Tim McVeigh might have put in there to . . . one of the ingredients of a bomb, I guess."

They asked about the washer and the dryer, and the mixer out in the shed that the government was beginning to believe Terry had used to grind ammonium nitrate.

"Is it okay if we take it?" Agent Dobson asked.

"You can take the whole house," Marife said. "As long as you're going to, you know, give me my money and send me to the Philippines."

And they probably would have taken the house if they could have gotten a court order to put it on a flatbed and drive it east to the FBI lab in Washington. Then they would have torn it apart shingle by shingle. Because Terry Nichols was a pack rat; he kept everything. In the garage was the fuel meter and several fifty-five-gallon plastic barrels, along with a safe deposit box key belonging to Arkansas firearms dealer Roger Moore. In the house was a sales slip for one of the large ammonium nitrate purchases. It still carried McVeigh's fingerprint, and the receipt was wrapped around some coins from Moore. Also found were a cordless drill and a set of drill bits believed used in the break-in at the Marion, Kansas, rock quarry.

One of the searches uncovered a small spiral notebook. Flipping through the pages, FBI agents found what seemed like a combination phone book and diary.

There were dates and amounts for the storage lockers, and the aliases Joe Kyle and Ted Parker. There were also notes about "Tim" and "places to camp."

Marife also confided in the little book. On one page she described a quarrel she had had with her husband in March about the clothing that had belonged to her dead son, Jason. Her husband had promised that she could keep the clothes, and now she was upset.

"Dear Diary," she wrote. "Terry and I argue about the clothes of Jason because he sold it to others. Only the blue jacket left."

The FBI assured her she did not need a lawyer, and they were so good at hiding Marife that even her husband's attorneys, including renowned criminal defense lawyer Michael Tigar, could not find her.

"They told me that you're okay as long as you're . . . you're telling the truth," she said. "You're not a suspect, so you don't need a lawyer unless you're not telling the truth. Then you need a lawyer."

Just two days after that trip with her husband to the Herington police station, she telephoned one of Terry's attorneys, desperate for someone who could help. But the lawyer, Ron Woods, was out; the phone call message noted that "she said the FBI would not let her leave."

She tried to reach her aunt, Lori Lastema, but had difficulty there too. Her aunt was a housekeeper, and Marife ended up talking to her aunt's boss, and all he wanted to know was whether Terry Nichols was innocent. She answered him the only way she could. "I think he's innocent," she said.

She was a mother who was expecting another child. What did she know of lawyers and vacuum cleaners and fertilizer bombs big enough to fill an oversized rental truck? And still they took her to Oklahoma City, where she was escorted before prosecutors busy that summer preparing federal grand jury charges against her husband and McVeigh. She tried to cooperate; but it was the $5,000 in cash and the nine gold coins and the three pieces of silver hidden in the house that she wanted most of all.

Finally, on one of her FBI-chaperoned trips back to the house, she slipped into her bedroom, rushed for the bed, and fell to her knees. She lifted the top mattress and reached in, but her hand felt nothing. The money was gone. The government had taken it.

She put on tears for an FBI supervisor, Gene Thomeczek, asking him to give the money back. What else was she to do? "I did cry for that," she recalled, "hoping that he would feel like, you know, I'm his daughter. And this is my money anyway, so maybe would he give it to me. But no."

The FBI said the money first had to go to the FBI lab to be examined for fingerprints.

The government would contend that Marife actually was never held against her will. They recalled a phone conversation she had with Terry's father, Robert Nichols, on April 30. The FBI later produced a transcript of the phone call, because, of course, they listened in.

Marife asked Robert Nichols about his other son, James, and how he was doing in jail in Michigan. Then the old man asked about her and the baby, Nicole.

"Oh, we're doing fine," she said. "Everything is okay. I mean, they give us anything that we need here, and we're fine."

She told him she wanted her freedom back, and a plane ticket out of America. "Go home to Philippines," she said. "It would be a lot better for me to, uh, since you know I, I need to talk to my parents. I wanted to go home, too. Uh, but I think they need to ask me a lot of, uh, questions about activities that we did ever since I got back here from Philippines."

And because FBI agents were listening, naturally they wanted to see what connections she could develop between Terry and James Nichols about the bombing, and maybe tie some new knots around McVeigh too. It was FBI agents that had handed her the telephone; now they told her to work for them, be an undercover agent.

"Um, about Terry," she said. She was scared. She faltered. What was she doing?

"I, I only talked to him once, on the telephone, and uh, he mainly just want me to go home. He, um, same as, as, you been watching the news?"

"What I can, yes," the old man said.

"Yeah it's, it's all the same as what, uh, James is, has, you know he's just a material witness."

"Uh huh."

"Yeah, did he ever talk to you before when we visit in your house about that?"

But Robert Nichols, with two sons now in jail in connection with America's worst terrorist attack, and the press and the FBI circling his own Michigan farm door, was too smart to bite; he was a shrewd man, and he knew better. He could almost hear the FBI breathing on the other end of the phone line.

"No," he said. "It's all news to me."

So Marife dropped it; she went back to saying how well the FBI was treating her. Flatter them, she thought, say what they want, maybe then they would give her the cash and a ride to the airport.

"Yeah, do, uh, I don't know what else can I say," she said, winding up the phone call. "I mean that we are okay. We're, we're fine. Nicole is fine. We are in this hotel right now. They, this FBI agent that I have, they're very nice."

After more than a month, when they were done with her, when they had repeatedly sifted through her home and clothes and the baby's toys too, had cleaned out the garage and sifted through the lawn and poked through the bushes, the FBI finally returned all but $200 of the cash. The $200 they kept for more evidentiary analysis.

When they parted company in late May, the government hoped there were no hard feelings. For Mother's Day, five female agents in the FBI's Kansas City field office sent her a greeting card. They wrote a long message on the card, pouring on the sympathy.

"We all hope the best for you. Please don't believe that the government workers are the bad guys no matter what anyone tells you. We are here to help you. We have all fallen in love with Nicole. We all wish the best for you and your new baby. Don't let all this latest news affect you. We are all here for you. If you ever are lonely, if you ever want to talk, if you ever want to cry, just call us. We'll be here for you."

They underlined, twice, the words "lonely" and "talk" and "cry." They penciled in their phone number, and urged her to call collect. They signed the card with "Love."

What a game they played, she thought. It began that first day, that moment they drove into the Herington police station lot and those first FBI agents rushed in after them. The world raced past her that day.

Why had she played along? For her money; for her children. "I was cooperating mainly because I want them to know that I have nothing to hide."

The abandoned wife eventually returned to the Philippines exhausted and lonely. She felt destroyed by her husband, used by the government, unclear about her future. Next, her husband's lawyers lobbied her hard to stay married to her husband; it would help them present Terry Nichols as an upstanding, caring family man when his case ultimately went to trial. "I was only trying to be truthful with everyone," she said. "I want to please with everyone."

Her brother-in-law, James, the family farmer, the older sibling that Terry looked up to and admired, fared no better. At least she got out of the country, away from this crazy business in America. He spent much of the spring, prime planting time in Michigan, behind bars as the FBI sought to hold him in custody for the bombing.

At first they theorized he might be the "mastermind" behind the blast, that his sharp tongue and angry anti-Washington diatribes might have been enough to sow in McVeigh's mind the idea of striking back at the federal government.

James Nichols was indeed a talker. He claimed to have first heard of the bombing that day, April 19, when he was visiting a self-serve lumberyard in Decker—a small Michigan crossroads with nothing much more than a church, post office, and tavern. Two days later, that fateful Friday, when his brother and McVeigh were being rounded up by federal agents, Nichols joked with a neighbor that there was supposed to be some kind of a raid on a Decker farm-house. The town was abuzz that morning.

"I was overwhelmed with laughter at this far-fetched notion," he wrote in a series of reminiscences. "Decker? The Oklahoma City bombing? I mean, everyone knows that's the kind of thing a terrorist or an intelligence agent would do in a foreign country, not something a hick from Podunk, U.S.A., would do to his fellow citizens, his own countrymen. Not a chance!"

But this was no joke; the government in fact was coming. That day, Nichols set off on a few errands, including a stop at an auto parts store twenty miles over in Marlette. He put $2,000 down for a tractor engine he was having rebuilt. Driving home, he noticed traffic was picking up. "It was obvious that whoever the feds were raiding lived somewhere near here," he said.

As he drove closer, he pulled up to a local police officer working a roadblock. He could see the white sedans and the vans, and the federal agents in black dress swarming around his farm home. He motioned the officer over, and the cop quickly realized that this was James Nichols, the one McVeigh had left as a reference in both Junction City and Perry. Nichols said of the officer, "It almost seemed as if he didn't quite know what to do with the most wanted criminal on the planet, now that he'd 'caught' him."

The policeman turned Nichols over to the federal agents.

"The government agents surrounding my farm possessed enough firepower to easily defeat a small planet," Nichols said. "As I approached my driveway, an ATF agent who mistakenly thought he was in a Ninja movie—I could tell by the way he was dressed and by the way he acted—jumped in my car and ordered me not to move, while pointing an assault rifle at my face in a nervy menacing manner. This guy seemed to be a recruit from the KGB or Gestapo or something, and was obviously a loose cannon who was also a few bricks short of a full load—a prerequisite for any adult who wants to dress and act like a Ninja turtle."

The FBI had come in dark SWAT uniforms.

"It appeared as if I was left hung out to dry," Nichols said. "Staring down the barrel of a fully automatic assault rifle—and into the cold eyes of a fanatic who had been trained to kill unarmed citizens who could not fight back—sent a shudder up my spine. Many thoughts raced through my mind. Does this guy want to take it out on me because he wasn't fortunate enough to be involved in the turkey shoots at Waco and Ruby Ridge?"

They took him into custody, and he too was seen on the nightly news, like his brother and McVeigh, being escorted in handcuffs from one jail to another. While they could not tie him directly to the bombing, they held him on unrelated federal charges of conspiring with his brother and McVeigh "to make and possess . . . destructive devices." As the FBI bought time to review what his full role might have been in planning the attack on the Murrah, they kept him in prison for making bombs and tossing them off into the fields at his farm in Decker.

According to a court affidavit, James Nichols told agents that over the past several years he had seen his brother and McVeigh building and setting off "bottle bombs," using brake fluid, gasoline, and diesel fuel. Sometimes, he said, he joined in on the bomb-making, and he had made small explosive devices with prescription vials, blasting caps, and a safety fuse. McVeigh had been around the house a lot, Nichols said; he even had his own back bedroom.

Nichols denied that he had ever personally purchased ammonium nitrate, but added that "McVeigh had the knowledge to manufacture a bomb."

Neighbor Dan Stromber told the government he had seen the Nichols brothers making small bombs by mixing fertilizer, peroxide, and bleach in plastic pop bottles. "We're getting better at it," James had bragged. Stromber said the brothers complained about the federal government and what had happened at Waco.

"The judges and President Clinton should be killed," Nichols had told Stromber. "The FBI and the ATF are to blame for killing the Branch Davidians in Waco."

Stromber also recalled a young man named Tim who had moved in last spring, a guy who "wore camouflage clothing frequently and carried a pistol." Another neighbor, Paul Isydorek, remembered this man as McVeigh, and said that McVeigh had a hand in the bomb experiments.

A confidential source told the FBI that two men, one using the name Terry Tuttle, had visited the Thumb Hobbies store in Marlette some time back and asked about buying liquid nitro model airplane fuel and, oddly, two hundred heavy-duty zip-lock bags. And then stepped forward Dave Shafer, the Indiana seed dealer, who told the agents the story about James Nichols and his little drawing of the Murrah building.

They locked James Nichols away, hoping to sweat him while they continued to study whether he had any involvement in Oklahoma City, even if it was just in planning the attack, or if it was just planting an idea with McVeigh that the combination of April 19 and an explosion at a federal building would trigger a second people's revolution in the United States.

For three days they searched his farm. They found large tanks with diesel fuel and twenty-eight fifty-pound bags of fertilizer. In a field by the outbuilding they discovered jagged-edged metal fragments which appeared to be bomb shrapnel.

In his large white home and his faded-red barn, they found the trappings of an American extremist. On the kitchen table lay a copy of the *Spotlight*; nearby was a paper envelope with a document quoting Adolf Hitler; near that was a paper bag containing twenty-eight blasting caps and a safety fuse. In a kitchen cabinet, third drawer from the right, lay a book titled *Ditching and Field Clearing with Dynamite.*

On top of the living-room television set, where two years ago McVeigh and the Nichols brothers had watched in horror the scenes of the suddenly blazing Waco compound, the agents recovered a videotape titled *Secret Societies and the New World Order.* In a first-floor den were copies of David Koresh pamphlets, and next to them two photographs from the Waco siege. Nearby were discarded envelopes addressed to James Nichols from a T. Tuttle in Kingman, Arizona.

The FBI recovered dozens of videotapes and audiocassettes. On the floor in the laundry room lay a *Bay Area News* with a special feature on the Michigan Militia. They even scoured the cab of Nichols's John Deere tractor and seized cigarette butts from the ashtray.

In a three-count indictment on May 11, the government charged James Nichols with conspiracy to possess unregistered destructive devices, but not with anything related to Oklahoma City. Ten days later, U.S. District Judge Paul Borman held a hearing into just what evidence the government really had compiled against Nichols.

Assistant U.S. Attorney Robert Cares said the defendant had prior knowledge of the Oklahoma City bombing, that he knew it was being planned and did nothing to stop the destruction. He pointed to a letter from McVeigh to James Nichols that agents found on the farm. "Keep me posted on any 'trouble,' " McVeigh had written. Cares saw it as a direct reference to Oklahoma City. He also noted that the day before the bombing, the Nichols brothers spoke for thirteen minutes on the telephone.

"If released, this defendant poses a risk of flight and a danger to the community," Cares warned the judge.

Defense attorney Robert R. Elsey argued otherwise, saying his client was just a forty-one-year-old farmer who needed to get back to his fields. He escorted into the courtroom a number of Decker neighbors who one after the other vouched for the good name of James Nichols. The client himself sat at his counsel's table, in a three-piece gray suit and a big-knotted tie. He occasionally would turn around and glance at friends and family members; he smiled when talking to his lawyers and passed them notes.

American justice was on the side of this man who hated the government. Judge Borman sent him home; the only restriction was that he wear an electronic tether and remain under house arrest until federal agents could sort out their next move. "There is not an iota of evidence of dangerous acts toward others," said an obviously put-out Judge Borman.

Learning that he was going home, Nichols picked up a jail telephone and jubilantly called a friend. "I'm innocent!" he shouted. He walked out of a federal lockup in Michigan and appeared nervous but grateful before the television cameras. "I'm an average American farmer, an average guy," he declared. At first it seemed like the same old James Nichols. But then he spread his fingers over his eyes and broke into tears; for once, he could not continue.

"My friends, my family, my neighbors really came through for me," he said in choked words. "I can't thank everybody enough."

He called the raid on his farm "a big show," but said he held no bitterness. "No," he said. "I've cooperated fully." He described the Oklahoma City bombing as "a bad tragedy," and he added: "Everybody should cooperate. I've cooperated fully to get to the bottom of it."

The FBI now had other concerns. If they could not hold James Nichols, and if they could not keep his sister-in-law, Marife, under wraps and use her to trap others, then it was time to move on past the Nichols family. It was best to return to McVeigh, and to Pendleton. Their next stop was his sister Jennifer.

She too found herself suffocated by the presence of federal agents. She adored her older brother, she had bragged to friends about him; now the government wanted her to tell all.

Jennifer McVeigh was still on her Florida vacation in Pensacola and driving a friend to pick up his paycheck when the car radio announced her brother's name in the Oklahoma City bombing. Stunned, she pulled over, and soon was chain-smoking. Her friend had to take the wheel. They drove to his house, and she called her father. She picked up some of the clippings her brother had sent her, the ones from *The Turner Diaries* that she had carried with her to Florida, and she stepped out into the laundry room behind the garage at her friend's home and burned them, all of them. "I was scared," she told the government later. "I just heard Tim's name announced, so I figured you would come around sooner or later to talk to me."

The FBI found her in Florida, and they talked to her several times. When she returned to the Buffalo area the Monday after the bombing, they spoke with her there too. She was met at the airport by her father; the FBI was there too. They all drove straight to the local FBI field office. But when Jennifer would not talk, they sent her home with instructions to return the next day. And then she talked, for eight or nine hours, and for the next eight days too. She hired a local lawyer, and she would joke with him about "camping out" at the FBI office. But inside the FBI interrogation room there were no smiles. "They told me Tim was guilty," she said, "and that he was going to fry."

On the wall hung large posters making up an evolving timeline of her brother's life. There was a second timeline for her, including her high school picture, taken by the FBI off her kitchen wall. The photo was enlarged, and next to it was a list of criminal charges that they were considering filing against her. They also handed her a law book that laid out the federal criminal code.

Page 57: "Whoever commits an offense against the United States or aids, abets, counsels, commands, induces or procures is punishable as a principal." Next to it they wrote the word "death."

On the next page, at Section III, Clause 1, they referred her to another offense: "Treason." And below it they wrote, "Penalty equals death." They underlined it too.

The FBI copied those pages and placed them on the wall next to the posters. She was in deep now; she knew what was coming next. They asked her to give up her brother. Don't you want to see Tim? they said. Visit him for us, ask him about the bombing, help us nail him. Even her parents asked her to cooperate, but she refused. Later, when the government drew up a written statement for her to sign, an affidavit in return for a grant of immunity against prosecution, they left out that part about asking her to pin her brother.

She talked, but only around the edges. She told them about his work at gun shows, about his strong beliefs in the Constitution. She said he loved guns and hated gun control; she said he hated the federal government and loved, most of all, *The Turner Diaries*. He had sent her the book too, and copies of antigovernment literature, and sometimes he highlighted in yellow the passages he wanted her to remember.

"He had people he knew around the country," she told the FBI.

She mentioned "Mike and Lori and Terry."

Once, she told them, he came home to Pendleton with a videotape about Waco, and the two of them sat in the living room of their father's house and watched the scenes from the FBI siege. The movie was called *Day 51*.

"It depicted the government raiding the compound, and it implied that the government gassed and burned the people inside intentionally and attacked the people," she said. "He was very angry. I think he thought the government murdered the people there, basically gassed and burned them."

By the government, he told her, he meant the FBI and the ATF. "He felt that someone should be held accountable," she said.

Did he think the government was ever held responsible?

"No," she said.

She showed them the letter he had written to the American Legion on her word processor, the one complaining about the "power-hungry storm troopers of the federal government" who marched on Waco. She gave them the file he had left in the processor too, the one called "ATF Read," with the warning "Die, you spineless cowardice bastards!"

What had he told her about himself?

He'd said he would no longer just talk and preach against the government. "Now I'm in the action stage," he said. He described the car wreck, and how he had been frightened that the explosives in the trunk would go off. He had sent her his personal effects. He had told her the Fortiers were trustworthy.

That summer, hemmed in by the agents, she signed a statement outlining in detail what Tim had said to her and given her, and what she had heard about his plans for something big to happen in the spring—how "there's going to be a revolution." She gave them what she had kept of her brother's writings, but she insisted he had never told her about ammonium nitrate or anhydrous hydrazine, never asked her about the part in *The Turner Diaries* where a truck bomb explodes at FBI headquarters, and never ever spoken about the Alfred P. Murrah Federal Building in Oklahoma City.

They searched her pickup and home; they took her cassette tapes of patriot music and some of her own antigovernment literature. They seized her *Citizens Rule Book*, a small handbook Tim had given her so she could speak the language of the revolutionary.

The FBI still wondered how much she really knew, or whether Jennifer McVeigh—tall, thin, and under the spell of her older brother—was just a braggart, a show-off; maybe like James Nichols, all talk. She was a community college student, thinking about a career in psychology or education, but what she really liked to do was party. She loved to kick her head back and laugh. And she wanted to be like her brother.

She went to Oklahoma City and testified before the grand jury, and at one point she burst out of the jury room flailing her arms and crying hysterically. But she always felt she did not betray her brother. She simply gave them his own words, to do with them as they would.

And still the FBI was not quite there. The investigators had built a largely circumstantial case, and that seemed unsatisfactory; they had no one who could put McVeigh in the Ryder truck that morning, no one who could positively identify him in front of the Murrah. They next turned to Michael and Lori Fortier. The young Kingman couple had been there at the beginning; McVeigh had told them how he planned to reawaken America, had even asked Michael for his help. But the Fortiers had hidden his secret, and their silence had helped make it happen.

For that, they would pay.

Marion Day Laird, a friend of the Fortiers, was at their home the night before the bombing. She stayed well past midnight, and returned for more festivities around eight in the morning. The television was on—it was always on in the Fortier trailer—and every channel was broadcasting the news from Oklahoma City.

Laird would recall that the Fortiers seemed uninterested. "They acted the same," she said. "They didn't act any differently that I would notice."

"The same" for the Fortiers was to shrug off the outside world. Okay, so it had happened; McVeigh had made good on his promise. They distrusted the government too. They watched the world search for the man in the Ryder, and not once did they pick up the telephone. Michael Fortier and Tim McVeigh had driven together down that white line of highway, they had stopped at the Murrah building, and he, Fortier, had seen those windows covering the entire north front; in his mind he could almost hear the glass shattering. Still neither he nor his wife bothered to call the authorities.

And then the FBI spotlight swiveled to them. Suddenly Kingman was all the talk; FBI agents and the nation's press were pouring into the desert town.

The agents were collecting outside Fortier's white trailer, knocking on his door and pestering his neighbors. They talked to his relatives, visited his high school, and interviewed his former coworkers at the hardware store. Agents followed behind as he drove his new black Jeep around town, even out to the desert where he liked to walk or jog, and the agents in their company cars followed his pounding footsteps. For the longest while, the FBI investigators believed Fortier or others had buried evidence somewhere out there in the sand, and they hoped he would lead them to a duffel bag full of bomb components, military gear, or more of the loot stolen in the Arkansas robbery.

Michael Fortier could not run fast enough, he could not drive far enough away. There was nowhere to go, not from the instant he saw the pictures on television. "Right away, I thought Tim did it. I think I thought, Oh my God, he did it."

He said he and Lori had talked later that day about calling the police, or at least maybe talking to her father about what they should do. But then they saw Janet Reno and Bill Clinton on television and there were vows from Washington about the death penalty. Seeing themselves as accessories to the bombing, they decided to tell no one of their involvement; only when the heat blew their way did they step forward. And then they lied.

They would use McVeigh as their shield. "I felt Tim was like a buffer zone," Fortier said. "If people thought he was guilty, then that would bring suspicion down on myself. But if he was innocent, then surely I would have no knowledge of it."

When the first agents stepped up on his front porch, "I told them I didn't think Tim was capable of it." And when they asked about Terry Nichols, "I just gave a negative answer that I didn't know nothing about Terry. I just wanted to push him aside and not even have to think about him."

He lied about their drive east through Oklahoma City, and said instead that he had thumbed a ride to Kansas to buy some weapons from McVeigh. But the agents could read the dishonesty on his face.

"How did you get there?" they asked.

"Hitchhiking," Fortier said.

"Who picked you up?"

"A trucker."

"What color was his truck? What did his truck look like?"

"It was like, uh, red."

He was just making up answers out of the thin desert air.

On April 23, he told the FBI that he had never heard McVeigh talk about bombs. In a second interview, he said he had only talked to McVeigh about guns and the government. He never, he said, "never, ever," picked up any indication that McVeigh was going to blow up the Murrah building.

The following day he again told the FBI he knew nothing of the bombing. On May 6, he asked them to leave him alone. "I don't want to cooperate," he said. "I can't be of any more help. I don't know anything."

The press camped outside his home became too unnerving, and the local media, particularly the *Arizona Republic*, were profiling him as a key member of the bombing conspiracy. He believed the FBI was leaking information to corner him, and so he and Lori drove out to the FBI headquarters and tried to dig a way out. But that did not work either. The agents were hostile, they accused him of lying and said they considered him a co-conspirator. One special agent leaned into his face and called him a name. It was the same epithet the crowd at Perry had yelled at McVeigh. "Baby killer."

More heated words followed—the FBI men in suits and ties in the bristling Arizona heat, the boy-man Fortier with his grunge look, the shaggy hair and beard stubble, wearing a T-shirt without sleeves. He asked his wife to leave the room and he and the agents yelled some more. Because now the agents were planning to search his home, and Fortier did not want an incident like the raid on the James Nichols farm in Michigan.

"There's no need to do that," he told the agents. "I will cooperate."

They set up a time for the agents to arrive, time enough for him to get Lori and their two-year-old daughter, Kayla, and the cats too out of the trailer. He also wanted to hustle five firearms from the Arkansas cache over the backyard fence. But guns, and drugs too, were not foremost on the FBI's list. In fact, they were there to do more than just palm through his belongings; they planted court-authorized telephone taps and electronic bugs inside the home. Then they sat back and listened for where Fortier might lead them.

Fortier suspected they were listening, but he did not seem to care.

In a phone call to an old army friend named Lonnie Hubbard, Fortier compared himself to Kato Kaelin, a star witness in the O. J. Simpson double-murder trial. If he was called as a witness in McVeigh's trial, Fortier told Hubbard, he knew just what he would do.

"I'd sit there and pick my nose and flick it at the camera," he said.

"Pick your nose and shit?" Hubbard asked.

"Flick it and then like kind of wipe it on the judge's desk."

"Scratch your ass and sniff your finger and stuff?"

Fortier laughed. "Yeah, really," he said. "Or wait just a second. Pull my finger. To the lawyer asking me questions. Come here. Pull my finger."

Hubbard was laughing too.

Fortier was on a roll.

"Oh, I don't know, dude. Once I get up there, I get comfortable, if there's like a camera. I don't know if they're going to do it like the O. J. Simpson trial or not. If they do, oh, my God, I'll be fucking fucked with the camera, hard core."

More laughter.

"And I'm the key," Fortier said. "I'm the key."

"'Cause you're the key," Hubbard said.

"The key man," said Fortier.

"That can unlock the whole mystery."

"The head honcho," Fortier boasted.

The two young men were roaring now. "You can unlock the mystery," Hubbard repeated. "Some guy that sits around his trailer with his wife and daughter . . ."

"Yep," Fortier said. "I hold the key to it all."

"Oh man, that just trips me out, 'cause I just know what a mellow dude you are. I mean really."

To his brother, John, Fortier bragged about his instant celebrity.

"I've been thinking about trying to do those talk-show circuits for a long time, and come up with some asinine story and get my friends to go in on it," Fortier said.

He added, "I found my career, 'cause I can tell a fable."

He burst out laughing. "I could tell stories all day."

He told his friend Glynn Bringle, "I want to wait till after the trial and do book and movie rights. I can just make up something juicy. Something that's worth the *Enquirer*, you know."

Money was hot on his mind. He figured he could sell some photographs of McVeigh for $50,000. Probably make more than that too, maybe a million if he marketed his entire story, his life with America's most hated man. "Make one cool mill," he boasted.

First he had to deal with the press outside his trailer. A week after the bombing, with the federal investigation focused on the Fortiers and Kingman, he spoke briefly with the *Los Angeles Times* and CNN.

"I do not believe that Tim blew up any building in Oklahoma," he said. "There's nothing for me to look back upon and say, yeah, that might have been it, I should have seen it back then. There's nothing like that.

"People cannot make a judgment on his guilt by what they read in the paper," he said. "But by what I see on TV, they have. They want his blood. In America, we believe people are innocent until proven guilty. Everyone must remember that. Whoever says forget the judiciary system, let's just hang him now, those people are not Americans. They may think they are, but they are not Americans."

The reporters asked him about John Doe No. 2, but he was only interested in defending McVeigh.

"I just want to tell him to be strong," Fortier said. "You are not alone. Right now, he might feel like there isn't anyone on this earth who is in any way supportive of him. But there is. Everyone should be supportive of him because he's an innocent man."

That is what Fortier told the press, the FBI, even his own family. His parents, Paul and Irene Fortier, begged him to tell the truth, to give the government everything he knew about McVeigh. "My father was taking this very hard," Michael remembered. "He was going through a nervous breakdown about it. He asked me one night if I had any involvement with it or if I knew anything, and I lied to him." Once the FBI microphones caught Fortier screaming at his mother when she brought up the problems that had fallen on the family. "Shut the fuck up!" he yelled.

Michael and Lori were subpoenaed to appear before the federal grand jury in Oklahoma City. Hurried written statements, sidewalk press conferences, big money talk on the telephone . . . none of that could help them now. They drove east and, on the morning of May 17, over breakfast in Oklahoma City, told each other it was time to make some decisions. They rented a room at the Motel 6 and there, alone and with no one else to point the finger at, they called the number on the subpoena and asked how to find a lawyer. Michael had signed a written statement in Kingman, but it was mostly lies; he knew it, so did the FBI, and he did not want his dishonesty held against him in the grand jury room. The FBI came out to see them, and they all talked, briefly, on the motel-room balcony.

"Then we asked them to leave and then me and Michael discussed between ourselves if we should really talk to them and what we should do," recalled Lori. "The agents came back about an hour later and we began to correct our statements."

They were given separate lawyers, two criminal defense attorneys from Oklahoma City, and both Michael and Lori agreed to cooperate now. The couple would talk for hours to the FBI, going over every detail, beginning with the Thanksgiving seven years ago when Michael first brought McVeigh home to Kingman.

Michael told them McVeigh had whispered about his plans with Terry Nichols to blow up a federal building, and at one point had grown angry when Fortier would not join his crusade. Fortier told them about the Kansas quarry burglary and the Arkansas gun robbery, and the trip he had taken with McVeigh to case the Murrah building.

Lori described that day in her kitchen when McVeigh had arranged soup cans on the floor and showed how he was going to fashion his bomb.

But her husband talked the most. Once, during a six-hour session, the FBI would not let him out of the interview room; for food they brought him a pack of M&M's, and he joked about feeding the little candies to the mice. The agents smiled. And when the Fortiers were done talking to the FBI, they told it again to the grand jury. And when the couple were done with the grand jury, the government had the last laugh: they charged Michael Fortier anyway.

He gave up his friend and he damned himself. It was a bitter trade. Lori would be given a grant of immunity, and she would testify when the case went to trial; that was the only favor the gov-

ernment gave in return. Michael could draw a sentence as high as
twenty-three years in prison for transporting stolen weapons, conspiring to transport those weapons, making false statements, and
failing to alert authorities about a pending felony—in essence, the
bombing itself. He signed the deal to save his wife, and because the
government told him that if he continued to cooperate and testified
truthfully, and Lori too, maybe prosecutors would later ask for a
reduced sentence for Michael.

By the middle of August the government had what it needed.
Marife could describe that sudden Easter Sunday trip her husband
made to Oklahoma City where McVeigh left his getaway car. James
Nichols told them of McVeigh's early experiences with bomb-making. Jennifer gave them his writings. And Michael and Lori Fortier
gave them his head.

On August 10, the federal grand jury sitting in the Western District of Oklahoma returned three indictments. The first two
charged McVeigh and Terry Nichols in an eleven-count conspiracy
case for the bombing of the Murrah building that killed 168 people.
Because eight of the dead were federal law enforcement officers, the
maximum penalty upon conviction could be death by lethal injection. The announcement of the indictments was carried live on
television, but McVeigh and Nichols were not there at the courthouse. There was no need for them to be there; they remained—
alone and apart from each other—in their cells at the El Reno
penitentiary. Afterward, their attorneys, Stephen Jones for McVeigh
and Michael Tigar for Nichols, held press conferences at a downtown hotel proclaiming their clients' innocence. While most of the
reporters were listening to the defense lawyers, a brief hearing was
underway in the federal courthouse.

Here now was Michael Joseph Fortier. He was twenty-six years
old, and he pleaded guilty before Chief Judge David L. Russell. He
would be formally sentenced after McVeigh and Nichols went to
trial, and on his mind was the knowledge that if he served the full
twenty-three-year term, he would be nearly fifty before he breathed
freedom again. How important to cooperate now, to get some of
that time shaved off.

So he told Judge Russell that he had lied, that he had indeed
known for months that this horrible crime was coming, and yet he
had done nothing to stop the tragedy.

Gone now was the bravado; there were no cameras, and Fortier was not picking his nose. He was not holding up a dirty finger. He stood with his head bowed, and he addressed the judge as "sir."

Chapter Sixteen

The Order of Battle

A few days after a fresh-faced Timothy McVeigh appeared on the cover of *Newsweek* magazine that summer, Chief Judge Russell of the federal court in Oklahoma City convened a closed-door hearing inside the El Reno prison. Government prosecutors wanted to know whether McVeigh's new defense attorney should not be punished for allegedly lying to the prison warden. It appeared that Stephen Jones had slipped the *Newsweek* crew—David Hackworth and Peter Annin—into the prison by claiming they actually were members of McVeigh's new legal defense team.

Judge Russell did not sanction Jones, but he asked McVeigh to think hard about whether he really wanted this man to continue as his lead defense attorney. Was Jones honestly acting in his best interests?

"Obviously, you don't want somebody representing you that is not going to give you their all; would you agree with that?" Judge Russell asked.

"Yes," said McVeigh.

"I mean, you're in serious trouble," the judge continued. "I think you understand that."

McVeigh nodded his head.

The judge pressed him. He wanted assurances that McVeigh was satisfied with Jones.

Then McVeigh spoke up. "We are trying to determine, I guess,

whether Mr. Jones would have any—in layman's terms—any reason
to not give me a hundred percent, something that would distract
him from fully focusing on my defense," he said. ". . . That is the
whole crux of the reason that we are here then."

Still Judge Russell was not sure. He asked McVeigh whether he
fully comprehended what he was saying, whether he believed himself to be "mentally competent" to understand that Jones already
might have violated the basic rules of conduct for a lawyer by making false representations to a federal prison warden.

This time, McVeigh did not hesitate in his answer. "I have no
doubt as to my mental competence," he said.

Two years passed before Timothy McVeigh went on trial for the
bombing. It was a time of intense legal wrangling, with bitter fights
over such basic issues as where the trial should be held—whether
across the street from where the Murrah once stood or perhaps not
in the state of Oklahoma at all. Defense lawyers and prosecutors
argued vigorously over who best should hear the case—an Oklahoma judge or someone from outside the state who might be less
affected. They sparred over whether McVeigh and Nichols should
be tried together, or whether the alleged crimes of one defendant
might bring down the other.

Reaching out to the press, Jones tried to erase or at least soften
the image of McVeigh that had become a popular icon: the prisoner
in the orange jumpsuit with the unrepentant stare. Jones was
roundly criticized for his motives, especially since he also displayed
an uncanny and unabashed talent for keeping the media spotlight
focused on himself as well as his notorious client.

Stephen Jones was born in Louisiana and raised in Texas, and
came to Oklahoma to practice law. His clients were big oil and gas
and the insurance industry. He had once worked in Washington as
a young Congressional aide, and also as a personal assistant to
Richard Nixon, during Nixon's wilderness years before the White
House. He is a diehard Republican, and his law office walls are cluttered with photos of him with one dignitary or another. In 1990 he
was the GOP nominee for the United States Senate from Oklahoma; but he was running against Senator David Boren, perhaps the
state's most popular Democrat ever, and he took just 17 percent of

the vote. "If only my son had voted, at least it might have been a tie in my home precinct," he joked.

Jones was in a very unpopular spot, of course, being an Oklahoman himself. But he had been here before. On his fifty-fifth birthday, shortly after taking the McVeigh case, he sat in the death house in the McAlester, Oklahoma, state prison during the last hours in the life of another of his clients, Roger Dale Stafford, the "Steak House Murderer," who had killed a family of three and, later, six people in a south Oklahoma City restaurant. Jones walked out of the prison afterward and found some kind words that balanced the way he felt about his client with the harsh feelings of most of his fellow Oklahomans.

"He was a man with dignity at death," Jones said, "even if the jury found him to be a serial killer."

Stephen Jones was no stranger to lost causes.

He was sitting at his desk in downtown Enid the morning the bomb went off. One of the lawyers in his firm rushed in and told him to turn on his television. He flicked it to Channel 9, and he immediately recognized the chaos. When he was a young man working at a funeral home in Houston, his old elementary school had been firebombed, and he had been with the first ambulance rushing to the scene.

"I recognized it as a bombing right away," he recalled. "And the minute I heard about the day care center I thought, That's it. Because I remembered the babies at Waco. And later that night I heard about old man Snell and I thought, Yes, that's relevant too.

Richard Wayne Snell was executed in Arkansas that very same day—April 19. Also an Oklahoma man, Snell was a white supremacist who had murdered a pawnbroker; he had an active following, and he was notorious for hating the government.

Even on that first evening, Jones was thinking conspiracy theories.

When he heard Coyle and Otto wanted out of McVeigh's defense, Jones wrote a letter to the judge recommending Rob Nigh, a public defender in Oklahoma. He assumed a team of public defenders would get the nod. He then drove an exchange student who had been living in his home down to the Dallas–Fort Worth airport, and when he returned, he found a note taped to his chair at the office. "Call Judge Russell."

They spoke, the lawyer and the judge, and Russell asked him if
he would be willing to take a federal appointment for anyone
arrested in the bombing. Jones had never been named to a federal
case before; all his clients in federal court had been paying customers. They talked for a couple more minutes; he asked when, if
he agreed to serve, he might get some word from the court. Then he
called friends, other lawyers, associates at Phillips University in
Enid. He telephoned Governor Frank Keating's office, because he
had done some legal work for the governor and he wanted to make
sure that his representing someone for such a reprehensible act
would not hurt the governor's standing in the state. Keating told
him it was fine; he added that Jones should be more worried about
his own safety.

Jones called Judge Russell on a Saturday night. "Your honor," he
said, "I've thought about it, and if it's your desire to appoint me, I'll
accept."

"Great," said the judge. "I'll appoint you to represent Timothy
McVeigh. Be in my chambers at one-thirty Monday afternoon."

Jones was there, and after their meeting, according to Jones, the
judge walked up behind him and said one thing more. "I hope I
haven't signed your death warrant."

Added Jones, "That makes two of us."

He drove out to El Reno. Coyle and Otto were there, and they
introduced McVeigh and handed over their client. Then they left,
and the two men, Jones and McVeigh, sat there, alone in the quiet,
looking into each other's eyes.

"I remember he was friendly and polite and eager," Jones said.
"We shook hands."

Jones stood up to leave. "We'll start working in the morning," he
said.

Then off he went to meet with the press.

The day Jones announced his appointment, a clerk in Coyle's
downtown Oklahoma City law office suddenly shrieked when she
heard his name on the radio. "You watch," she warned. "He will
make it all about himself."

But Jones, in his formal announcement, demurred. "I was drafted,"
he said. He read a four-page typewritten statement to the press in
Enid, a copy of which included two pages from a lawyers' guide about
his firm and his own credentials as listed in *Who's Who in America*.

He compared the McVeigh matter with the never-ending cycles of conspiracy theories that grew up around the assassinations in Dallas and Memphis in the 1960s. He urged against a rush to judgment. "There will be no *Ox-Bow Incident* in Oklahoma City," he declared.

Then came his pledge: "I will seek, for my part, to avoid the circus atmosphere that has prevailed in certain other well-known jurisdictional proceedings, which have included the self-promotion and self-aggrandizement of some individuals. I am a small-town county-seat lawyer."

He ended with a curious statement of principle for a man with such a public relations flair: "There is a well-recognized tension between the need for a free press and a fair trial, so I hope the ladies and gentlemen of the press will understand that I will defend this case in the courts of law."

But then, because not enough reporters could get to little Enid that morning, he drove an hour to Oklahoma City and met with CNN at its local studios. Then it was on to dinner with the *Los Angeles Times*. He became, from the start, Mr. Accessibilty.

In Oklahoma City, the government was passing the baton too. Merrick Garland was leaving, heading back to Washington, where Janet Reno wanted him to resume his duties as a senior manager at the Justice Department. In his place, Reno created a trial team that came to be known as the OKBOMB task force. At its head she put a little-known prosecutor named Joseph Hartzler.

Hartzler was then trying cases in central Illinois. Now in his mid-forties, he had a young family and he had left Chicago in the hopes of spending more time watching his boys on the Little League field. Instead he gave up the next two years with his children. He loved his family but was committed to his work. When Hartzler's selection was announced, a criminal defense attorney he knew asked him what he thought about the case.

"Whoever did this should spend some time in hell," Hartzler said. "I just want to accelerate that process."

He was the consummate bureaucrat, a government lawyer representing other government employees killed at their desks in the Murrah building. He was a deeply religious man, a good practicing Lutheran. He parted his dark hair down the side and combed it over; he wore dark suits; he liked to stay home with his children and sing songs around the piano. He donated chunks of his time in

volunteer work to support research into the cause of multiple sclerosis, a muscle-and-nerve disease that strikes young adults in the
prime of their busy lives. He knew this because it had struck him
too, and he was now confined to a wheelchair.

He was so unlike Jones. Hartzler vowed there would be no press
conferences, and there were, in fact, very, very few. When he did
speak, he was direct and quick; by the time reporters had turned to
a new page in their notebooks, he was gone. He always seemed so
busy with the work at hand and uninterested in shenanigans outside the courtroom. But while Hartzler and his team members pri-
vately derided Jones for his coddling of celebrity journalists, they
too had their favorites, most notably Jeffrey Toobin, a writer for *The
New Yorker* and a legal analyst for ABC News. He once had worked
in the U.S. attorney's office in Brooklyn with two of the government lawyers who joined the OKBOMB prosecution; now Toobin
rarely missed an opportunity to champion the prosecution.

Sometimes Hartzler could seem a bit arrogant, and he was
known to alienate some members of his team, such as the federal
prosecutors from Oklahoma City who found themselves relegated
to menial tasks. But no one doubted his dedication.

Hartzler had an intense dislike for McVeigh, and he worked
unendingly—nights and weekends—to assemble what Washington
was calling the most complicated prosecution of its kind. In pretrial
sessions in the judge's chambers, as the lawyers droned on about
arcane legal points, Hartzler and his assistants could sense they
were getting the better of McVeigh. They could tell because sometimes he would stare at them, tightening his hand into a fist, the
veins throbbing visibly.

In the fall of 1995, Jones spoke at the University of Oklahoma. He
talked about the personal impact the case had already had on his
own life. But he also tackled what he believed this case was all
about—the emergence of the dangerous, radical right. This was the
world of Timothy McVeigh, and Jones would try to persuade America, and ultimately the jury, that McVeigh could not have avoided
being influenced by that culture. It was a dangerous position to
take; it could so easily backfire in a country deeply angry over the
deaths in Oklahoma City. The argument went something like this:
blame Tim McVeigh, and you blame all of America.

"There are today a large number of individuals whom people on the two coasts would refer to as the far right, the fringe group, the militia community," Jones said. "At least in the interior of the country, the views of these individuals on subjects as diverse as taxation, the jury system, government regulations, police power, the schools, the family, gun control, corruption, and citizen militia represent not the fringe but increasingly the mainstream."

He spoke to the crowd in the room with the words that McVeigh might have used. "This is not just a dissatisfaction with the government of the day," he said, "but a more deep-seated resentment under the cirumstances and with the immediate backdrop of Ruby Ridge and Waco.

"Waco and Oklahoma City have this in common: they have increased the polarization between impenitent federal officials and disenfranchised social groups such as bankrupt farmers and ranchers and a dislocated working class. One common thread that ties Waco and Oklahoma City together is the shared outrage of the federal government's failure to acknowledge the full extent of their responsibility for Waco. Not until the Waco matter is satisfactorily resolved can a regenerative process begin to repair the damaged trust between millions of disaffected citizens and their government."

This was heady talk—was he saying that the government, through its failures at Waco, had allowed Oklahoma City to happen?

He described the tanks and the smoke and poisonous gas hurled at the Branch Davidians on Mount Carmel. "Little wonder then," he said, "that Tim McVeigh, along with millions of other people, shares the outrage of the blunder at Waco."

But Jones argued that McVeigh was not a monster. "That is not the Tim McVeigh I have come to know," he said. And even though his client had drifted in and out of that world of government haters, that did not automatically make him a killer.

"Tim is not without faults," Jones said. "He is well read, but he lacks formal disciplinary training. Simply because he wrote in for information on a variety of controversial political issues no more makes him a bigot or a neo-Nazi or a racist than the fact that when I was in high school I went to the Soviet embassy in Washington and for three years subscribed to *Soviet Life* magazine makes me a Communist."

Jones challenged his listeners to watch closely as events

unfolded and McVeigh moved closer toward judgment day. "This case has the drama of a great trial," he said. "It is not my intention by these remarks tonight to magnify my office. But it is hardly possible, for the reasons I have stated tonight, to exaggerate the importance of this case and what it means for our country. Someday when you know what I know and what I have learned, and that day will come, you will never again think of the United States of America in the same way."

With that as the heart of the McVeigh defense, Jones set out first in search of a new judge.

As it had turned out, Wayne Alley, a former military courts-martial judge sitting on the federal bench in Oklahoma City, had been chosen by lot to preside over the McVeigh case. He had been away from the courthouse on the morning of the blast, but his courtroom, like much of the courthouse itself, had been damaged. Jones, joining forces with Nichols's lawyer, Michael Tigar, argued that no judge in Oklahoma was untouched by this tragedy and all of them should be recused.

The courthouse was less than a thousand feet from "ground zero," as Jones put it. The building was seriously damaged—walls and doors cracked, windows shattered, bookshelves toppled. The damage ran to more than $2 million. But he and Tigar cited other reasons, more human reasons, why neither Alley nor anyone else in the federal Western District should hear the case.

More than thirty-three of the dead had conducted regular business affairs in the federal courthouse, most prominently the eight federal law enforcement officers. Some of the judges attended as many as seven funerals. Other judges helped in the rescue effort. An employee in the court clerk's office lost her baby in the Murrah day care center. Many other court employees were hurt either in the blast or running from the courthouse.

Fund-raising drives for the victims were set up inside the courthouse itself. T-shirts were sold, flowers were delivered, and lapel ribbons were worn. One T-shirt was simple in design but resonant in its message: it carried a logo of a federal law enforcement badge and next to it the inscription

In Memory
April 19, 1995
Oklahoma City

Judge Alley argued that he could be impartial. He said his court-room and chambers were only slightly damaged, and that only one of his staff members was injured, and then only slightly. He had lost no family or friends, "and I attended no funerals." But Jones and Tigar appealed to the Tenth Circuit in Denver and prevailed, and a new judge, Richard P. Matsch in Denver, was selected.

Matsch was sixty-five years old, with a reputation for being tough. Eight years earlier, he had presided over the trial of white supremacists who had gunned down a Denver radio talk show host. When they were convicted, Matsch sentenced them to 150 years in prison. He gave them that specific number of years because, he said, "unfortunately a life sentence doesn't mean a life sentence under the existing law."

"This is a society of ordered liberty, a free people under the order of the Constitution and the laws which implement it," the judge said. "It is not a society of one race or one creed.

"And the very core of the Constitution of the United States is the concept of the preservation of human dignity, the sanguinity of every life . . ."

And to make sure the world understood Judge Richard P. Matsch, he added: ". . . and it is also the right to continued existence."

He ran his courtoom on time, on track, and on his terms. He was a son of Iowa with a streak of Prussian authority in him. He once jumped on Hartzler during a pretrial hearing. Jones was arguing that the prosecutors were not turning over enough of their evidence, so Matsch ordered Hartzler to get on with it. But then Hartzler complained about "Mr. Jones's definition" of proper disclosure under the law.

The judge had heard enough. "What I think is the law is going to be the law for now," he snapped.

Another time Matsch took on Jeralyn E. Merritt, one of McVeigh's assistant defense attorneys, when she asked for more time to prepare for a witness.

"Well," the judge said. He often started his sentences with "Well" when he was annoyed. It was kind of a squeaky, impatient "Well." And if that didn't move things along, he would start playing with the pencils on his benchtop.

"Well," the judge asked, "why can't you get ready for her?"

"Because I don't have her material here," the lawyer said.

The judge whirled from his chair and pounded toward the door, calling for the noon recess. Left hanging in the air was his final bark at the defense lawyer: *"You get ready for her!"*

Controversy seemed to be Matsch's natural element. He infuriated the media with his orders sealing much of the case file before McVeigh's trial, and he also angered many of the victims by ruling that those who planned to testify at the trial should not be allowed to watch the proceedings. But he granted the first-ever closed-circuit television feed in federal court, which allowed victims in Oklahoma City to watch the case unfold in a theater setting at the Will Rogers Airport.

Stephen Jones had a new judge; now he wanted the trial moved out of Oklahoma. Working again with Michael Tigar, Jones showed not only that there had been an inordinate amount of press coverage in Oklahoma, but that the people there—from which the jury would be chosen—harbored deep resentment against the defendants.

Patrick Ryan, the new Clinton-appointed U.S. attorney in Oklahoma City, said moving the trial would be too much of a hardship for the victims and the families of the dead. They wanted to watch this trial; they had to see and hear and feel justice from a front-row seat. No newspaper story, no television report, would do it for them.

Ryan urged Matsch to keep the trial in the state; to move it to Tulsa if he had to, but let Oklahomans dispense justice. In his closing argument on the defense motion for a change of venue, he spoke eloquently, even tearfully—don't make these people victims again, he said.

Matsch moved the proceedings to Denver anyway.

In Denver, the defense team scored again when they persuaded the judge to order separate trials for McVeigh and Nichols. Here the sticking point was the nine hours of interviews Nichols had given the FBI. He had implicated McVeigh, and the government wanted to use Nichols's words at a joint trial, not only against him but against McVeigh too.

Tigar, a tall, scholarly lawyer with a booming voice and a pleasing Texas courtliness about him, argued that Nichols's statements had been coerced. He claimed the FBI had never fully apprised Nichols of his rights and that the agents wrenched those nine hours out of him while holding him against his will in the basement of the police station. Tigar said the nine hours should be thrown out.

Jones saw it a bit differently—just don't use it against my man, he said. His argument was that it was unfair, in any setting, joint or separate trials, for a jury to hear Nichols's words from the police station without McVeigh's defense team being given the opportunity to put Nichols on the witness stand. But that would be unfair to Nichols, because if he took the stand, in any kind of proceeding, wasn't he opening himself up to questions from the prosecution too?

The question was clearly a muddle; Matsch could see that. So he split the case in half and ordered separate trials, ruling that the Nichols statements could not be used against McVeigh in any fashion. He also set a trial date of March 31, 1997, with McVeigh up first.

By the end of 1996, with a new judge, a new trial location, and separate trials, Jones seemed to have the hot hand. He was also beginning to make some headway not only in remaking his client's image, but in raising the specter of other deeper and more diabolical conspiracies that he would contend were behind the Oklahoma City bombing. He was becoming a household name, for he had been on all of the network talk shows, repeatedly, and in all the newspapers. He had been to dinner with Barbara Walters at a black-tie affair with the president in Washington. He had had Diane Sawyer out to his house.

On December 22, three months before the trial was to start, he placed a large ad in his local Sunday paper, the *Enid News & Eagle*. The ad showed him marching into court in Denver, looking very determined, aware of his place in history. Below the photo he wrote a farewell message headed "To the people of Enid and Northwest Oklahoma."

"It has been a year and a half since I was appointed by the United States District Court to represent Timothy McVeigh, charged with the greatest act of revolutionary terror and murder in American history; 168 dead, including one of Enid's own sons, 500 injured, and a billion dollars worth of property damage. The bombing of the Alfred P. Murrah building altered forever the physical, intellectual and emotional structure of Oklahoma City and the state of Oklahoma."

He said that before departing for Denver, he wished to speak personally "to you, my fellow townspeople."

"No one, not in my situation, can appreciate my feeling of sadness at this parting, which I hope may only be temporary. To this place, Enid, and to the kindness of these people, I owe everything. Here I have lived more than a quarter of a century, and have passed from a young man to one whose life journey is more than half over. Here my children have been born, and my father is buried.

"I now leave, not knowing when or whether ever I may return, with a task before me greater than that which has ever rested upon any lawyer entrusted with the defense of someone where the decision on his liberty and life depends upon twelve strangers sworn to find a fair verdict. Without the assistance of that Divine Being whoever attends any of us, those charged with responsibility in the matter of *United States of America vs. Timothy James McVeigh*, whether the prosecution or the defense, cannot succeed. With that assistance, we cannot fail and the truth will emerge. At this time of year I ask for your prayers, not only for those of us associated in any way with this case; the law enforcement personnel, prosecution, the Court, the witnesses, but also the defense, and most importantly, the survivors and the family of those who perished.

"Trusting in Him who can go with me, and yet remain with you, and be everywhere for good, let us confidently hope that the truth of this tragedy will emerge and that justice will be served. To His care commending you, as I hope in your prayers you will commend me, I bid you an affectionate farewell with a grateful heart for your many acts of personal friendship, affection and esteem."

But Stephen Jones could not fool all the people; his farewell address was immediately recognized because he had taken many of the phrases from the greatest political leader of his own Republican Party, a man who had uttered those sentiments a century earlier when he left his home on the prairie to move to the capital at Washington.

Ironically, that man's picture was on Timothy McVeigh's T-shirt the day of the explosion at the Alfred P. Murrah Federal Building. His name is Abraham Lincoln.

Chapter Seventeen

Meet John Doe No. 2

Jones moved to Denver and began to prepare for trial, and he brought with him the best friend Timothy McVeigh never had. Nameless but not faceless, the man had appeared on thousands of wanted pictures—the baseball cap, the eyes that didn't move, the lips that didn't open, the jaw at perfect right angles. For the defense, he was their ideal poster boy.

The FBI knew nothing about the man, except that they wanted to find him, even if that meant proving that he never existed at all.

He was called, simply, John Doe No. 2. His description was spare—a white male, late twenties to early thirties, 175–180 pounds, medium build, five-nine to five-ten, with dark hair combed straight back and a snakelike tattoo on his left arm. "CAUTION," the poster said. "Subject is considered armed and extremely dangerous."

John Doe No. 2 either got away with the biggest crime in U.S. history or is a man who never lived. Fact or figment, he complicated the government's attempts to pin the responsibility for Oklahoma City on one key individual, McVeigh, and also on his old friend Nichols.

But if there ever was such a man, then some puzzling questions come to mind, such as why McVeigh never gave him up to help himself. And why didn't Nichols, so quick to turn on McVeigh that day of his surrender in Herington, mention this other figure? Wouldn't that have deflected some of the blame that was being heaped on Nichols himself?

Discounting the crank or "hysterical" sightings, only three people ever saw John Doe No. 2. Eldon Elliott, Vicki Beemer, and Tom Kessinger, the three Ryder employees, would recall only minor details about the man, and their recollections were as shadowy as his face. They remembered that he neither spoke nor acted; he simply waited in the office lobby as the truck was picked up.

"They just came straight to the counter," is how Beemer would remember seeing two men. "They were both in the office. I really don't recall what the other guy—he was in there, but I don't really recall where he was standing exactly."

The FBI was able to show that McVeigh had ridden alone in a taxi that afternoon from the Dreamland Motel to a McDonald's restaurant near the Ryder agency. And at the McDonald's, McVeigh was caught on camera—again alone. From there, the FBI assumed, he walked along the frontage road to the Ryder shop. Why would he need anyone with him at all?

On the night following the bombing, the bureau sent Agent Raymond Rozycki to the Ryder shop to interview the employees and draw composite sketches of both men. The next morning, in downtown Oklahoma City, Weldon Kennedy of the FBI was holding up Rozycki's drawings, urging anyone with information to contact authorities immediately.

The race was on.

In Georgia, Scott Sweely was stopped by a local sheriff and ordered to crawl out his car window. Once outside, he was made to lie facedown on the asphalt. He had been spotted at a gas station by someone who thought Sweely resembled Doe 2. The sheriff had noticed the Oklahoma plates on the back of Sweely's red BMW. He handcuffed his prisoner and brought him to the police house, where he was interviewed by federal agents for four hours. He was from Oklahoma, sure enough; he was from Del City, actually, a suburb of Oklahoma City next to Tinker Air Force Base. But he finally was let go when authorities became convinced that he was telling the truth—that he was merely a thirty-two-year-old who had just left the air force and was on his way to Florida.

Sweely was one of the first. In Minnesota, a Doe 2 look-alike was stopped at gunpoint near the giant Mall of America. In California, a man AWOL from the army was rousted out of his home and transferred to Los Angeles, where crowds yelled for the coward's head.

For a while, investigators theorized that Doe 2 was actually Josh Nichols, Terry's boy, who, large for his age, was certainly around central Kansas during his visit with his father in Herington. They questioned him, and once he joked about being the famous mystery man. He was just a kid, after all, and kids believe in myths.

In Oklahoma, finding Doe 2 became the new sport, or obsession. Mike Moroz, a downtown Oklahoma City garage mechanic, would swear not only that he saw McVeigh pull into his station shortly before the bombing, but that McVeigh had also asked directions from the window of his Ryder truck. The driver wanted to know how to get to 5th and Harvey streets, the Murrah site. Moroz also remembered another man—someone he would say he did not get that good a look at, but nonetheless would describe as close to Doe 2, with short brown hair and a build larger than McVeigh's.

In Spiro, Oklahoma, agents concentrated on Roger Barnett, an army buddy who had soldiered at Fort Benning with all three of them—McVeigh, Nichols, and Fortier. Barnett was stocky, and he wore a skull-and-crossbones tattoo on his left forearm. He also lived not too far from the Arkansas state line, and Roger Moore's horse farm. The FBI sat him on a polygraph box and later cleared him, after time cards showed he was at work at a Fort Smith, Arkansas, paper company the week of the bombing.

A second friend from the army, Ray Jimboy, was also questioned at length. The FBI knew about him early on; agents had even asked Nichols about Jimboy when they had their little discussion at the Herington station. Jimboy was working as a fry cook in Okemah, Oklahoma, east of Oklahoma City, and he too bore some likeness to the poster sketch. He had the square jaw and the dark hair. But he parted his hair down the side, and it flopped over his left eye. And there were no tattoos. He too was hooked up to a lie detector, and he too was cleared.

The calls to the FBI poured in, hundreds in the first week alone, thousands in the weeks ahead. A second and a third sketch were released, showing him in profile and wearing a baseball cap with lightning streaks on the side. The phone calls increased; so did a reward, finally topping out at $2 million. The FBI listened patiently, and took many of the calls seriously. But not all of them, not the ones from women anxious to be rid of ex-husbands or ex-boyfriends, a father-in-law too maybe. One man called and said that when he saw that baseball cap, the picture fit perfectly. Who is it? the FBI asked. "My wife," the man said.

There were two strong possibilities in the Kingman area, where agents by now were digging through Fortier's past. One was Jeffrey A. Martin, who ran a tattoo parlor in a building that housed a security company where McVeigh had briefly worked. Martin generally fit the description, so like the others he was interviewed and fingerprinted, and he too was released, once he convinced agents that he had never met McVeigh.

The second was not so lucky. Steven Colbern, with addresses in California, Arizona, and Nevada, was traced to the desert outside Kingman. He was wanted for possession of a number of unregistered firearms, including an SKS assault rifle. He was arrested but then skipped bond in an attempt to avoid trial, and was being sought as a fugitive. He was a gun nut, like McVeigh, and, according to U.S. marshals, he also was trained in survival skills and was a biochemist by trade.

Moreover, when agents searched his light brown Chevy pickup in Bullhead City, Arizona, they found a plastic bag containing ammonium nitrate. He also had used aliases and had rented a storage locker there, all of which sounded familiar. The FBI recovered a letter Colbern had written to his parents in Oxnard, California, in which he vowed that he "would not go to jail and would fight when the time came." That too had the ring of a McVeigh follower.

Colbern wore his hair longer than Doe 2, and he sported a mustache. He had a scar on his right wrist, but alas no tattoo. When he was found on May 12, he was arrested—not for the Oklahoma City bombing, but on the outstanding firearms warrant. The FBI snuck up on him sitting on a bench in Oatman, Arizona, where burros are allowed to mosey up and down the main drag to give it "that Old West feel." Like a desperado, Colbern did not go gently; he tried to pull a loaded .38-caliber revolver but was wrestled to the ground by three federal marshals. He kicked one of the marshals in the jaw, and they finally had to double-handcuff his wrists behind his back. He was returned to California for trial, with some residents in Kingman and Oatman swearing that if he wasn't Doe 2, he darn sure seemed a lot like McVeigh.

The low point in this comedy of errors took place in a little strip motel in a tiny Missouri town called Carthage. The town sits on

the edge of the Ozarks in southwestern Missouri, not far from the
borders of Oklahoma and Arkansas. This time the agents really
thought they had their man. Or men.

Gary Alan Land and Robert Jacks were the objects of an FBI all-
points bulletin. They were a Mutt and Jeff of the highway, a Laurel
and Hardy roadshow. They were drifters like McVeigh, and they also
had the unhappy talent of being in the wrong place far too often.

A driver's-license photo of the thirty-five-year-old Land showed
he bore a close resemblance to the most wanted man in America.
He also had come from Arizona. In fact, Land and his touring companion, the sixty-year-old Jacks, were driving east across country in
a white and roomy 1981 Ford Thunderbird. The car had new tires
and was relatively rust-free, though it had some 160,000 miles on
the odometer. Police officers across the nation were instructed to
find this tourmobile and stop its occupants.

Land and Jacks would stay in cheap motels like McVeigh, and
smoke all night; Land preferred Marlboros, Jacks was content with
generic cigarettes. They loved their cold beer—any kind, as long as
it came by the case. And they never knew for a moment that they
were wanted for anything. That was because each evening, relaxing
in the motel room they always shared, they passed up watching the
news in favor of reruns of *Kojak* and *Streets of San Francisco*.

They had originally paired up six years ago in San Francisco.
They took to the road, sometimes sleeping at rest stops to conserve
the money they received from government disability checks. Jacks
had never recovered from an injury to the tendons in his left hand,
the result of a bar fight. Land said alcoholism was why he could not
work.

That did not mean that Land could outdrink Jacks. "I'm a
drunk," Jacks once boasted to a crowd of reporters. "I just pick up
. . . I just pick up work or . . . or anything I want as I go, you know."

"I'm sorry, you said what?" asked one reporter.

"You said what?" asked another.

"You said you're a drunk?" asked a third reporter.

"I'm a drunk, yeah," Jacks said. "I drink off . . . off . . . off . . .
and on."

For a while they lived at the El Trovatore lodge in Kingman at
the same time that McVeigh was staying across the street in
another cheap motel. The week of the bombing, they overnighted

at Deward and Pauline's Motel in Vinita, Oklahoma, and on the very night of the bombing, they happened to be staying at the Dan D Motel in Perry—the same town where McVeigh was spending his first night in jail.

The T-bird at last was spotted by a local cop on the night of May 1 at the Kel Lake Motel in Carthage. The FBI was alerted, and soon another strike force was being assembled. The cop's wife, who lived near the motel, stayed up most the night to fix the agents pancakes as they prepared to raid Land and Jacks's room at dawn. She was already bragging that her husband was a hero for finding Doe 2, the most dangerous man ever loose in America.

At first light, the FBI quietly roused the other guests and evacuated the motel. Then a dozen agents in riot gear and brandishing shotguns and automatic weapons took their positions out front. They telephoned Land and Jacks's room and startled them awake, ordering them to get out of bed, throw on some clothes, and walk slowly backward out the door, with their hands held high over their heads. So Gary Land and Robert Jacks did just that—they walked backward into history. They were promptly arrested and spent the next eighteen hours being questioned by the FBI. The T-bird was examined too, but only after the FBI used a remotely controlled robot to open the doors.

There was no bomb in the car, and Land and Jacks had no bombshells to tell the FBI. They just wanted back out on the road. But when they were released, there was one quick detour—their debut on national television, ABC's *Nightline* program. Quite a treat for a pair of drifters who never watched the news.

"They treated you all right, didn't they?" asked anchor Ted Koppel. He meant the FBI.

"Well," said Jacks, "as long as I didn't get shot coming out of that motel. If I'd have stumbled or they'd have had some . . . some trigger . . . some trigger-happy rookie . . . I'm . . . I'm . . . I'm dead, you know."

What about Land? He was the one who was supposed to be Doe 2.

"Yeah," the younger man said. "I didn't think I looked anything like him. I wasn't, you know, I wasn't worried about getting, you know, blamed for this stuff. But I don't know. It sure took that turn. Because he was arrested in Perry and we were there that night, and . . ."

The absurdity of it all stayed behind to mock the government. By midsummer the FBI had begun to realize that their witnesses at the Ryder shop may have been mistaken. Now what they had to do was make him go away—make Doe 2 dissolve from the nation's consciousness.

The FBI investigators had to come up with another story. They had to prove the Ryder people were wrong. So they went to Fort Riley and they found Private Todd Bunting.

He too had the lantern jaw and the deep-set eyes; he had a Carolina Panthers cap with lightning strikes down the sides. On his upper left arm, just under the short-sleeve line, right where Kessinger had said it would be, was a tattoo. He had been to the Ryder agency on Tuesday, April 18, the day after McVeigh, and he had gone there with another man—his sergeant.

But before the FBI could formally unveil the man they now thought was the true Doe 2, the story leaked and the press converged on Fort Riley. But he was not there; he was in Timmonsville, South Carolina, attending the funeral of his wife's mother, who had been killed that week in an auto accident. The press, determined to clear up the Doe 2 question, highballed it to Timmonsville. Bunting, attending his mother-in-law's wake, was besieged by reporters, including some television cameramen who barged their way into the funeral home.

He eventually returned to Fort Riley and took his place before the hot lights. He said he had simply gone to the Ryder shop with Sergeant Michael Hertig to get a truck and pack up his belongings to transfer to Fort Benning. He told how the FBI had questioned him thoroughly, and he described the chill up his spine at the thought of his brush with the Oklahoma City tragedy.

Bunting was a good sport. Around the barracks, other soldiers had kidded him that he looked a lot like that Doe 2 figure with the $2 million price tag on his head. "The hat looked like my Carolina Panthers hat, and we kind of joked about that," Bunting recalled. "And I said, 'Well, shoot, if that was me, I'd turn myself in.' "

That should have ended the debate over Doe 2, but it did not. Almost two years passed before the FBI officially closed its investigation into that second individual and took down the wanted posters. Still he lingered; soon he had his own Web site on the Internet, the "John Doe Times," posted there by an Alabama militia-

man. It was basically a bulletin board for antigovernment types to
continue their criticism of the FBI investigation, insisting that others, rather than McVeigh and Nichols, were the true bombers. The
Spotlight newsletter, as late as the fall of 1996, was carrying ban-
ner-headline stories that said the feds had employed "dupes" to
bomb the Murrah building. They reported that Doe 2 was alive and
well, living on an Indian reservation in, of all places, upstate New
York. He had to remain in hiding, though, because he actually was
a government provocateur—a double agent, if you will.

Of course, Stephen Jones continued to breathe life into Doe 2. As
long as the second man lived, so did Jones's client, and the lawyer
was quick to spin out conspiracy yarns. For a while, Doe 2 was a
German neo-Nazi named Andreas Strassmeir, who admitted that
he had lived in Oklahoma and, in an affidavit, said that he had once
met McVeigh at a Tulsa gun show. The next Doe 2 was Michael
Brescia, a near ringer for the man in the FBI sketch, who had stayed
with Strassmeir at a radical religious compound called Elohim City
in far-eastern Oklahoma, and who later was indicted along with a
larger group in a string of bank robberies in the Midwest. Brescia
ultimately pleaded guilty to robbery and conspiracy, but denied, as
did Strassmeir, any involvement in Oklahoma City.

Nor was Jones alone in pursuing the ghost. J. D. Cash, a chain-
smoking sleuth from eastern Oklahoma, crisscrossed the Midwest
in search of the real bombers, never believing that McVeigh had
acted alone, if at all. Cash joined forces with Glenn Wilburn, the
grandfather of two boys killed in the Murrah day care center. Cash
began writing articles for a small newspaper in Idadel, Oklahoma,
near Elohim City. His stories and Wilburn's relentlessness kept the
Doe 2 myth alive.

The best Cash and Wilburn came up with was a bizarre episode
at a Tulsa topless club called Lady Godiva's. On the night of April
8, eleven days before the bombing, two strippers erupted into a
shouting fit in the dressing room. The scene was caught on a security camera. One of the strippers was heard boasting about a male
customer who said someday he was going to be famous.

"I'm a very smart man," she claimed the man had told her.
". . . And you're going to remember me on April 19, '95. You're
going to remember me for the rest of your life."

But the tape's sound quality was poor. Was it truly "April 19,

'95," or just "April 1995"? And why would someone put the year on a date that was just eleven days away? Why not just say "April 19"? Why not just "next week"?

The dancer would contend that the man was McVeigh, and that two men with him that night were Brescia and Strassmeir. But if that is true, McVeigh did a lot more driving than even the FBI knew about, because on March 31 he had checked into the Imperial Motel in Kingman and on April 7, the day before he was supposed to be making boasts inside Lady Godiva's in Tulsa, he paid for another five days. A maid in Arizona would say she saw him there every day, and that his car, that old blue Pontiac station wagon he later swapped for the yellow Mercury, never left the lot.

The story had the stuff that sells—intrigue, sex, and McVeigh. But it was just one story that Jones was pushing in the media; another involved a former Tulsa debutante who, using the alias Freya, became an ATF undercover informant and infiltrated Elohim City.

Carol Howe was working inside the compound before the bombing, and government agents decided to keep her there after the blast, even though they were deeply concerned about her state of mind, particularly when she grew suicidal and slit her face, neck, arms, and hands with a knife.

Along with hating the government and answering to the word of their cult leader, the Reverend Robert Millar, the group at Elohim City also stockpiled weapons. And Howe found out that they brazenly discussed blowing up a federal building.

She agreed to sneak into Elohim City because she believed in her country. "I don't like America as she is today," she wrote in a letter to her parents in August 1994, explaining her decision to help the ATF. "But I don't think she is past saving. And if there's something I can do to help this country realize a glimmer of her potential greatness, then I must do it.

"These people intend to start a war here within the next few years," she added. "They have the power, means and support to do it. This war would especially devastate America."

Inside the compound, she met Strassmeir and Brescia, and Millar too. She learned about *The Turner Diaries*—"the bible of the organization," she said. She watched as the men dressed up in night camouflage and practiced paramilitary exercises. Their "plans," she told the ATF, "are to forcibly act to destroy the U.S. government with direct actions and operations such as assassinations, bomb-ings, and mass shootings." They believe "the biggest enemy to be the United States government," she said.

She told her ATF handlers that Millar, who repeatedly disavowed any connection to the Murrah building blast, was spoiling for a new revolution, and his antigovernment rhetoric was ratcheting up in the months before Oklahoma City.

According to an ATF investigation report in January 1995, "Dur-ing a Sabbath meeting, Millar gave a sermon soliciting violence against the U.S. government. He brought forth his soldiers and instructed them to take whatever action necessary against the U.S. governement. It is understood that ATF is the main enemy of the people at EC [Elohim City]. He further stated that they would be gaining territory and expanding throughout the midwest. He stated that certain groups from Texas, Missouri, Arkansas and Oklahoma would be uniting as one front to fight the government.

"He told 183 [Howe's informant ID number] that EC considers itself a separate nation of Israelites which happens to be located in the continental United States. He especially told 183 that they were preparing to fight a war against the government. He also stated that they had been close friends of the Weavers [in Ruby Ridge] and that they agreed with what they did. He stated that they were friends with some of the Branch Davidians in Waco, Tex., and that the Branch Davidians have set up another community in Colorado."

In a separate ATF report dated February 1995, two months before the bombing, Howe reported that she and "several individuals from Elohim City," including Millar, traveled to Oklahoma City to inquire about setting up contacts with a church there. The purpose, she told the ATF, was "to create a more powerful adversary oppos-ing the U.S. government."

Howe was deactivated as an informant after her near suicide. Then, the day after the bombing, she notified the ATF that the Doe 2 picture resembled one of the Elohim City residents. So again they slipped her in under the Elohim City gate, and she reported that there was talk about the bombing, mostly about their own ali-bis for where they were on April 19. But after McVeigh's arrest, she no longer was of much use to the government. She later waffled about whether she ever saw McVeigh in the compound, or even heard his name.

But Jones would not let go of the Elohim City story; to him, this seemed the most likely base for the real perpetrators. He suggested that at most, McVeigh might have been a "patsy" for those in Elohim City who hated the government.

The religious compound also had connections to another conspiracy theory, and this one seemed the most intriguing of all. It involved Richard Wayne Snell, the white supremacist who had killed the Texas pawnbroker.

A dozen years before the Oklahoma City bombing, a group of white separatists devised a plan to blow up the Murrah building, according to government evidence collected at that time. In 1983, Snell was encouraging others to destroy the Murrah and actually had talked one of his followers into casing the federal building. But the plans never took hold, and Snell suddenly had far greater concerns.

In 1984 he was stopped for a traffic violation by a black state trooper near De Queen, Arkansas. Snell shot and wounded the trooper, then shot him to death as he lay on the ground. He was chased across the state line to Broken Bow, Oklahoma—authorities theorized he might have been trying to make it to Elohim City—and he was arrested after a gunfight that left him wounded. Inside his car, police found the gun that had been used a year earlier in the slaying and robbery of that Texarkana pawnbroker. He was convicted in both murders; for the death of the pawnbroker, he was sentenced to die.

From his prison cell, "old man Snell," as Jones liked to call him, raged on. He published his own newsletter, *The Seekers*, which swore that a "war to establish righteousness" was coming. In that war, the sixty-four-year-old Snell considered himself the first POW. His execution date was set for April 19, 1995.

That spring, in March 1995, the Militia of Montana took up his cause. In their publication, *Taking Aim*, they warned their readers of that date—April 19. This is what they said:

"April 19, 1775—Lexington burned.

"April 19, 1943—Warsaw burned.

"April 19, 1992—The feds attempted to raid Randy Weaver, but had their plans thwarted when concerned citizens arrived on the scene with supplies for the Weaver family, totally unaware of what was to take place.

"April 19, 1993—The Branch Davidians burned.

"April 19, 1995—Richard Snell will be executed, unless we act now!!!"

The newsletter did not suggest violence; there was no call to blow up a federal building; Oklahoma City was not mentioned. Snell's wife, Mary, in a note published by the militia newsletter, suggested that readers should act by writing the Arkansas governor's office and pleading for her husband's life.

When April 19, 1995, arrived, Snell waited out the clock with his friend from Elohim City, the Reverend Robert Millar. The preacher later said that the two of them watched television reports that morning of the bombing of the Murrah building. Then Snell was led away to meet his own doom. "Look over your shoulder," he warned as prison officials strapped him to a gurney and prepared the lethal injection. "Justice is coming."

Millar brought Snell's body back to Elohim City, but that did not bury the conspiracy theories. Jones postulated that others may have blown up the Murrah building as a present for Snell. McVeigh's lawyer could be like that, seizing on any morsel of conspiracy to deflect blame from his client. When an extra leg was found inside the Murrah rubble, he argued that it was all that was left of the real bomber; it turned out it belonged to a black female who had been visiting the federal building that morning. When Hoppy Heidelberg, a federal grand juror and horse farmer south of Oklahoma City, complained that prosecutors were rushing the case with no grand jury testimony about other potential suspects, Jones sought to have the indictment thrown out; he failed.

Jones's finger-pointing at other possible bombers did have some effect. Many among the public were beginning to doubt the government's claim that only these two men had had any criminal role in the bombing. The indictment had read that McVeigh and Nichols had conspired "with others unknown." Who were those others? Where were they?

The hullabaloo continued. Even as McVeigh was going to trial, a new investigative grand jury was gearing up in Oklahoma City to answer two fundamental questions: Has the government fully investigated this crime? And had the government known that the building was going to be hit?

These were troubling questions, and with just weeks to go before trial, Jones had hit a crest. That ugly memory of McVeigh walking out of the Perry jail had been blurred by new pictures and a video showing him relaxed, smiling, eager to go to trial. "I'm trying to show him as he really is," said Jones. "He's a home-grown American boy."

All that hard work by the defense was blown apart a month before the trial when the *Dallas Morning News* published a story alleging that McVeigh had confessed to his defense team. The paper excerpted what it said were defense memos in which McVeigh tells a member of his team that bombing the federal building during normal working hours would ensure a high "body count" and that that would send a strong message to the government. The thunder from that story rocked Jones's case, and he immediately sought a delay in the trial. He was turned down. He also tried to explain it away, saying first that there was no confession, later that it was simply internal paperwork and not a confession at all, and finally that the reporter, Pete Slover, had stolen the documents.

Slover later filed an affidavit in court all but admitting that he did not even know if his story was true or not. "Although the *News* and I believe the documents are authentic," he said, "I have no personal knowledge of the preparation of the documents or the matters recorded in the documents."

But the damage had been done. Jones held a series of hurried press conferences, including one outside the courthouse in a raging snowstorm, hoping to bat down the alleged confession, obviously worried that the jury pool about to be summoned to Judge Matsch's courtroom could now never give his client a fair trial.

Then came a second salvo, this one from Ben Fenwick, a Reuter's reporter in Oklahoma City who claimed to have his own set of "confessions." Fenwick's document appeared to be an internal summary of the case that had been put together by the McVeigh defense team. Fenwick had obtained the document a year earlier, but had held on to it in the hope of turning it into a book about the criminal case. When that failed, and after he saw the ruckus over the first confession story, Fenwick sold his material to *Playboy* magazine. He also was hired by ABC News as a consultant, an arrangement that allowed the network to quote extensively from Fenwick's document for a special on the eve of the McVeigh trial.

Fenwick also would later acknowledge that he did not authenticate his material. His document stated that McVeigh ran from the Ryder truck that morning and that the explosion knocked him against a wall. He then met a deliveryman who looked at him and said, "Man, for a second I thought that was us that blew up." McVeigh responded, "Yeah, so did I." It made for high drama, but Fenwick never checked to see if such a delivery man ever existed. Other reporters tried to find him, but they came up empty.

However, another anecdote from Fenwick's story did bear fruit— for the government. That is how the FBI learned about Timothy Chambers and VP Racing Fuels, and how McVeigh dressed up like a Harley biker and visited the Chief Auto Parts races in Ennis, Texas, to buy the fuel.

Whatever the mix of fact and fiction, the confession stories were a double blow to Jones. Matsch denied Jones's request for a delay in the trial. Jury selection began as ordered on March 31, and a panel was chosen in just over three weeks. The tension was thick, particularly on the last day of jury selection, when the lawyers were making their final picks and reading out numbers like A5 and B17 in place of using the names of jurors.

Wasn't that a bingo? chief prosecutor Hartzler joked to the judge.

Matsch was clearly not amused. "It's a lot more serious than a bingo game," he snapped.

Chapter Eighteen

Trial

Each morning Timothy McVeigh was escorted into the second-floor courtroom by grim-faced guards in suits and ties and wearing tiny earphones to follow the security arrangements that had turned the federal district courthouse in downtown Denver into a modern-day fortress. He always seemed cheerful. A smile lit his face as he shook hands with members of his defense team, and then he would settle into a chair next to Jones.

He was the last one brought into the courtroom before the judge and the jury, and when Matsch called each day's proceedings to order, McVeigh's smile suddenly vanished. Then he would lean back in his chair or prop an elbow on the defense table. He would stretch his long index finger sideways across his lips, and hold that pose for hours.

In the nine weeks of the capital murder trial, from jury selection to final verdict, McVeigh rarely revealed a hint of emotion. His face was blank, his big blue eyes unfixed. Victims of the bombing came away from the courtroom frustrated, unable to find any answers as they searched his face.

The first phase of the trial began on April 24, 1997, the day after McVeigh turned twenty-nine years old. Early that morning, a light midspring snow fell on Denver.

The courtroom was packed; every day it would be jammed full. Prosecutors and defense lawyers crowded around their respective tables, making room for assistants and investigators and support staff. In the half-dozen rows behind them—often squished together—sat the nation's press, and behind them victims and members of the general public. Each dawn, lines would form outside Courtroom C-204 of people wanting one of the few precious unassigned seats.

Outside, roads were blocked off, sidewalks too. Special credentials were required to walk in certain areas around the courthouse. Because the building is adjacent to the Denver federal office building, a high-rise taller than the old Murrah, that meant a lot of pedestrian traffic, which in turn necessitated guards in uniforms, police cars, police on horses, and police with dogs. The area at 20th and Stout streets became perhaps the safest corner in America. Even the manhole covers were sealed shut, and any motorist slowing on Stout Street to crane his neck toward the spectacle out front was hurried along.

Occasionally a protester would appear, angry over taxes or warning of God's wrath; for a while a tall man in a beard and an Abraham Lincoln costume marched in front of the building. When one group held a rally against the death penalty, they drew a small crowd mostly made up of reporters—but then it was press coverage they wanted anyway. When a deliveryman double-parked across the street and rushed inside to drop off a package, his truck was suddenly surrounded by armed SWAT men. The man was admonished and sent on his way.

The judge and the lawyers had gone through a hundred prospective jurors before deciding on their twelve. For most of April, these prospective jurors were asked what they knew of McVeigh, what they thought about the government and Waco, and—perhaps most important of all—whether they could set aside any personal morality and sentence McVeigh to death if first they voted for conviction.

Some were disqualified because they believed McVeigh already guilty. Some had made their own personal pilgrimages to Oklahoma City to visit the Murrah site, now surrounded by a chain-link fence covered with flowers and other mementoes.

The jurors selected—Coloradans all—were a fair cross section of America. A navy veteran of the Vietnam War. An elderly housewife. A marketing manager. A middle-aged man a little hard of hearing after attending too many Grateful Dead concerts.

Their foreman was James Osgood, the marketing manager, who was the son of a career air force serviceman. Each day Osgood wore a tie, and usually a suit or sports coat too. He sat in the middle of the jury box, the center aisle, and had perhaps the best view of McVeigh across the room. When victims testified, telling stories of lost loved ones, their words followed by tears, the jury foreman would stare directly at the defendant.

The snow was still lightly falling that first morning when the jury was sworn in and the lawyers introduced themselves. Jones also introduced his client.

"Good morning," McVeigh said.

He would not speak to them again.

Matsch read from the federal indictment, the three counts of conspiracy and the eight charges of murder for the deaths of the federal law enforcement officers. He reminded the jury that McVeigh had pleaded not guilty, and that the government must prove beyond a reasonable doubt that McVeigh planned and carried out the bombing of the Alfred P. Murrah Federal Building.

"We start the trial, as we are today, with no evidence against Timothy McVeigh," the judge said. "The presumption of innocence applies."

Hartzler was the next to speak. Sometimes during the trial he would come to court in a relaxed mood, talking about the latest Chicago baseball score or greeting the victims and their families with a smile and a thumbs-up.

"Ladies and gentlemen of the jury," he began. The chief prosecutor had wheeled his chair around to face the jury box, and they could see him perfectly. He wore his customary dark suit, his hair combed to the side, his voice not loud nor emotional, but clipped and forceful.

"April 19, 1995, was a beautiful day in Oklahoma City. At least it started out as a beautiful day. The sun was shining. Flowers were blooming. It was springtime in Oklahoma City. Sometime after six o'clock in the morning, Tevin Garrett's mother woke him up to get him ready for the day. He was only sixteen months old. He was a toddler, and as some of you know . . ."

In his opening statement Hartzler served notice that this case would not be solely about McVeigh but would encompass victims too. He told them of Tevin Garrett and his mother, Helena, about their drive to the Murrah day care center, and then Tevin's small hands against the window, waving goodbye.

"Across the street, the Ryder truck was there to resolve a grievance," Hartzler said. "The truck was there to impose the will of Timothy McVeigh on the rest of America and to do so by premeditated violence and terror, by murdering innocent men, women, and children, in hopes of seeing blood flow in the streets of America.

"At 9:02 that morning, a catastrophic explosion ripped the air in downtown Oklahoma City. It instantaneously demolished the entire front of the Murrah building, brought down tons and tons of concrete and metal, dismembered people inside, and it destroyed, forever, scores and scores and scores of lives, lives of innocent Americans: clerks, secretaries, law enforcement officers, credit union employees, citizens applying for Social Security, and little kids."

Hartzler spoke directly to the jurors; he did not rely on notecards.

"The only reason they died, the only reason that they are no longer with us, no longer with their loved ones, is that they were in a building owned by a government that Timothy McVeigh so hated that with premeditated intent and a well-designed plan that he developed over months and months before the bombing, he chose to take their innocent lives to serve his twisted purpose.

"In plain, simple language, it was an act of terror and violence, intended to serve a selfish political purpose.

"The man who committed this act is sitting in this courtroom behind me, and he's the one that committed these murders."

He did not turn to look at McVeigh; he did not point. McVeigh did not react at all.

Hartzler continued, "He fled the scene. And he avoided even damaging his eardrums, because he had earplugs with him."

Through the morning, Hartzler outlined the government's case—the arrest in Perry, the envelope found in the car, the storage lockers, the fertilizer purchases. He previewed his star witnesses, Michael and Lori Fortier.

He reminded the jury of the Branch Davidians disaster.

"The tragedy at Waco really sparked his anger. And as time passed, he became more and more and more outraged at the government, which he held responsible for the deaths at Waco. And he told people that the federal government had intentionally murdered people at Waco, they murdered the Davidians at Waco. He described the incident as the government's declaration of war against the American people. He wrote letters declaring that the government had drawn 'first blood' at Waco."

He described McVeigh's revolutionary zeal.

"He expected and hoped that his bombing of the Murrah building would be the first shot in a violent, bloody revolution in this country."

In America, a country of laws and with courts to enforce those laws, McVeigh had gone too far, Hartzler said.

"Everyone in this great nation has a right to think and believe, speak whatever they want. We are not prosecuting McVeigh because we don't like his thoughts or his beliefs or even his speech; we're prosecuting him because his hatred boiled into violence."

His voice rolled on. Hartzler took the jury from the lake regions of New York and Michigan, out West to the Arizona desert, back again to the plains of Kansas and Oklahoma.

He led them into McVeigh's world—the gun show circuit, the crowded farm road outside Waco, *The Turner Diaries*. He told them how easy it was to buy fertilizer, how simple to rent a truck. He suggested that McVeigh flipped the Yellow Pages in search of detonation cord and racing fuel. He told them of the long winter nights in December and January, of McVeigh at his sister's word processor, patiently waiting for the April thaw.

"McVeigh liked to consider himself a patriot, someone who could start the second American revolution," Hartzler said. "The literature that was in his car when he was arrested included some that quoted statements from the founding fathers and other people who played a part in the American Revolution, people like Patrick Henry and Samuel Adams. McVeigh isolated and took these statements out of context, and he did that to justify his antigovernment violence.

"Well, ladies and gentleman," the prosecutor said, "the statements of our forefathers can never be twisted to justify warfare against innocent children. Our forefathers didn't fight British women and children. They fought other soldiers. They fought them face to face, hand to hand. They didn't plant bombs and run away wearing earplugs."

Hartzler returned to the prosecutors' table. The judge called a short recess, and in the hallway outside, through the high windows that looked out upon the courthouse plaza, the crowd watched the light snow turning to drizzle.

When court reconvened, it was Jones's turn to address the jury. He stood before the lectern and would remain there until nearly four in the afternoon, sometimes leaning on it, repeatedly putting on his glasses and taking them off. Like Hartzler, Jones began with the story of a mother, one who had lost two children in the bombing. It seemed an odd place to start for someone trying to defend the accused bomber, but he promised that this witness would remember seeing someone other than McVeigh outside the Murrah building that morning.

"I have waited two years for this moment," Jones said. Then came his vow, that the government's evidence, from witnesses and documents, from videotapes and wiretaps, "will establish not a reasonable doubt, but that my client is innocent of the crime that Mr. Hartzler has outlined to you."

This was the largest criminal investigation in American history, he said. "But the question is: did they get the right man?"

He suggested that once the government had isolated McVeigh in Perry, there was no need to look further. They closed their case, he said, on the wrong man.

"So let me begin first with Timothy McVeigh."

He told the story of Pendleton, the boy McVeigh, his parents' separation and ultimate divorce. He spoke of the restless young man, his jobs at the local Burger King and as an armored car driver, his enlistment in the army and then combat as a tank gunner under the harsh desert sun. He described McVeigh's grueling attempt at making the Special Forces.

His client came home to Pendleton, Jones said. "McVeigh was a political animal. He studied history, the Constitution, the amendments to the Constitution. He carried [copies of] them on his person. He carried them in his car, he carried them in his briefcase, and they were stacked in his house and he laid them out on tables at gun shows."

But McVeigh's political ideas were not evil. The John Wilkes Booth quote *Sic Semper Tyrannis*, Jones said, was the official slogan of the Commonwealth of Virginia, chosen by two of the new nation's leading lights, George Mason and Richard Henry Lee. And the "something big is going to happen" had nothing to do with Oklahoma City.

"Those words and expressions and communications and conversations were all over the Internet, in which thousands of people exchanged communication back and forth because they believed that the federal government was about to initiate another Waco raid, except this time on a different group."

There: Waco.

"Our proof will be that Tim McVeigh believed that the federal government executed seventy-six people at Waco, including thirty women and twenty-five children. That was his political belief. He was not alone in that opinion."

Jones continued, "We will prove to you that the evidence that the government brings to you which they call the motive for blowing up the building proves nothing; that millions of innocent people fear and distrust the federal government and were outraged, and that being outraged is no more an excuse for blowing up a federal building than being against the government means that you did it."

Even *The Turner Diaries*, Jones said, with 200,000 copies sold in this country, was not enough to spark McVeigh into turning its fantasy into fact. That book was no more a blueprint for Oklahoma City than the works of some of the greatest writers, men like William Faulkner and D. H. Lawrence, were written to inspire violence.

In the afternoon session, Jones derided the Fortiers, their drug habits and their cycle of lies, their cowardly desire to wipe their hands clean even if it meant forever dirtying a friend. "Mr. and Mrs. Fortier could only be expected to say whatever the government wanted to hear, and we will prove they tailored their testimony to fit what they already knew about the prosecution's case and theory and save their own skins at the expense of the truth."

He spoke of the unreliability of the telephone credit cards, of the mystery man Doe 2, of the witnesses at the Dreamland Motel who insisted that they saw the Ryder the day before the truck was rented. He described problems in the FBI Crime Laboratory in Washington, and how significant it was that the forensics experts found so few traces of explosive material debris on McVeigh's belongings.

"If Tim McVeigh built the bomb and put it in the truck, our proof will be that his fingernails, his nostrils, his hair, his clothing, his car, his shoes, his socks would have it all over them. They don't. Out of seven thousand pounds of debris, there is less than half a dozen pieces of evidence of a forensic nature. They do not prove Mr. McVeigh guilty or a participant in this bombing."

The hour was straight-up four; Jones was weary. "I apologize for the time— I don't apologize," he said. "I take it back. I don't apologize for the time. This is an important case. You know it."

He too was finished. He shut his large notebook binder and, stuffing it under his arm, gave the jury one final piece of homely Oklahoma advice. "Every pancake has two sides," he said.

The first prosecution witness was Cynthia Klaver, the Water Resources Board attorney who caught the bomb's concussion on her tape recorder. The government's first piece of evidence was the copy of *The Turner Diaries* that McVeigh had given his cousin, Kyle Kraus, the Christmas he returned from the army.

Oklahoma State Trooper Charlie Hanger, in uniform, testified about arresting McVeigh and finding the hidden Glock under the young man's arm. Agent William Eppright, in the suit and tie of the FBI, described opening the envelope recovered from the front seat of the Mercury Marquis.

The government's case awed the jurors. Prosecutors and FBI agents brought in high-tech computer graphics, video presentations, chunks and bits of the blasted-away Ryder rental truck including that burned and deformed axle, hundreds of pages of documents, individual phone records, motel registration cards, ammonium nitrate tickets, storage locker receipts—even, for several days, a snazzy large-scale model of downtown Oklahoma City, complete with a plastic Murrah building that snapped apart.

Rescue workers—firemen and police—took the stand and told the jury of hearing the initial blast—was it prairie thunder? a gas main explosion?—and of rushing to 5th and Harvey streets, of the pandemonium and smoke in the air, of the thousands of tiny paper shreds floating in the Oklahoma breeze. Murrah building employees described each of the nine floors, using detailed video images that placed the jury inside individual offices and cubicles, behind individual desks. At the close of every employee's testimony, the witness identified the dead, and placed name plates under their photographs on a wide piece of poster board set up near the jury box. There was never any mistaking that this was not just about McVeigh. This also was the story of a wide swath of death.

At irregular intervals, usually at the end of the week, the prosecutors brought in more of the victims, and then the room became very still. Susan Gail Hunt testified about searching for her fellow HUD workers. Donna Weaver told of running toward the Murrah building, hoping to spot her husband at the top-floor windows. Helena Garrett described the anguish as rescue workers carried out the dead babies.

In the courtroom, tears could not be helped. Some of the jurors wept, some of the prosecutors too. Reporters hung their heads. In the back rows, victims cried openly. McVeigh did not flinch.

Patrick Ryan, the U.S. attorney in Oklahoma City, who handled most of the victim testimony, called to the stand retired army captain Lawrence Martin. He now worked as a substitute teacher in Oklahoma City, having left the service at the age of forty, the height of his career. In April 1995, he was assigned to the army recruiting station in the Murrah building. He described the offices, showing the jury the suites where two dozen military and civilian personnel regularly met around seven each workday morning.

On the morning of the 19th of April, Sergeant Vickie Sohn had come in early, around six. Wanda Watkins and Dolores Stratton were eating breakfast, which they had picked up from the snack bar across the hall. Sergeant Lola Bolden was working in the supply office. John Moss, Peggy Holland, and Karen Carr were going about their respective duties—public affairs, computer work, advertising.

Sergeant Bill Titsworth from Fort Riley had shown up, with his wife and two small daughters. He was reporting to his new job assignment and wanted to show his family around and introduce them to the more than twenty army staffers he soon would be working alongside. It was a minute, or two, after nine.

Then Ryan paused. He wanted to go slow here, to be sure the jury listened.

"Did you ever again see Sergeant Vickie Sohn alive?"

"No, I didn't."

"How about Dolores Stratton?"

"No.

"Wanda Walker?"

"No."

"Sergeant Lola Bolden?"

"No."

"Karen Carr?"

"No."

"Peggy Holland?"

"No."

"John Moss?"

"No."

Another pause. Ryan was composing himself; of all the prosecutors, he had the hardest time fighting tears. Defense attorneys stared at the floor; their client looked straight ahead.

Martin said he had been on the telephone at his desk just four feet from the windows when the bomb exploded. "I ended up about twelve feet from my desk, went through a wall, and ended up in the next office," he said.

"Did you ever hear anything?" asked Ryan.

"No. I—I did not hear a noise at all. When I looked up to what used to be my window, all I saw was fire and smoke."

Ryan handed him a photograph of what had been his office, and Martin drew a line, a long line, from where his desk had been to where he landed on the floor.

"All right," Ryan said. "What did you do now after you had found yourself in this position? You felt numb? What happened? What next event occurred?"

"Well," Martin said. "Two of my sergeants, female sergeants, were crying, and it wasn't like a normal cry. It was like a wailing sound and it was just very eerie, and I knew something bad had really happened. And then I looked at myself and noticed that my wrist was damaged real badly and blood was pouring out."

A three-inch chunk of glass was sticking out of his hand. "I started praying immediately. I started praying. I said, 'God, take charge of what's going on in this situation.' "

An army major who that day happened to be wearing a suit rather than his uniform offered Martin his tie for a tourniquet, and then the major took off his shirt too, and used that to cover the left side of Martin's bleeding face. Within twenty minutes they had him outside, and off to a city hospital. He underwent five surgeries on his wrist alone, and one on his eye, and he was medically discharged from the army.

"Virtually, my army career is over. If I had been still in the army two months ago, I would have been going through the majors' board."

Ryan asked about Sergeant Titsworth and his family, the visitors that morning to the building. He asked specifically about the little girl, Kayla, three years old.

"She died that morning on the floor?" he asked.

"Yes, sir."

Ryan moved ever so slightly from the lectern. "That's all, your honor," he told the judge.

Then he stepped back, his face red and wet with tears. He looked again at the judge. "I'm sorry, your honor," he said. Then the chief federal attorney from Oklahoma City walked back to his seat and buried his head in his hands.

At the close of each court day, McVeigh would rise, shake his lawyers' hands, and be taken back out of the courtroom through a door behind the judge's bench. Two years now he had been behind bars, and he knew the regimen. By May, when his sister Jennifer was called to testify, he showed up in court with a new flat-top buzz cut, his hair dark, even shorter than normal. His skin was turning a chalky white from the lack of sunshine.

During the trial he was housed in a special basement cell below the courthouse–federal building complex, a holding area larger than his normal prison lockup at a facility in the Denver area. Downstairs at night he could read his court files, and in the morning the newspapers, to follow the press accounts of his trial. He would drop to the floor and begin his series of push-ups, or hop to his feet to count off jumping jacks. He worried about losing his muscle tone; he fretted over developing a paunch. He read a book about Einstein's theories and Zane Grey novels, and he counted the steps of the guard walking past at each appointed interval. What McVeigh missed most was trees. He could not see any trees.

In court, he appeared interested when old army buddies would testify, for either side, perhaps to talk about his obsession with guns and right-wing propaganda, or how he passed around copies of *The Turner Diaries*. When experts droned on about bomb-making and the chemical components of ammonium nitrate, he might lean a bit forward, as though trying to concentrate harder. But he showed no sorrow or remorse at the tragic stories from the victims. When court ended each day, and McVeigh was led back downstairs, the spectators in the back rows would shake their heads. The man has no face, they said.

Jennifer McVeigh stepped up into the witness chair. Her brother nodded.

She was a government witness, and like Lori Fortier she had been granted immunity: what she said could not be used against her. She led the jury through her brother's writings, told them about his strong antigovenment views, said she shared many of his political beliefs. Under questioning by assistant prosecutor Beth Wilkinson, Jennifer McVeigh described Pendleton and her parents' breakup, her brother's departure for war, and his restless return.

Rob Nigh, Jones's chief lieutenant, took her gingerly through cross-examination, again about her and Tim's early years and his enlistment in the army. She said many of the personal belongings he had sent her were his own achievements, the certificate for the Bronze Star, the Army Commendation Medal. She read them out loud for the jury.

When Nigh asked about her FBI interview sessions and the pictures of her and her brother on the wall in the interrogation room, she broke down; the memories were overwhelming.

Lori Fortier came to court in a neat blue-black suit, her dark hair stylish, and she had an air of confidence about her. But when she spoke, she was still the trailer-park Lori. She admitted that she too had been distrustful of the government. But unlike Jennifer, she was a mother, and she knew what was coming that April of 1995; she saw on television the pictures from the day care center and heard the cries of other mothers.

From the witness box, Lori Fortier turned on her old friend Timothy McVeigh, the best man at her wedding, but she could not explain away her own inactions. With Hartzler asking the questions, she admitted laminating the fake Robert Kling driver's license, and told how McVeigh had squatted on the floor in her mobile home and laid out an array of soup cans.

Then April 19, 1995. "We turned the news on early that morning, and we seen what had happened," she said. "We saw that the building had been blown up, and I knew right away that it was Tim."

Hartzler asked about her personal responsibility.

"I could have stopped it," she said.

Her voice cracked, and she later again tried to make some sense of her inability, her carelessness, her decision not to stop McVeigh.

"Why didn't you say anything?" Hartzler asked.

"Because I guess on some level, I—Tim was my friend and I thought that he wasn't capable of it at that time. I don't know."

"He told you that he had the materials. Is that right?"

"Yes," she said.

"He diagrammed the bomb. Is that right?"

"Yes."

"He told you what his target was. Is that correct?"

"Yes."

"He indicated he was capable, didn't he?"

"Yes, he did."

"Why did you think he wasn't?"

"Because I guess on some level I was in denial that he really was capable of this."

"You recognize today that you could have stopped this from happening, do you not?"

"Yes, I do."

"Do you feel responsible?"

"Yes, I do."

"Why do you think you didn't stop it?"

"I don't know," she said, crying now. "I mean, I wish I could have stopped it now. If I could do it all over again, I would have."

Hartzler was through with her. It was five o'clock, and the judge sent the jury home. Tomorrow she would belong to Stephen Jones.

The chief defense attorney made her describe the deal that her husband had signed, possibly twenty-three years in prison so she could remain free. He went over their drug-filled nights before and after the bombing. How could she claim to be scared of McVeigh when she freely allowed him into her home, let him sleep on her couch, let him baby-sit her daughter?

"You didn't think he was serious?" Jones asked. He meant his client, he meant the bomb. He was hoping to get her to say that McVeigh could not have done this.

"I didn't want to think he was serious because he was a friend of ours," she said.

"Well, did you think he was serious or not, Mrs. Fortier?"

"Yes," she said. "Because I had seen all this stuff." She meant the blasting caps she had wrapped for him in Christmas paper.

Then she changed her mind. "No," she said. "He was a friend of ours and I didn't want to believe he was capable of doing something like this."

Jones continued to jab. "Well, what more would he have had to tell you for you to believe that it was serious, if everything you've said is true?"

She breathed hard. "I believed he was serious," she said.

"Then you would agree with me that if your testimony is accurate, all you had to do to prevent the death of these one hundred and sixty-eight people was to pick up the telephone?"

"Yes."

"And you did not do that, did you?"

"No, I did not."

Her husband took the stand in a light brown suit, his hair combed. He was repentant now; prison can do that. Speaking earnestly, he seemed at times like a truly sorrowful young man. When he told how he had lied to his father, Michael Fortier wept.

For Fortier, there were no cameras, no floodlights; there were no fancy book deals, no *Geraldo Show*. Just he and the judge and the jury, and McVeigh off to the side, listening with great interest because Fortier, the fellow patriot, the gunrunner, the bigmouth, was alone now. He was not the "key man."

It was obvious that he had been coached at length by the prosecution team; Hartzler's questions and Fortier's answers were well rehearsed. And he told it all, all the way through to his trip with McVeigh to case the building.

"You realize," Hartzler said, "that as you sit here today that you might have stopped this bombing, had you called someone?"

"Yes, sir," he said. "I live with that knowledge every day."

"Why didn't you?"

"There is really—there is no excuse that I could offer that would compensate for why I didn't. I think one would have to look at my lifestyle and my friendship with Tim. I—I had known Tim for quite a while, eight years up to that point, maybe less than that, six years. But Tim—well, if you don't consider what happened in Oklahoma,

Tim is a good person. He would stop—he would stop and help somebody that's broken down on the side of the road."

Fortier had spent much of his adult life looking up to McVeigh, admiring his skills as an army sergeant on the gun range, jealous of McVeigh's courage in war, delighting in his bursting antigovernment fervor. Fortier wanted McVeigh as a buddy, he needed him as a friend. McVeigh paid him for running the guns, and he provided an opportunity for Fortier to feel like part of the game. It allowed Fortier some measure of self-respect to say that he had partaken of the revolution, that he counted for more than just flying that black flag with the coiled snake in front of his desert trailer.

Court was recessed, and when Fortier later resumed the stand, Jones stood up and mocked him with his own words, reading for the jurors from the FBI wiretaps. They heard the braggadocio, the foolish boasts Fortier had made, while down the highway in Oklahoma a whole city was filling its cemeteries.

Jones played the tapes, too.

"Oh, my God, I'll be fucking fucked with the camera, hard core."

"I'm the key."

"The key man."

Fortier left the courtroom, his figure disappearing through the door behind the jury box, returning to prison. Soon the government's case would be concluded. FBI Agent Louis Hupp testified about taking McVeigh's fingerprints, but defense attorneys were able to show that Hupp had not found their client's prints on the Ryder truck lease, the body shop counter, or even the storage lockers. Steven Burmeister, chief of the FBI crime lab's Chemistry and Toxicology Unit, described a half-dozen "hits"—traces of explosive materials found on McVeigh's clothing, and his earplugs too. Defense lawyers, led by Christopher Tritico, did not fare as well in their attempts to discredit the lab. During jury selection, the Justice Department's Inspector General's Office in Washington had determined widespread problems with examinations and record-keeping at the lab, and those findings led to the announcement of a new crime lab that would be built at the bureau's training academy. But Judge Matsch limited them from a full-scale attack on the lab.

At the end of its case the government presented Dr. Frederick Jordan, the medical examiner in Oklahoma City. To him it fell to describe not only the horror of that morning, but the tragic hours and days that followed as the people of his city clamored for any scrap of news about their loved ones. He was the one who approved their death certificates, all 168.

Then the government was done.

Jones's case was brief, lasting but a few days. He presented his own experts, suggesting that a bomb composed of ammonium nitrate and fuel oil would not have caused the type of damage seen at the Murrah site; the brunt of the blast would not have shot upward as it did, but would have moved outward from ground level, taking the whole building down, perhaps. FBI crime lab whistleblower Frederic Whitehurst testified about shortcomings at the lab, but he could not say for certain that any of the evidence against McVeigh was tainted.

As promised, the defense also called its own victim, Daina Bradley, the young mother who was gravely injured and whose two small children and mother were killed, and her sister seriously injured. Daina Bradley was used by the lawyers for Timothy McVeigh to help the man who had taken so much from her.

She now was twenty-one years old, but so nervously soft-spoken that defense attorney Cheryl Ramsey repeatedly had to ask her to raise her voice. She was an Oklahoma City native who liked to read and to build models of cars, and who cared only for "spending lots of time with my son," a new child born since the bomb of two years ago.

"You don't want to be here, do you?" Ramsey asked.

"No."

She once had another son, Gabreon Bruce, and he was four months old, the youngest to die that day. She had gone to the Murrah's Social Security office to change his ID card and to make an appointment to review her own benefits. She was there with her daughter, too, Peachlyn Bradley, three years old, and her mother, Cheryl Hammon, and her sister, Felicia Bradley.

"You looked out the window, and what did you see?"

"I seen the yellow Ryder truck drive up."

She thought that very unusual because "downtown, they do not allow moving trucks as far as those kind of vehicles being parked down in that area."

She continued, "I went back and I looked up and I started talking to my mother again and I looked back out. I seen two men get out of the truck."

She turned from the windows, to finish filling out a Social Security form. "All I know is that when I was talking to my sister, that a flash of light came over the desk, and that's—that's where I—I don't know how long that it was there."

"And what is that you remember next?"

"That I was trapped."

Ramsey asked her now about her meetings with the FBI. She reminded Bradley that she had told the agents about the truck's passenger, a clean-cut, olive-complected man with short, curly hair, dressed in a blue Starter jacket, blue jeans, and tennis shoes. And a white hat with purple flames.

She believed he resembled the man in the sketch of John Doe No. 2.

"I told them that he had got out of the truck, went to the back of the truck, and proceeded to walk very fast forward in front of the truck," Bradley said. "He went back on the sidewalk and left."

The driver she would remember only as a "white male and that he had walked off very fast across the street." And she was "absolutely positive" that that man was not McVeigh.

Prosecutor Ryan next questioned the witness. "I am sorry to have to be asking you some questions now," he said, "but if you'll bear with me."

He reminded her how the other day, in an interview with prosecutors, she had said she was really only "not certain, probably and probably not, yes-and-no" about her statement that the driver was not McVeigh. He reminded her also that the first time she talked to the FBI, she told the agents, "I've been through a lot of trauma, I've been through a lot of things in my life. I just don't have a good memory of these events."

"You had a really rough childhood, haven't you?" he asked.

"Yes, I have."

"You were in a psychiatric home, hospital, when you were seven years old?"

"Yes, I was."

"And you were in a mental health facility from the age of seven until the age of sixteen, is that right?"

"Yes, I was."

"Were you given a lot of medication during those years?"

"Yes, I was. A lot."

"Excuse me?"

"Lots."

"How would you describe the effect the medication had on you?"

"It had caused me to lose memory of who I was and people around me."

"And you were depressed?"

"I was depressed."

"And you were there for a very long time."

"Yes."

"And have you received any therapy since the bombing in which you lost your mother and two children?"

"At a shorter time but not long enough to speak of. A lot—to explain—to tell people what is really going on and how exactly I feel. I didn't get the time to do that."

"Do you think you need some more counseling and treatment?"

"Yes."

Larry Mackey presented the government's closing argument. The assistant prosecutor from Indiana, big and rough-hewn, hand-chosen by Hartzler as his chief deputy, revisited the government's key points. But this was more than just what ingredients make up a gunny sack of ammonium nitrate, more than the sum of the exploding parts of a rented truck van.

"America stood in shock," Mackey told the jurors. "Who could do such a thing? Who could do such a thing?"

Mackey gave them their answer.

"Tim McVeigh has been at the helm of two weapons of mass destruction. In the Gulf War, he was a good soldier. He was a soldier who manned a Bradley tank, a vehicle of mass destruction that's built for that reason. It's built to kill other people. And on the side of that tank are the words 'U.S. Army,' and an American flag. Those are words and symbols meant to declare its purpose, its killing power. That was one weapon of mass destruction that Tim McVeigh manned.

"The second one was a Ryder truck, a Ryder truck that he delivered to the door of the Murrah building on April 19, 1995. On the side of that truck was the name 'Ryder,' were the words '18,000 pounds' for its capacity, and a 1-800 number. Those are words meant to disguise the purpose that was packed in the back of that truck by Tim McVeigh.

"That truck crawled to a stop in front of the Murrah building on that morning, right in front of the children and women and men, and then Tim McVeigh ran away."

Mackey spoke too of the victims.

"The law enforcement officers that died that morning were not 'treasonous' officials, as Tim McVeigh had declared, not 'cowardice bastards,' as he had described.

"The credit union employees that disappeared that morning were not tyrants whose blood had to be spilled in order to preserve liberty.

"And certainly the nineteen children that died that morning were not storm troopers that Tim McVeigh had said must die, innocent storm troopers who must die because of their association with an evil empire.

"In fact, the people who Tim McVeigh murdered on April 19, 1995, weren't one thing. They were bosses and secretaries, they were executives and others. They were blacks, they were whites, they were mothers, they were daughters, they were fathers and sons. They were a community.

"So who," he asked, "are the real patriots, and who is the traitor?"

Jones followed as best he could. He tried to attack the government's evidence directly; at other times he rambled on about a biography of an old English barrister or gave the jurors another dose of Oklahoma folklore. When he was on point, such as when he was once again discrediting the Fortiers, he was quite good, but in the end, his thunder had been stolen by Mackey.

"Someone blew up the Murrah building," the defense lawyer said. "But more likely than not, several people were involved. They had skill and training, and they didn't get it out of some book that talks about mixing it in an oven."

In closing, Jones offered up another obscure anecdote, this one about the fall of communism in Eastern Europe, brought down not by one leader but rather by individuals, a lawyer, a Polish priest, a shipyard electrician.

"Ultimately, justice will be done in this case by the men and women from ordinary lives who have been summoned here and empowered to make the decision.

"And now," he concluded, "we will be silent and we will listen to you."

The jurors took the case at nine-thirty the following morning, May 30. Three days later, shortly after one-thirty on the afternoon of June 2, they returned to the courtroom, their faces grim, the first part of their task completed. The court already had announced that a verdict was imminent, and outside, hundreds of people, many of them federal employees from the office high-rise next door, the American public too, gathered, waiting for the verdict. Behind them, from a second-floor window of the U.S. Custom House, a federal government worker with the benefit of a transistor radio leaned out and shouted: "Guilty!"

From the crowd arose a great cheering that grew louder as the courtroom emptied and the prosecution team marched out into the street, heading toward a nearby Catholic church where the victims often gathered. This was the winning team, and they paraded with hands waving, thumbs in the air, smiles widening their faces.

Suddenly a woman pushed her way out of the crowd. Crying uncontrollably, she threw her arms around Hartzler and said, "Dear God, thank you for what you have done."

Chapter Nineteen

One of Ours

When the jury returned to court to weigh an appropriate sentence for Timothy McVeigh—life without release or death by lethal injection—America was still not at peace. There remained sharp divisions, and while the patriot community did not act out McVeigh's call for revolution, some were certainly with him in spirit.

Some actions would have pleased McVeigh that spring of 1997.

At Fort Davis, Texas, a tiny dot of a town an hour away from any urban center, nearly ninety miles from the closest Wal-Mart even, the self-styled Republic of Texas, a group believing that their state was not a state at all but an independent nation, held a weeklong standoff against federal authorities, surrendering only when one of their members was fatally shot.

In the steel orchard of Pittsburgh, about fifty members of the Ku Klux Klan, wearing the familiar white hoods but also waving Nazi swastika banners, marched in anger through the downtown streets. "The solution is white revolution," announced their leader, the group's National Wizard.

Two men were arrested in Yuba City, California, an old mining burg north of Sacramento, where authorities seized five hundred pounds of explosives. The detainees were acquaintances of a member of the antitax Freemen organization that had held the FBI at bay in Montana the year earlier. Not far away, in Redwood City, California, police arrested a homeless man for shooting up a power substation. No one was injured, although the gunfire did knock out power to nearby homes. The shooter had an "extreme dislike" for the federal government, police said. Authorities found more than fifty-five rifle shell casings, a Confederate flag flying from the substation fence, and a newspaper bearing the headline "McVeigh Guilty."

Anger over Waco continued to flare in America's heart. In Dallas, relatives of Branch Davidians killed in the 1993 raid were dealt a major blow in their bid to sue the government. An appeals court ruled against them, denying their request to remove the same judge who had earlier presided over the criminal trial of eleven of the cultists. "If he is our judge, we are dead," proclaimed Mike Caddell, the Branch Davidians' lead counsel. "That's about how bad it is."

And the debate over gun control raged on. In Washington that June, the Supreme Court scored a victory for those who hated the Brady bill, ruling that the federal government cannot force local police departments to conduct background checks on handgun buyers. That judicial order did far more for the gun lobby than all of McVeigh's white-and-blue barrels full of ammonium nitrate.

And in Colorado too, tensions were building. Ronald Cole, who had distributed literature at the start of the trial suggesting that McVeigh might not get a fair accounting, was arrested along with two others. FBI agents seized seventy-five pounds of rocket fuel from their Denver suburban home, three land mines, six fully automatic AK-47s, and other weapons and ammunition. Cole had long claimed ties to the Branch Davidians; he had insisted that in the last two years hundreds of the cult members had contacted his Colorado First Light Infantry militia about establishing a common base of operations in the Rocky Mountains.

According to the FBI, Cole kept his firearms hung on the wall of his bedroom at night. He particularly liked his MP-5 assault rifle; he carried it in a black backpack and called it "my baby." Cole also loved to roam the Internet under his "misc.activism.militia" newsgroup. The favorite topic of chat was Waco.

For the ten days after McVeigh's guilty verdict, a judge and a jury and two dozen lawyers grappled with a very fundamental question. This was the sentencing phase of the trial, the penalty phase, and there were but two options. The jury had to decide whether Timothy McVeigh should spend the rest of his life in prison with no hope of freedom, or should be executed by lethal injection by the very federal government he had sought to overthrow.

McVeigh apppeared on the cover of *Time* magazine, his lips pursed, his gaze front-and-center, in his prison-gray sweatshirt with the sleeves rolled up. "Should He Die?" asked the headline.

He made the cover of *Newsweek* again, but only his eyes this time, and below his eyes, the federal death chamber in Indiana, with a picture of the leather gurney, the Velcro straps and the armrests splayed out in the sign of the cross. "Should He Die?" asked the headline.

A *Newsweek* poll that first week of June showed 67 percent of Americans favored the death penalty for McVeigh. In general, 56 percent thought a convicted murderer, one driven by political or ideological beliefs, should be executed. A *Time*/CNN poll came up with even more ominous numbers: 78 percent said he should die. And yet that same poll asked the respondents whether they thought law enforcement officials had captured and identified all of those responsible for the Oklahoma City bombing, and a startling number—77 percent—said no.

In Denver, Archbishop Charles Chaput of Colorado posted a message on his own Web site. He was upset by a local radio station's theatrics in setting up a kind of drive-by jury system in which motorists passing an intersection a few miles from the courthouse were to honk if they wanted McVeigh to "fry." By the evening of June 4, just the first day of testimony in the sentencing phase of the trial, more than 24,000 Coloradans had pounded their horns.

The Catholic cleric and others opposed to capital punishment were equally annoyed with a man who called himself Citizen Scott and rolled a billboard out in front of the courthouse. Mr. Scott wore dark sunglasses and slicked his hair back; his billboard carried a caricature of McVeigh, his arms bound and dynamite sticks wedged into his ears and mouth. Three hands approach with lit matches, the message yelling: "Let Us Have Him."

Archbishop Chaput was not amused. "Killing the guilty is still wrong," he said. "It does not honor the dead. It does not ennoble the living. And while it may satisfy society's anger for a while, it cannot even release the murder victim's loved ones from their sorrow, because only forgiveness can do that."

Judge Matsch reminded the jury of the new federal law allowing victim-impact testimony, giving those hurt by a crime the chance not to lash out against their assailant, but rather to tell and show the jury the suffering they have endured, so that the jury can consider that pain when weighing the proper punishment.

The defense team would be permitted to speak too. "We're not here to seek revenge on Timothy McVeigh," the judge said. "We're here to consider these lives and what's happened to these people and also, as you will hear later, his life. Hard as it is, you must wait now and withhold judgment. Don't overreact. And I know you are human beings, and so am I. So is everybody here."

Jurors were given long lunch breaks and provided backgammon boards, playing cards, and Chinese checkers. Some of them, including seventy-eight-year-old Ruth Meier, passed the noon hour walking for exercise and to relieve their anxiety, trudging up and down a narrow courthouse hallway.

The lawyers too were battling their inner demons. Defense attorney Chris Tritico, who handled most of the evidence and testimony on the bomb forensics and the FBI crime lab, began dropping pounds; by the end of the trial he was wearing suspenders to keep his suit pants up.

Pat Ryan, who had such a difficult time controlling his emotions, was fretting over Judge Matsch's repeated concerns that his crying was affecting the jury. At night he tossed in bed, his mouth and skin parched from the dry Denver air. In court, the defense lawyers complained that Ryan's crying was turning the jury against McVeigh.

"I'm going to do everything that I can to restrain myself," Ryan promised the judge. "This is, of course, involving the death of one hundred and sixty-eight people."

Matsch ordered both sides to shield their emotions from the jury. "We ought to have poker faces," he said.

The best such face in the room belonged to McVeigh.

Ryan began the sentencing phase of the trial when he stood to address the jury. He often came to court in suits of soft gray or light brown. He would wear a large white cowboy hat into the courthouse, and sometimes he arrived in the morning with his daughter in tow, her small hand wrapped tightly in her father's much larger one.

Speaking to the jurors, he sometimes faltered, his voice breaking; but he did not cry this time. He began, "My name is Pat Ryan. I'm the United States attorney in Oklahoma City, where these crimes occurred."

Crimes, plural.

He outlined the aggravating factors in the case, recalling McVeigh's rage over Waco, his purchasing a book on how to build a bomb with nitromethane a month after the Waco inferno. He talked about *The Turner Diaries* too, and McVeigh's phony Robert Kling driver's license, and his choosing April 19 as his new birthday.

"As the defendant gathered his bomb components and thought about his plan, he knew exactly what the effects of his bomb were going to be," Ryan said. He reminded the jury of the eight federal law enforcement officers killed in the Murrah explosion, and he reminded them too of McVeigh's pledge to see federal agents "swinging in the wind," his plan to "rip the bastards' heads off."

He described again the Ryder truck rolling east on 5th Street, pausing twenty-three seconds in front of the Regency Tower security camera. "As Mr. McVeigh got out of his truck, the children in the day care center were playing. Their cribs were up against the north wall. Right up against the glass where they were visible from the street."

Ryan tightened his chin. "As Mr. McVeigh got out of the truck," he said, "and as the defendant crossed the parking lot on his way behind the YMCA, Kathy Ridley, a young lady, was walking across the parking lot. He would reach the safety of the YMCA behind the building and she would burn to death from the blast and the fire that crossed 5th Street."

He took them back to the Murrah building, up the stairs to the second floor, into the brightly colored rooms of the America's Kids day care complex. And what of the children who lived?

The government would show them videotapes.

Brandon Denny. "This is a child who had a ceiling tile pierced through his skull and deeply embedded in his brain. He had to have seven brain surgeries to remove this ceiling tile."

P. J. Allen. "A child who was terribly burned in the bombing. You will see the evidence of how he rasps as he tries to breathe through his tracheostomy."

Nekia McCloud. "A little girl who suffered profound brain damage. You will see her frustration as she tries and she fails to follow the simplest of commands."

And the many deaths, young and old, throughout the nine floors. Dora Reyes lost her husband, Tony, a HUD employee who volunteered his weekends to community causes around Oklahoma City. "The defendant killed many husbands," Ryan said.

Greg Sohn lost his wife, Vickie, in the army recruiting station. "The defendant killed many wives," Ryan said.

Suzanna Chavez-Pate lives on without her grandson, three-year-old Zachary, a child at the day care center. "The defendant killed many grandchildren." Cynthia Ferrell Ashford buried her sister, Susan Ferrell. "The defendant killed many sisters." Michael Lenz, Jr.'s, son was never born. "The defendant killed three unborn children." Todd McCarthy's father. Clint Siedl's mother. David Klaus's daughter. Laura Kennedy's son. "The defendant killed many fathers. The defendant killed many mothers. The defendant . . ."

Ryan was nearing the end.

"It would be easy for you as a jury to think of this as one mass murder," he said. "Don't. There are one hundred sixty-eight people, all unique, all individual. All had families, all had friends, and they're different. They went to church, they coached Little League, they designed highways, they liked to watch their children dance. They tried to prevent disease. They played on their beds with their kids. They enforced our nation's laws. They had unique smiles and ways of greeting people at the credit union. They had unique abilities to recruit men and women into our armed forces. Some knew how to run machinery and keep a building going. Some nursed and comforted the sick. Some helped others obtain Social Security. Some protected presidents and even popes. And all brought enjoyment and love to others."

At the morning recess, Ryan's colleagues stood and patted him on the back. Stephen Jones walked across the room and shook his adversary's hand.

For the next week, the stories of one community's great loss unfolded inside the courtroom. The jurors leaned forward, pulled back in their chairs, wiped their eyes and cried openly, without shame.

Greg Sohn, like his wife an army sergeant, described her as persistent and stubborn, a perfectionist. "She gave every minute of her day to something," he said, turning and speaking directly to the jury, one of the few victims able to do so without completely breaking down. "There was no wasted time for the day. And she at nighttime, after the kids went to sleep, cross-stitched little sayings for their room."

On the day after the bombing, his wife still missing, he and their five children held a family meeting. "I sat down with them and held hands on the living-room floor. And I started to tell them about how strong she is, that she would drink gasoline and eat concrete if she was there. That's just how she was. If she was alive, if there was somebody alive in there, it's going to be her and to always think that we're going to find her."

Her body was identified five days later.

"It didn't really hit me hard until they said it, and I broke down very, very hard, and that's—I didn't want the children in there at the time because I was one thing that they were leaning on for security."

The children were having bad dreams.

"Daddy, are they going to blow up our house next?" asked one.

"No," their father said. "Not as long as I'm here."

He could not let them know that he cried too; and when he did, "I dismissed myself to the garage or where they couldn't see me." Sometimes they all climbed into his now half-empty bed, or all five children gathered their sleeping bags and fell asleep as one on the living-room floor.

John Michael, their youngest son, still could not sleep. "He's dreaming about monsters in the night," his father said. "You might consider that as just a lot of young men, young babies, dream that way. Also he's still just—he just asked the other day to. . . . he just, you know, asked about his mommy. He was scared about his mommy. Sometimes it hits him as, well, Mommy's not there, and sometimes it . . . he knows she's not going to ever be back. But he still thinks about Mommy."

David Klaus came from the Denver suburb of Evergreen.

"How are you doing?" asked chief prosecutor Hartzler.

"Pretty well."

"Are you going to be able to go through this?

"Sure. A little nervous—"

Klaus and his wife had two children, and the oldest, their daughter Kimberly, had married Damon Burgess. They moved to Midwest City, which is a suburb of Oklahoma City. They lived in housing at Tinker Air Force Base, and she worked at the Murrah credit union.

"We talked at least once a week," Klaus said. "Sometimes more often. By telephone." He last saw her in February 1995; they last spoke, on the phone, that Easter Sunday before the bombing.

The morning of April 19 was his wedding anniversary, his thirty-second; he and his wife have since arbitrarily picked another date to celebrate. "Because it's—it's too hard to do on that date."

Klaus on the witness stand was thin and pale; Hartzler showed the jury a 1993 photograph of the Klaus family before the bombing.

"Have you lost some weight?" Hartzler asked.

"I've lost at least twenty-five pounds, and I've just never gained it back. My eating habits are fairly poor now. I just don't have the appetite I used to have."

"When was it you started losing weight?"

"I think probably immediately after the bombing. We just—I just did not have much of an appetite, and it just continued literally to this day."

"Mr. Klaus, have you experienced other physical difficulties or problems since your daughter's death?"

"Yes, I have," he said. He tilted his head back; it was his way to battle the tears. "I've had a number of physical ailments, including hepatitis and bronchitis twice and pneumonia, and suffer from depression, which I'm being treated for right now."

"I don't mean to offend you," said Hartzler, "but you appear older than from the photograph we saw."

"I feel like I've aged ten years in two years."

Hartzler could see, the whole room could tell, how difficult this was. "Mr. Klaus," he said, "could you describe in general the impact— This will be my last question, so you're holding up well. Can you describe in general the impact that the death of your daughter has had on you?"

"Well," Klaus began. "It's been physically and emotionally just devastating for me, and I've been in counseling and I—I'm just to this day not dealing well with this, this tragedy."

He tried to compose himself; he could not. "There is just this huge hole in my heart that is never going to get filled up."

He was crying; several jurors were crying. Hartzler could not look; Judge Matsch turned away. Osgood, the jury foreman, was staring at McVeigh.

"The loss of Kim is just—" Klaus broke again. "I mean, I think about her first thing in the morning, and the last thing I think about at night is Kim and the fact I'm never going to see her again, and trying to imagine how I get on with life without her."

Diane Leonard, whose husband, Don, a Secret Service agent, died in the bombing, said she had never turned her anger against McVeigh.

"The first few days after this occurred, I had some general anger. The first time I saw him on TV, I did not get angry. I decided early on that it took a lot of energy to be angry, and I had too many other places—I didn't have that much energy left. And what I had left, I had too many other places to put it."

She testified about one of her three sons, Jason. Late one night, after his father's body was found but before the funeral, Jason came to her. He was crying very hard.

"I want my dad back," Jason told her. "I want him to see me graduate from college. I want him to meet my wife and be at my wedding. I want him to see my first child."

Jason was twenty-four now, the middle son. "He's getting married next month," she said. "And there will be a rose where his father should be."

One after another, the Oklahoma City victims took the witness stand.

Mathilda Westberry's husband, Bob, worked for the Defense Investigative Service. Their grandson, David, was four years old at the time of the blast. When he started school, he became very aggressive.

"He would sit in the classroom and put his hands over his ears and ask the kids to be quiet," she said. "He was very, very afraid because he was afraid his school was going to get blown up."

In counseling, he was told that his school was safe. It wasn't in a building where people worked for the government, they said. They had him build a replica of the Murrah with Lego blocks; he would not let anyone break it down. Sometimes in the car, he would ask his mother to run red lights so they could crash and he would die and join his grandfather, his "Papa," in heaven. He wrote messages for his grandfather and slipped them inside helium balloons, then

ran through the park and let them go, watching the balloons drift
skyward.

Mike Lenz described losing his wife, Carrie, and their unborn
son, Michael III, in what he called "one fell swoop."

"I did things that I'm certainly not proud of," he said. "Probably
drank more than I should, caused trouble. I had no regard for—for
anything. I'd lost everything. There was nothing. I mean a house,
it's bricks, mortar. Without a family in it, it's not a home."

He paused. "There was a point when I—I contemplated, definitely not being in the best of my judgment, but—there was a point
where I actually stuck a pistol in my mouth. I couldn't pull the trigger, thank God, but . . ."

He stopped again. "There is . . ." he said. "There is nothing, nothing, more dangerous than a man who has no reason to live."

Clint Seidl was seven when his mother died in the Murrah explosion; he put together a short statement he dearly wanted to read
from the witness box. But Judge Matsch thought it best Clint's
father, Glenn, do this for him. So Glenn Seidl, forty years old, a life-
long Oklahoma City area resident, mustered all of his courage and
took the witness stand to tell the world of his boy's sorrow.

Glenn Seidl met Kathy in the fifth grade. They married in 1986
and he went to work as plumber. She took a job as an investigative
assistant for the Secret Service.

"I worked out of town," he said. "I took the job so we'd have
more money to build a house. And my wife took care of everything
and taking Clint to day care, picking him up, taking him to
wrestling practice, keeping the woodstove going during the winter.
And she didn't take motherhood for granted. When we got married,
it was with the understanding that the chances of ever having a
child would be slim. Kathy had scarring of the tubular—the tubes,
and so she loved Clint more than anything in the world."

He adjusted himself in the witness chair. He could see across the
room the man who had taken all of this from him; he could see
also, in a back row, the little figure of his son, Clint, now nine, sitting straight and tall.

The day after the bombing, professional counseling teams from
Washington had met with the Seidls and other relatives of the dead.
The boy told a counselor that he was worried because he had not
seen his father cry yet. "I think the people that have done this are

after me and my dad," he said. He mentioned the $180 in his savings account. "I will pay you that money if you will help my dad."

The room was quiet. Glenn Seidl unfolded his son's typwritten statement. "This is the original one," he said. "It—words are misspelled. I'll do the best I can."

He began reading. "I miss my mom. We used to go for walks. She would read to me. We would go to Wal-Mart. Sometimes at school maybe a kid will bring something up for show-and-tell, something new that he got and someone would ask him or her where they got it. And they usually say, 'My mom got it,' and that makes me sad.

"After the bomb, everyone went to my aunt's house, and my grandma took me to the zoo, my cousin and I to the zoo. While we were there, I bought my mom a ring. I bought it for whenever they found her.

"Sometimes at school around the holidays, I will still make my mom Mother Days and Valentines like the other kids."

The rescue workers, who had labored even when there was no chance anyone was yet alive, had become victims as well. Don Browning, an Oklahoma City police officer for twenty-seven years by the time he took the witness stand, had seen, he said, "a lot of death" as a combat marine in Vietnam. But it was the Murrah explosion that kept him awake at night.

"I dream that I'm crawling through the rubble; that there is rebar," he told the jury. "It's dark, but I am crawling in more of a confined area, in a tunnel area, and I can hear children crying from in front of me and to my right."

He turned, shifting his arms and shoulders, showing the jurors how in his sleep he grappled with his inability to reach those he was sent to save.

"I see a darker tunnel; and as I crawl towards it, I begin to feel the ground tremble underneath me, which turns into a draw, almost a monstrous draw. And I turn and run, and the kids quit crying, and I feel very guilty that I didn't get to them."

Police Officer Alan Prokop also still could not sleep. Like Browning, he had marked more than twenty-five years in the Oklahoma City police department when he was dispatched to the fire and smoke at 5th and Harvey streets. In his nightmares, he said, "I saw the people coming towards us wanting help, and there weren't enough of us . . . there were not enough of us."

The tensest rescue of all was by Dr. James Andy Sullivan. He had been a doctor for twenty years, and was professor of orthopedic surgery at the University of Oklahoma hospital when he was summoned to the Murrah building. The call came after noon; there was a young lady still trapped in the basement. Dr. Sullivan ran for the operating room, scooped up an amputation set, requisitioned a police car, and rushed to the site. In the medical kit were two trays of sterile instruments, a saw, and some disposable blades. He also had nylon rope that he could use for traction, and a variety of knives and clamps. Before leaving, at the last minute, he also grabbed his pocketknife.

He made his way to the Murrah basement. "It was dark and foreboding. Full of smoke. Poor light, rubble. It was like walking through boulders, water on the floor, electrical lines that you had to step over, pipes, a lot of dust in the air, the smell of gasoline engines. And a lot of shouting."

At last he reached the young woman. "It's kind of like when you go in a parking garage and the roof above you has concrete beams and one of those beams had fallen. And then the floor above it had collapsed, so that formed kind of a triangular crevice, like a cave. And the patient was at the end of the crevice."

His patient was Daina Bradley. She was packed so tight back there in the heavy rubble that Dr. Sullivan had to remove his hard hat just to scoot in. Rescue workers had hooked up a portable light-bulb and he could see her face, dazed and dusted. "I crawled on top of her. Her left leg and arm were free. Her right arm had been freed by that point. And then if you traced her right leg down, it disappeared beneath the beam that had fallen."

"Right onto her leg?" asked assistant prosecutor Scott Mendeloff.

"Right onto her leg," the doctor said.

She was cold and clammy and wet, lying in water, exposed, and she was in shock.

Tell us again, said Mendeloff.

"I had to get down on my belly, and crawl in on my belly, kind of a combat crawl. It was not—it wasn't enough space to crawl in on my hands and knees, so you had to go in on your elbows."

He examined her quickly, her broken ribs, her one collapsed lung, blood in both lung cavities. Beyond her right knee, he could

not feel anything. So with help they moved some of the rebar and
Dr. Sullivan crawled in closer yet.

Starting an IV was impossible. He also realized that he would
need the traction rope now, because to cut the leg without a tourniquet would only leave her bleeding to death. Wearing his surgical
gloves, he dug through the small gravel and pieces of metal, then
wrapped the rope around her leg and pulled tight.

Then, suddenly, from nowhere and from everywhere, came
panic: another bomb scare.

"I scurried out. And we ran."

"As you left," asked Mendeloff, "what reaction did Daina
Bradley have?"

"She screamed, 'Don't leave me! Don't leave me! I'm going to
die!' It was gut-wrenching. You don't leave somebody to die."

He returned in forty-five minutes. She was still unmovable
under that giant beam, coughing dust, spitting water. He told her
what he would have to do.

"She initially cried and refused and said that that would—she
couldn't tolerate that."

"What did you tell her?"

"I told her in that instance that we'd have to leave, that we
couldn't stay, the building was in danger of collapsing and we
couldn't stay. And I was very concerned that I would kill this lady;
that in the process of cutting through the leg, that she would lie
there and bleed to death in my hands."

She was screaming, even before the first slice of skin. It made
him hesitate. He could not give her morphine or any other drug to
deaden the awful pain that was coming because she was in shock
and breathing poorly, and a painkiller might kill her. So he crawled
out again, and another doctor, an emergency room physician,
crawled in and gave her a different kind of drug, an amnesic. She
would feel everything, every cut through her skin and bone and the
marrow too. She would learn later that her two babies and her
mother were dead in what had been the Social Security office, that
her sister was seriously injured, and that she herself must learn to
walk again. But this drug would give her temporary amnesia; would
make her unable to remember what Dr. Sullivan did to her.

"I prayed," he said. "I prayed that she wouldn't die as a result of my treatment, and that if I died, my family would remember me."

He knotted the tourniquet, raised a long blade, "like a bread knife," and began cutting. With each stroke, the end of the blade hit the concrete, dulling the knife, and still he kept cutting; he dug deep and then he tossed the blade away and reached for another, and he cut some more and he went through all four disposable blades and still he was cutting.

"I tried to go as rapidly as I could. I took a deep breath. And once I started cutting, she started kicking and screaming so I had to more or less pin her against the wall while using my left hand."

Dr. Sullivan cut through Daina Bradley's leg to save the rest of her. "I cut my hands too, and all my shoulders and neck and everything were scratched. I had a patient I didn't know anything about, didn't know her background, working in an unsterile environment with cuts now on my own skin, so I was concerned about the possibility of getting hepatitis or AIDS or other infectious diseases."

When he thought he was done, when he could cut no more, when his four blades were broken, he crawled out. In fact, he twice crawled out thinking he had removed the leg, but when they pulled on Daina Bradley, she did not come out; she was still attached, and screaming.

In the courtroom, the doctor closed his hands and looked straight ahead. He was not proud of what he was about to say. Sometimes we do the best with what God gives us.

"I remembered that I had my pocketknife," he said.

So he went back in, and he removed her leg completely this time, and then she was swiftly taken to an ambulance. He rode with her to the hospital too, because he was her doctor, and with only a mile or two to go, she was lapsing into unconsciousness. Then he screamed at her and slapped her, and he shook the life back into this young woman. Breathe! he shouted. Breathe! Dr. Sullivan saved Daina Bradley's life twice that day—once in the hell of the Murrah ruins, and once again in that desperate ambulance ride.

The victims had spoken.

Attorney Richard Burr rose for the defense. He and his wife, Mandy Welch, a fellow lawyer, were death-penalty specialists from Texas, where they had run a coalition fighting state executions. They would spearhead McVeigh's plea to live. He would not talk, so they would speak for him. Sometimes he wanted desperately to talk to the jury, not to beg forgiveness or apologize but to express his feelings about Waco and the ATF and the growing antigun lobby. He would argue endlessly with his lawyers, insisting they allow him to climb up in that tall chair and explain himself.

But his lawyers urged him to sit still, to be quiet, because anything he said could be used against him later by the county prosecutor in Oklahoma City, Bob Macy. And Macy was declaring, loudly and publicly, that no matter what happened to McVeigh in Denver, life or death, he was going to retry him with an Oklahoma jury, and that he would prosecute him repeatedly if that was what it took to win a death sentence.

One day McVeigh asked his lawyers, "How many times do they want to kill me?"

"How did this come to be?" Burr asked the jury. "What could have caused this unthinkable thing, this unspeakable tragedy, to have happened right here in the heart of America? What could have happened to bring about so much suffering?"

There are, he said, two Timothy McVeighs. The first comes from the stories of his boyhood in Pendleton, his rise to manhood in the army, his search for his place in America. "You will be able to see him for who he is. A person not very much unlike your brother, who could be your brother, who could be your son, who could be your grandson. You will find that, because that is who he is."

The second McVeigh broods; he loves guns and despises the government. "He went on a search, a search to find more information and to glean what he thought was the truth about what had happened at Waco, to try to come to understand."

Burr described again the horror of Waco, no less an American tragedy than was Oklahoma City, he said, only differently directed, one a beginning, the other an end. As he talked, he had a habit of leaning to his left, his head tilted, his brow furrowed, a devout liberal trying to appeal to the jury's respect for human life.

"These realities are clearly connected," he said of his client, McVeigh. "There is violence, there is much death, there is tremendous suffering. But there is also a person at the center whom you will not be able to dismiss easily as a monster or a demon, who could be your son, who could be your brother, who could be your grandson, who loved his country, who served it, who had a number of admirable human qualities, and a number of frailties, just like any of us. . . ."

Yes, Burr said, that was it. Timothy McVeigh, with his boyhood smile, his basement hideout; his army duffel bag, his rusting old cars, his "Warriors" pounding down America's highways. "He is," Burr repeated, "just like any of us."

The defense brought in soldiers who had served with McVeigh, and while each offered warm stories of his short years with the army, his command of the Bradley cannon and his love of the infantry, they could not get past the cross-examination by the prosecution. Just a few questions from the government lawyers were enough to discredit McVeigh's service record.

"When you were in the army with Mr. McVeigh," assistant prosecutor Beth Wilkinson asked former Sergeant Jose Rodriguez, "were you schooled on the rules of engagement and the law of war?"

"Yes I was."

"And," asked Wilkinson, "were you taught as the first rule that you were never to kill noncombatants, including women and children?"

"That's part of the rules."

"And is that something that every soldier learns when they're trained in the United States Army?"

Rodriguez cleared his throat. She had him; more important, she had McVeigh.

"Yes, it is," Rodriguez said.

Sergeant Major Bob Harris, twenty-two years in the army, decorated in combat, testified about McVeigh's heroics in war. Wilkinson cornered him too.

"Have you said in the past that Bronze Stars were handed out left and right in the Gulf War?" she began.

Harris seemed relaxed. "Yeah," he said. "The Bronze Star was frequently awarded to just about—to many people. Yes, ma'am."

"Was that in part because there hadn't been a war for a while and a lot of soldiers hadn't received awards?"

"Ma'am, I do not have the answer to that. . . ."

"But it was your opinion that they were handed out quite frequently?"

"Yes, that was my opinion," he said. "Absolutely."

Jones tried to repair the damage. He asked Harris about the brilliant U.S. military victory in Kuwait, the short ground offensive, the quick surrender by the enemy.

Did McVeigh deserve the Bronze Star? Jones asked.

"Absolutely. We submitted him for it, and we thought he deserved it. Yes, sir."

"And I take it the secretary of the army doesn't have a reputation of just carrying them in his pocket and handing them out, does he?"

"No. No, sir."

Jones sat down; Wilkinson stood up.

"Very few American soldiers were killed due to direct combat with the Iraqis during the Gulf War," she said. "Isn't that true?"

"That's correct, ma'am," said Harris.

"In fact, under one hundred and thirty-seven American citizens were killed in combat during the Persian Gulf War; isn't that right?"

"I do not know the stats, ma'am. I couldn't tell you yes or no to that. . . ."

But the point was made—fewer Americans had been killed in this country's last war than died the day McVeigh set off the bomb in Oklahoma City.

Still his defense lawyers forged ahead, They brought in schoolteachers and childhood friends. They read letters McVeigh had written home during the war. The parents of his friends from his Pendleton boyhood, the McDermotts and the Drzyzgas, offered personal reminscenses.

Elizabeth McDermott recalled how McVeigh would baby-sit her children. "I love Tim," she said. "I think he's—I love Tim."

Her husband, John, who encouraged him in his comic book collection as a way to make an investment for college, broke down. "I liked him very much," he said. "I trusted him. I can't imagine him doing anything like this. I can't."

Lynn Drzyzga, his dear "Mrs. D," told the jury about the chocolate-covered cherries he gave her each Christmas and the little tin with the flip lid that he rescued for her from the garage sale. "Tim is my friend," she said, holding her head high. "And I will always cherish all our memories. It was a relationship that was special because it was my son's friend and I was a mom, and really friendships like that do not come along, and that's why I feel it is so special."

Next spoke her husband, Richard, who had encouraged McVeigh to join the army and then delighted in his enlistment, and who also had watched from the window as his wife and McVeigh cried together that day McVeigh worried that he might come home from the war in a body bag.

Richard Drzyzga knew this would not be easy. He said he felt torn about McVeigh. "Confused," he said. "There's a part of me that still remembers Tim, a little kid. And then there's a part that sees what everybody else sees on TV and gets angry. And I can't put the two together. I mean it just—hearing and listening and reading all that was being said might have been true, but it wasn't the Tim that I knew. I mean in me everything was just kind of going in circles. As a kid growing up, you know, I was there along with some of the other neighbors, and some of his teachers, and we virtually prodded Tim to do good, and he did do good. He was a great kid. He wasn't mischievous. He didn't get in trouble. He was always there.

"I mean he kind of closed himself off a little bit, you know. He kept his feelings to himself."

And you still care about Tim?

Richard Drzyzga was crying, for himself, for McVeigh. What had gone wrong that something this bad could have happened?

"Yeah, I do," he said with a great sigh. "And it's a hard situation for me. It really is. Because, you know, I have to face people every day, and there are people out there that detest him. And they detest me because I knew him. They detest me because I still have feelings for him."

The last to defend Timothy McVeigh were his parents. Mildred Frazer wore a plain dress. She told the jury about the divorce and her move to Florida; she now worked as a bus driver's assistant transporting emotionally disturbed and physically disabled children. "I love my job," she said. "It's very rewarding."

In her hand she held a small piece of paper, a short note she had written. It had taken her three copies to get it right, to make it perfect.

"Tell the jury what you'd like them to know," said Burr.

She turned to the jurors. "Can I look at them?" she asked Matsch. But her voice was muffled, hard to pick up.

"We can't hear you," said the judge.

She spun back around, turning her eyes away, back to the page in her hands, and she began to read. "I cannot even imagine the pain and suffering the people from Oklahoma City have endured since April 19th of 1995," she said.

Timothy McVeigh's mother was crying.

Burr stopped her. "Mrs. Frazer," he said, "let me just interrupt a minute. Why don't you take a breath."

"Okay."

"Relax," he said.

She paused, but just briefly; she wanted this over. "This tragedy has affected many people around the world," she read, "including myself. I also understand the anger many people feel.

"I cannot tell you about Tim McVeigh, the son I love, any better than it already has been told the last three and a half days. He has— he was a loving son and a happy child as he grew up. He was a child any mother could be proud of. I still to this very day cannot believe he could have caused this devastation. There are too many unanswered questions and loose ends. He has seen human loss in the past, and it has torn him apart. He is not the monster he has been portrayed as. He is also a mother and father's son, a brother to two sisters, a cousin to many and a friend to many more.

"Yes," she said, now trying to turn back toward the jury, "I am pleading for my son's life. He is a human being, just as we all are."

She had borrowed Burr's theme, that her son belonged to all of us.

"You must make this very difficult decision on my son's life or death, and I hope and pray that God helps you make the right one."

She stepped down, wadding the paper in her tight, thin fist.

She was followed to the stand by her ex-husband, William McVeigh. He came in wearing brown slacks, an open-neck shirt, and white shoes, like bowling shoes. He sat down, and the eyes of this painfully shy man seldom left his lap; even his hair fell down over his forehead, making it difficult to tell if he was seeing the room at all. He answered a few questions about his own army service thirty years ago. With prodding from Burr, he told about a videotape he had helped make for the jury. It would be much easier for him to talk to the jurors that way, describing Pendleton and their home and Tim's school, and the Good Shepherd Catholic Church, which he attended until the eleventh grade, and the Burger Kings where he worked as a teenager. The video had been shot last fall, around Veterans Day.

Burr played the tape, and the scenes came flickering onto the courtroom television monitor, shots of Tim's great loving bear of a grandfather, of the family's backyard pool, of Tim and Jennifer riding on their father's tractor as Dad tended his giant garden full of corn and squash and big ripe red tomatoes. The camera panned through the town, and there were the green open spaces, yards with no fences, grass as high as a little boy.

"When I grew up, it was all farms. When Tim grew up, it was half and half." William McVeigh was narrating on the tape, sitting in the yard, squinting into the camera. "My grandfather himself comes from Buffalo. His parents, I guess, were Irish from Ireland. My grandmother, I ain't sure where, but her parents were from Germany."

The tape whirred on. "It's a wonderful neighborhood to grow up in. The whole town of Pendleton is like that. That's why you see so many houses going up around here. Everybody likes the town of Pendleton. It's a rural town. Houses ain't too close together."

There was the walkway that straddled the Erie Canal; and Kenan Arena, where it cost fifty cents to ice-skate; and Darien Lake, for summer vacations; and the Tonawanda Sportsman Club, where Tim learned to target-shoot.

"He come home one day and says he was going in the service. And I said, 'When?' And he says, 'Tomorrow.' That's about all I can tell you about when he went in the service or over to the Persian Gulf. He didn't seem to mind going. He was ready to go when the time came. They went to Kuwait."

William McVeigh told how he was still working at the auto plant when his son returned from the army at Christmas 1991. "He was welcome, but we thought he was going to be in the service for three more years so we had changed his room over to my daughter's room. My daughter, Jennifer, had come home from Florida. When I was working nights he'd sleep in my bed, and then finally he moved downstairs. He seemed to be happy when he come home."

When the tape ended, Burr held up a photograph of a smiling William and Timothy McVeigh, father and son, their arms around each other as they laughed in the family kitchen, sometime around 1992. Burr wanted his client's father to speak now to the jury; the photo was his prop.

"Looking at this photograph and just focusing on it, does it bring back memories?"

"Yes."

"Can you tell us about some of the memories that it brings back?"

"Well, it's—to me, it's a happy Tim. It's a Tim I remember most of my life."

Burr was leaning to the side of the podium, trying to draw the words out. "Can you tell us about that Tim that you remember?"

"Oh, he's always good-natured, fun, always fun to be with, always in a pretty good mood."

"Is the Tim that we see in this picture the Tim that you know?"

"Yes. The Tim that I know most of my life."

"Is the Tim that we see in this picture still alive to you?"

"I believe so."

"Do you love the Tim—"

"Yes, I love Tim."

"—in this picture? Do you love the Tim in this courtroom?"

"Yes, I do."

"Do you want him to stay alive?"

Burr was thinking: Speak to us. Be proud. He is your son. Save your son. But the old man just looked at his lap, his hair fallen over his eyes, his face ruddy, his ears turning red.

"Yes, I do," he said again, and that was all he could say.

With that came the lawyers' closing arguments. Wilkinson was insistent in her call for the death sentence. "Look into the eyes of a coward," she said, pointing at Timothy McVeigh. "Tell him you will have courage." She pointed again. "Tell him he is no patriot. He is a traitor and he deserves to die."

The defense split their closing argument. Jones again talked at length and often rambled. He conjured up the images of other mass murderers, Charles Manson in California, John Wayne Gacy in Chicago, Charles Whitman atop the University of Texas tower. Ted Bundy, too. Totaling up all of their victims still would not surpass the number of dead in Oklahoma.

Give him a life sentence with no parole, Jones said; there lies the harsher punishment. "Day in and day out until sometime pretty close to the half-century mark, he will die an old man, carried out by the coroner. And every day of his life, he can never escape, never escape what has happened here. You can't watch that much televi-

sion or play that much tic-tac-toe or write that many letters home.
You can't run from it."

Jones recalled the indictment had stated that "others unknown"
were involved too, that perhaps more men were still out there, men
in baseball caps, men with tattoos, men like John Doe No. 2. Kill
McVeigh, and you end any chance of resolving that mystery. "Dead
men do not tell tales," Jones said. "I say again, the government may
not be the only people that want my client executed."

Burr, as always, was moving. "You know that Tim is not an evil
man, not a man who was somehow defective in the way he
thought or felt or dwelt among us in his lifetime. But instead a
man who embodies much of the best that we call 'human,' and a
young man who loved his country and proudly put his life on the
line for all of us."

McVeigh, he said, echoing those who had spoken up for him, had
embodied all of the virtues found in all of us. So how do we then,
as a nation, respond to this man within our midst?

"How do we teach love and compassion when what we are confronted with is hate?" Burr asked. "What is the response to hate
that is guided by love and compassion? When hate leads to killing,
do we abandon our commitment to love and compassion by killing
the killer?"

Timothy James McVeigh was one of our young men; his crime
was our bombing; it came from within the borders of our own
nation.

"Mr. McVeigh's beliefs about Waco and Ruby Ridge and the
threat presented by militarization of federal law enforcement did
not arise in a vacuum, did not arise out of thin air. These are not
the delusional fantasies of a madman. Somehow, in the midst of
Mr. McVeigh's misplaced, mistakenly acted upon, horrifyingly out-
of-proportion beliefs, there is a reason for all of us to have concern.
That we have not expressed that concern before this tragedy means
that we all bear some responsibility for Oklahoma City."

And so, said Burr, "we should not feel a clear conscience if we
kill Timothy McVeigh."

The last word was Hartzler's; the government always goes last.
He spoke again of the victims, particularly the children. Feel no sorrow for McVeigh, Hartzler said; unlike McVeigh, these nineteen
dead children will never get to have a haunted house in their base-

ment or run barefoot through the grass. "I'm sorry you have to do this," he told the jury. "I'm sorry you have to do it. But you do."

The chief prosecutor mocked Burr's suggestion that "he's one of us," that McVeigh could be your son or grandson or brother. Nor did he accept the hidden message from the elder McVeigh's home movie about his son coming from a middle-class home and attending public school. "So what?" Hartzler said. "Where does that take us? That means that his life should be spared because he had a background similar to ours?"

Hartzler looked into the faces of the twelve; he had told them when they were chosen that they must be strong enough to look into McVeigh's eyes and have the courage, if the government prevailed, to put him to death.

Timothy McVeigh was never one of us, Hartzler said. "That is not America."

The jury met for eleven hours over two days. They cried, they held hands, and they took one vote. They came back into the courtroom on Friday, June 13. They did exactly as Hartzler had asked in that all of them, not just foreman James Osgood, resumed their courtroom seats and stared into McVeigh's eyes. Osgood handed over the verdict, and the judge reviewed it quietly. In the back of the courtroom, one of the Oklahomans knelt while another recited the rosary. Stephen Jones cradled a copy of the Book of Common Prayer.

Then Matsch read the verdict, again just one word that mattered, written this time by Osgood in large, dark capital letters pressed deeply onto the page: "DEATH."

McVeigh received the sentence with no visible reaction, his hand on his chin, his elbow on the counsel table, his eyes on Judge Matsch. Almost immediately the prisoner was led away by federal marshals. He flashed a peace sign to the jury, then turned quickly toward his parents and his sister in the front row, searching them out. Just before he disappeared through the courtroom's rear door, he mouthed: "It's okay."

Chapter Twenty

Life After Death

Sunday was Father's Day, and Bill McVeigh had returned
to Pendleton. He drew up the blinds, opened the windows, and
changed into his shorts. He put on an old baseball cap against the
afternoon sun. Soon he was back on his garden tractor, mowing the
grass, tending to the marigolds and his sweet alyssum. There was
much work to be done, much to keep his hands busy. The garden
was about a week behind, he guessed. He had plenty to do.

A *New York Times* reporter wandered up to the McVeigh house
that weekend, and Bill agreed to talk, relieved at least to be away
from the swarming press crowds in Denver. "Father's Day was
nothing special in our house," he said. "And Timmy ain't much at
the sentimental stuff. I don't think he even knows when my birthday was, to tell you the truth."

He showed his visitor a bucket of old golf balls. "My son found
them a long time ago. He went scrounging in the ditches. He gave
them to me. He sold all the good ones."

Bill McVeigh was back that night on the late shift at the Harri-
son Radiator factory. Life was the same, and it was not the same. "I
know it's never going to be over," he said.

Another reporter, this one from the *Los Angeles Times*, knocked
on the door of the McDermott home. John McDermott appeared at
the screen. Even if Tim had gotten life, he said, he never is going to

last in prison. His courtroom tears welled up again. "We just loved
the kid," he said.

In Washington, moving with uncharacteristic speed, the United
States Senate voted 98–0, less than a week after the trial ended, to
bar Timothy McVeigh from ever being buried in a military ceme-
tery. The measure also stripped him of any veterans' benefits. "This
is one further statement of national resolve," announced Senator
Robert Toricelli, a New Jersey Democrat and cosponsor of the bill.
"We will deny you honor in death."

In a part of America forever changed those two Aprils ago, the
people of Oklahoma City, their neighbors too, and visitors, tourists,
complete strangers, kept making daily pilgrimages to the corner of
5th and Harvey streets. The chain-link fence still carried the teddy
bears and cards, the poems too. Some of them now also wished a
swift death for Timothy McVeigh. It would be a long summer. On
the first day of July, just before the American celebration of liberty,
a design was unveiled for the construction of a permanent memorial to the bombing, featuring 168 stone-and-glass chairs, each one
inscribed with the name of one of the dead.

Someone had once suggested to Governor Frank Keating that
maybe they ought to rebuild the Murrah on the same spot, make it
a phoenix and show the world that life endures. No, said the governor. That is hallowed ground.

Stephen Jones had visited briefly with his client moments after
the final verdict. They had hoped the jury would split on the question of life or death. That would have bound Judge Matsch to sentence McVeigh to life. "But it was not to be," said his lawyer.

In the weeks ahead, as Jones prepared to return to Oklahoma, he
and his client squabbled over his representation. McVeigh asked
Judge Matsch to remove Jones from his appeal. Jones complained
that McVeigh was being unresponsive.

One August evening, McVeigh picked up a prison telephone and
called Lou Michel, a *Buffalo News* reporter who had befriended his
father in Pendleton.

McVeigh complained about the press leaks over his purported
confessions. He said he bore no grudge against the jurors, although
"I thought they ruled too much on emotion." He defended his
demeanor during the trial. "I tried to be a perfect gentleman in the
courtroom when people called me a coward."

He was asked about his quarrel with Jones. "It's a cultural clash between us," McVeigh said. "Jones would be a politician, and I'd be a statesman."

He added: "The truth is this guy [Jones] only succeeded in getting the death penalty."

Ultimately, Jones was taken off the case. He went home to Oklahoma and announced that he had signed a book deal.

Hartzler too had gone home, and was reunited with his family in Illinois. He was no longer poring over legal briefs; instead that summer he picked up *Les Misérables*, the story of another criminal case. Soon he was watching his kids out on the Little League diamond.

The chief prosecutor did grant one of his few interviews to *The Lutheran*. The religious magazine ran his picture; underneath they saluted him with a banner headline: "Good job, Joe."

In the interview, he sought to square his religious views with his task as a federal prosecutor seeking to put a man to death. He was reminded of Martin Luther's precept that government acts on God's behalf to bring order to society. He said that "God works through each of us," and, while he did speak with some modesty, it was clear that he sensed the Almighty sitting with him at the prosecution table, right there between the jury and McVeigh.

"I serve the people in my capacity as a prosecutor," he said. "I serve God in doing what I think He believes is right and just in this world."

Justice for Terry Nichols was bittersweet. He was tried separately before Judge Matsch and a second jury, in the same courtroom, and although much of the government's evidence against him was similar to that used in the McVeigh trial, the outcome was decidedly different.

Nichols was found guilty of conspiring with McVeigh in the blast, but he was acquitted of using the bomb or destroying the Murrah building. The jury also found him not guilty of first- or second-degree murder in the deaths of the eight federal law enforcement officers killed that morning, and instead convicted him only of involuntary manslaughter.

Like McVeigh, Nichols did not speak during his trial. But several times he broke down and cried when his ex-wife, Lana, described their past life with their son, Josh.

The jury was unable to agree on whether he should live or die, and so Terry Nichols escaped death. By law it fell then to the court to decide how long he should remain in prison.

For McVeigh a sentencing hearing was held on August 14. The court reassembled, along with lawyers from both sides. McVeigh was making his last public appearance.

Before the hearing began, he again was laughing it up with his lawyers. "Look at my shoes!" he said, pointing to the ugly prison-issue flip-flops the marshals had given him to wear. "Look at my shoes!"

But he turned cold and silent when the judge entered and took the bench. Matsch asked both sides for comment, but none of the lawyers desired to speak.

"All right," said the judge. "Mr. McVeigh, you have the right to make any statement you wish to make. Do you wish to make a statement?"

"Yes, your honor," he said. "Briefly."

He rose and walked to the center of the courtroom, dressed in the drab, cream-colored uniform of a federal prisoner; he stood at the lectern, his fingers clasped but twitching nervously behind his back.

"If the court please," he began. "I wish to use the words of Justice Brandeis dissenting in *Olmstead* to speak for me. He wrote, 'Our government is the potent, the omnipresent teacher. For good or ill, it teaches the whole people by its example.' "

The room seemed perplexed. Victims were here again, hoping for some explanation from this man's mouth. But what was he saying?

"That's all I have," McVeigh said.

Matsch seemed entirely unimpressed. "All right," he said. Then the judge sentenced McVeigh to die and the marshals took him out.

On the courthouse plaza, lawyers discussed the quotation. Defense attorney Tritico said he had never heard it before; he planned to retreat to his law library and look it up. He would find that the citation was from a 1920s Supreme Court case dealing with the use of government wiretaps during Prohibition. Justice Louis Brandeis had felt that government agents broke the law to make arrests.

Some of the victims said McVeigh's quotation just showed that he was unrepentant. Paul Heath, speaking for many of the victims, said it was clear that McVeigh still considered himself a revolutionary.

Hartzler joined those in the plaza. This time he turned eagerly to the cameras. "Don't interpret his words as those of a spokesman or a statesmen," he cautioned.

The reporter Lou Michel flew out from Buffalo. He was invited into the federal prison in Florence, Colorado, a super-maximum-security installation south of Denver known as the Alcatraz of the Rockies, and he spoke with McVeigh in a concrete basement cubicle.

"I want people to think about the statement," McVeigh said. "What Hartzler is trying to do is not have people learn. He wants to have them put their heads in the sand."

The Brandeis quote reflects upon the death penalty, McVeigh said; the government said it was wrong for him to kill and yet "now they're going to kill me."

"They're saying that's an appropriate way to right a wrong?" he asked.

They chatted for under an hour. McVeigh said he was grateful to the people of Pendleton for their support, his family too. He said he missed his gun, the big black Glock, the one strapped underneath his arm that morning he lost his freedom. He was not upset about Jones's suggestion at the close of the trial that if he was executed, the answer to the riddle of the Oklahoma City bombing would die with him. "I don't have a negative response to Jones saying that. We all have to die." He admitted his chances on appeal were "slim to none."

He told a story about the trip back to prison after the sentencing hearing. McVeigh knew he was a fast runner, always had been, from as far back as his days racing through the lawns of Pendleton.

"On the way down here in the helicopter, I said to the marshals, 'Just let me out and give me a head start. . . .' " He found the idea amusing.

But he said nothing of the lives he had taken. He showed no remorse, offered no apology. He did not even say whether the jury had it right, whether he was the bomber at all. He was a soldier to the end, and when it came time to leave, he stood and gave the thumbs-up sign. Then he returned to his seven-by-ten-foot cell—a bed, a stool, and a concrete shelf—and the prison door slammed shut on Timothy McVeigh.

If his legal appeals fail, he will someday die in prison, either as an old convict weary from a life behind bars, or as a young man, his sleeve rolled up the way he likes it, the executioner searching for a vein.

Printed in the United States
109542LV00003B/33/P

Made in the USA
Monee, IL
19 March 2022

93178692R00198